Isaiah Berlin's Liberalism

Isaiah Berlin's Liberalism

Claude J. Galipeau

CLARENDON PRESS · OXFORD
1994

Oxford University Press, Walton Street, Oxford OX2 6DP
Oxford New York Toronto
Delhi Bombay Calcutta Madras Karachi
Kuala Lumpur Singapore Hong Kong Tokyo
Nairobi Dar es Salaam Cape Town
Melbourne Auckland Madrid
and associated companies in
Berlin Ibadan

Oxford is a trade mark of Oxford University Press

Published in the United States
by Oxford University Press Inc., New York

© Claude J. Galipeau 1994

British Library Cataloguing in Publication Data
Data available

Library of Congress Cataloging in Publication Data
Galipeau, Claude, 1959–
Isaiah Berlin's liberalism/Claude J. Galipeau.
Includes bibliographical references.
1. Berlin, Isaiah, Sir—Contributions in political science.
2. Liberalism. I. Title.
JC571.G24   1933   320.5'1—dc20   93–1312
ISBN 0–19–827868–3

1 3 5 7 9 10 8 6 4 2

Typeset by Cambrian Typesetters
Frimley, Surrey
Printed in Great Britain
on acid-free paper by
Biddles Ltd
Guildford and King's Lynn

To Jane

Preface

Liberal theory and practice have fared rather well over the past two decades. In 1971 there was the publication of John Rawls's *A Theory of Justice*, which proposed liberal and egalitarian principles for modern statecraft; its success encouraged serious study of political and moral problems in the Anglo-American academic world. In politics, many governments in Western industrialized democracies attempted a return to *laissez-faire* policies of economic management, trying to overturn the achievements of the welfare state, defended by Rawls and others. Apart from economic matters, principles of individual liberty and democracy animated mass political movements, from China to South Africa. The demise of the Soviet Empire is the most spectacular political and military change of recent decades; yet the ethnic, racial, and national sentiments which fuel the civil wars in many of the former Soviet states and satellites, and similar strife in South Africa, have demonstrated the naïvety of those who were quick to proclaim the worldwide triumph of *pax libertas* as soon as the Cold War ended.

The latter events could not have surprised Sir Isaiah Berlin, whose work is the subject of this book; this is because Berlin, who is as staunch a defender of individual liberty as Rawls and his epigones, has made it a point to argue that human beings pursue a variety of ends other than liberty. Moreover, Berlin holds that values can be incompatible and in conflict, often tragically so; thus it is not out of the ordinary that oppressed people proclaim one day a belief in the universal principles of individual liberty and justice, but, once freed from the foreign yoke, seek liberty for themselves as a people only, without justice or liberty for others. Belonging to a people can conflict with individual liberty, with equality, with justice, with mercy, with compassion, and other values. A central message of Berlin's writings is that value pluralism is constitutive of our moral universe, rather than the result of intellectual error to be rectified by a better theory or system of thought. Once seriously taken into account, the idea of value pluralism limits the ambit of rational ethical theory.

It is this idea about pluralism, and the general sense of cultural and historical realism, that distinguishes Berlin from other contemporary liberal philosophers. Even though he defends liberal principles, he is critical of the rationalist and Enlightenment ideals and methods which guide virtually all liberal thought. At a time when the promises of rational contract theory, such as that promoted by Rawls, are proving less compelling (even to Rawls himself), it is opportune to focus on a thinker whose wide range includes studies that seek to explain our multiple affinities, defend core human values including liberty, as well as to give an account of the intricacies and paradoxes of human behaviour.

This book presents Berlin's ideas focusing particularly on his liberal thought. This is a systematic study about a set of ideas which have not, however, been systematically ordered by their author, principally because his personal credo is to resist all systems. In this respect, my project carries significant risk: namely, to render systematic that which is not, and possibly to gloss over contradictions and tensions; and to avoid dealing with incoherent positions. These dangers are always present when studying thinkers of Berlin's sort, and I plead guilty, at the outset, for ordering his ideas in ways he never did. However, as anyone who reads more than half a dozen of Berlin's essays will come to realize, his work does express a set of ideas about human nature, morality, and politics, and a unique kind of liberal philosophy—and these can be stated in a systematic way.

Throughout his published work and lectures, Berlin has developed his political and moral thought in historical, philosophical, and literary studies. It is these ideas that I have ordered to clarify and inform the debate about his political thought, especially with respect to his most famous lecture, 'Two Concepts of Liberty'. I have sought to link this lecture to most of Berlin's other writings, in order to locate the influences and the meaning of what is presented there. I have worked according to the principle that, in all cases, one must first come to understand a thinker before rendering criticism; and since all critics have written without full knowledge of his thought, at least I might prevent further conceit. At the very best, I might render more accurate any future debate about his work.

A book of this nature is possible only with the aid and support of teachers, colleagues, peers, friends, and loved ones. I thank Gerald

Tucker for introducing me to the work of Isaiah Berlin while I was an undergraduate. As a graduate student, J. A. W. Gunn and Doug Williams fostered my interest in the history of ideas and political philosophy. This book began as a dissertation project at the University of Toronto and owes much to the supervision of Ronald Beiner and Joe Carens. None of what follows would have been possible without the support and comments of Steve Andrews, Richard Barry, Michal Ben-Gera, Stefan Dupré, Neil Freeman, Chris Gould, Lloyd Hoffer, Namir Khan, David Knott, Will Kymlicka, Evert Linquist, Craig McFadyen, Ken Rasmussen, and Richard Sigurdson. During my research and writing, I profited greatly from conversations and correspondence with G. A. Cohen, John Gray, David Miller, and Larry Siedentop. They helped me avoid a number of errors. I thank Henry Hardy for keeping me informed of new additions to Berlin's bibliography, for his help in locating sources, and for his editorial support. I also thank Beata Polanowska-Sygulska for her interest and permission to use parts of her correspondence with Isaiah Berlin.

This dissertation would not have taken its present form without the support of Sir Isaiah. I thank him for listening, reading, and replying to my queries with interest and kindness. I will always treasure our conversations in London and Oxford. I also thank him for his generosity and permission to use our correspondence and the transcripts of our conversations.

The library staff at the Bodleian Library, Oxford, the British Library, London, and the Robarts Research Library, Toronto, were instrumental in gathering all the primary material for this study. Special thanks to Jane Lynch in the Interlibrary Department of Robarts Library: her detective work saved me much needless expense and travel. Tim Barton, of Oxford University Press, carefully guided this project from manuscript to publication. I should like to thank the Social Sciences and Humanities Research Council of Canada for giving me doctoral and post-doctoral fellowships.

Chapter 7 contains material originally published in 'Liberalism and Zionism: The Case of Isaiah Berlin', *Queen's Quarterly*, 97 (1990). I am grateful for permission to use this article.

Finally, I would like to express my gratitude to Jane Hargraft, for her editorial advice, as well as the love, support, and patience that gave me the time and energy to bring this work to completion.

Contents

Abbreviations

I. Books by Isaiah Berlin

AC   *Against the Current: Esssays in the History of Ideas*, edited by Henry Hardy, London 1979.

CC   *Concepts and Categories: Philosophical Essays*, edited by Henry Hardy, London 1978.

CTH   *The Crooked Timber of Humanity: Chapters in the History of Ideas*, edited by Henry Hardy, London 1990.

FE   *Four Essays on Liberty*, London 1969.

PI   *Personal Impressions*, edited by Henry Hardy, London 1980.

RT   *Russian Thinkers*, edited by Henry Hardy and Aileen Kelly, London 1978.

VH   *Vico and Herder: Two Studies in the History of Ideas*, London, 1976.

II. Interviews with Isaiah Berlin

All Souls   With C. J. Galipeau, All Souls College, Oxford University, 23 May 1989.

Athenaeum   With C. J. Galipeau, Athenaeum Club, London, 1 June 1989.

Jahanbegloo   With R. Jahanbegloo, *Recollections of a Historian of Ideas: Conversations with Isaiah Berlin*, New York 1991.

Certes, c'est un sujet merveilleusement vain, divers et ondoyant que l'homme. Il est malaisé d'y fonder jugement constant et uniforme.

Michel de Montaigne, *Essais*

I

INTRODUCTION

> When all is said and done, we are never too sure—not even the
> wisest among us—of what is good for men; in the end we can
> only be reasonably sure of what it is that particular societies of
> individuals crave for: of what makes them miserable and
> what, for them, makes life worth living.
>
> (Isaiah Berlin, 'The Three Strands in My Life')

Sir Isaiah Berlin is a British man of letters of Russian-Jewish
origins. Born in Riga, Latvia, in 1909, his family emigrated to
Britain in 1919, fleeing the Russian Revolution. He was brought up
and educated in Britain, and has spent most of his professional life
studying and lecturing at Oxford University, or at universities in
America and Israel while on leave. To the international scholarly
community he is best known as the author of 'Two Concepts of
Liberty' (1958),[1] yet his professional interests cover many fields in
addition to moral and political philosophy: music and literary
criticism, historiography, scholarship in the history of ideas,
cultural interpretation, translation, teaching, university and arts
administration, diplomacy, community work, and broadcasting.
His distinguished career has been recognized by many honours and
charges, including the Chichele Chair of Social and Political
Theory at Oxford (1957–67), the Presidency of Wolfson College,
Oxford (1966–75), a knighthood (1957) and the Order of Merit
(1971), the Presidency of the British Academy (1974–8), a series of
honorary doctorates, and trusteeships and directorships on academic

---

[1] Now included in *Four Essays on Liberty* (London, 1969), 118–72. Henry Hardy
has compiled a complete bibliography, which is included in its most complete form,
in the latest impression of *Against the Current* (Oxford, 1991). When referring to
Berlin's work, I will use the convention of citing his name for the first reference, and
then proceed to cite only the title of the work subsequently. For interviews and
collected editions, I will also use abbreviations, noted on the page preceding this
chapter.

and performing arts boards, such as the Royal Opera House, Covent Garden (1955–66, 1975–).

He has spent most of his life in the academic world at Oxford, but his influence carries beyond that university, into the cultural life of Britain and the Anglo-American and Jewish worlds. Berlin's travels, including his wartime diplomatic postings in New York, Washington, and Moscow, have allowed him to come into contact with some of this century's best-known figures from the arts, politics, and economic and social milieus. Some of these meetings are preserved in essays or in *éloges* and obituaries.[2] While he prefers scholarly pursuits, Berlin understands the world of action, of politics, debate, and artistic performance. He has entered the political fray, usually discreetly from the wings of the public stage: specifically, in battling fascism and communism, and in support of the Zionist cause, both before and after the founding of the modern state of Israel.[3]

This experience, married to his ability to understand others, to enter into world-views vastly different from his own, and express them to his listeners and readers, makes his work unique, informative, wide-ranging, and enlightened. It also gives substance to his defence of political liberalism. His range of knowledge in the history of ideas, his experience of the great debates of this century and its moral and political battles, which are conveyed in his writings, make for erudite, wise, and compelling prescriptions for politics and society.

Why Study Isaiah Berlin?

In addition to the above-mentioned considerations, there are four reasons for studying the work of Berlin. The first is the influence that his work has had on other scholars and philosophers, from Charles Taylor[4] to Bernard Williams,[5] from Joseph Raz[6] to John

---

[2] See *PI*, and Hardy's bibliography in *AC*.

[3] For a few autobiographical sketches, see the Jahanbegloo interview, 3–23; I. Berlin, 'The Three Strands in My Life' *Jewish Quarterly*, 27 (1979), 5–7; and I. Berlin, 'The Pursuit of the Ideal' in *CTH*, 1–19.

[4] See C. Taylor, *Human Agency and Language: Philosophical Papers*, i (New York, 1985); and *Philosophy and the Human Sciences: Philosophical Papers*, ii (New York, 1985).

[5] See B. Williams, *Ethics and the Limits of Philosophy* (London, 1985).

[6] See J. Raz, *The Morality of Freedom* (Oxford, 1986).

Gray.[7] The second is the relative paucity of concerted attention that his work as a whole has attracted amongst the scholarly community. This is surprising, given its originality and influence. The third is the intrinsic worth of his contributions to philosophy, to moral and political philosophy in particular, and to that modern and rich field of study, the history of ideas. In the latter, he has been a leader and setter of standards; in the former, his views on value pluralism, arguably his most original contribution to ethics, presage philosophy's current concerns with the limits of rational theory in ethics. The fourth reason is the contemporary relevance of his work. To take an academic example, Berlin is not guilty of the charges laid against contemporary liberal thinkers by so-called 'communitarian' theorists. His defence of political liberalism is neither abstract nor ahistorical, nor insensitive to community values; rather, it exhibits an awareness of the problems of abstract defences of liberalism. It is now, after the success of the work of John Rawls,[8] Robert Nozick,[9] Ronald Dworkin,[10] and Bruce Ackerman,[11] and the criticisms elicited by these works, that we need to return to Berlin.[12]

It is undeniable that Berlin is a towering figure in the world of letters, especially in the Anglo-American world; though, it should be noted that much of his work has been widely translated.[13] His reputation is that of a man of wide learning, eclectic tastes, ready wit, keen intellect—all of which are presented in the most charming of countenances. Anyone who has met Sir Isaiah quickly realizes the presence of all these virtues, and more:[14] he has been called 'the

[7] See J. Gray, *Liberalisms: Essays in Political Philosophy* (London, 1989); and *Post-Liberalism: Studies in Political Thought* (London, 1993).

[8] J. Rawls, *A Theory of Justice* (Cambridge, Mass., 1971).

[9] R. Nozick, *Anarchy, State and Utopia* (New York, 1974).

[10] R. Dworkin, *Taking Rights Seriously* (Cambridge, Mass., 1978); and 'Liberalism' in *A Matter of Principle* (Cambridge, Mass., 1985), 181–204.

[11] B. Ackerman, *Social Justice in the Liberal State* (New Haven, Conn., 1980).

[12] I deal with this link to the communitarian criticism of liberal thought in Ch. 7.

[13] See Henry Hardy's bibliography in *AC*.

[14] For testimonials, see Anon, 'Silhouette: Sir Isaiah Berlin' in *Jewish Chronicle* (5 June 1959), 11; A. J. Ayer, *Part of My Life* (Oxford, 1977), 97–8; Yorick Blumenfeld, 'Is Isaiah Berlin the Philosopher of the 1980s?' in *International Herald Tribune* (28 Dec. 1979), 7W, 10W; Maurice Bowra, *Memories: 1898–1939* (London, 1966), 182–6; Vera Weizmann, *The Impossible Takes Longer* (London, 1967), 258; and finally, Jonathan Lieberson and Sidney Morgenbesser, 'Isaiah Berlin' in Edna and Avishai Margalit (eds.), *Isaiah Berlin: A Celebration* (London, 1991), 1–30 (originally published as 'The Questions of Isaiah Berlin' and 'The Choices of Isaiah Berlin' in

greatest living lecturer in the English language',[15] some of his efforts being preserved on tape; even in transcriptions or in revised essay form, his thoughts come across in a lively, exuberant manner. However, he prefers the essay form, for it gives the best range to his nuanced, layered, mellifluous style.

Literature, music (especially opera), and philosophy have figured prominently in his life. As an undergraduate, he wrote literary and music reviews for *The Oxford Outlook*, and later became the editor of that journal, following W. H. Auden. But it was philosophy that he first undertook to practise professionally in the 1930s, first as a tutor at New College and then as a Fellow of All Souls College. In that 'golden period' of Oxford philosophy he was part of the privileged circle that included A. J. Ayer and John Austin and contributed actively to their debates.[16] The partial focus on conceptual analysis in his famous later lecture 'Two Concepts of Liberty' (1958) indicates his debt to this Oxford tradition and those early philosophical debates. The lecture itself helped continue the analytical tradition within moral theory, for it opened the gate to a flood of debate and writing about the correct meaning of the contestable concept 'liberty'.[17] The influence of that essay continues to this day, over thirty years after its publication.[18]

Berlin relates that he turned away from a career in philosophy because he became convinced towards the end of the Second World War by the Harvard logician, H. M. Sheffer, that progress in philosophy is impossible. Wanting to progress in matters of the mind, Berlin decided to pursue his love of literature and ideas, and began studying the thinkers of the past, and their influence on contemporary affairs. He had already moved in this direction, with

the *New York Review of Books* (6 and 20 Mar. 1980), 38–42; 31–6. Some brief testimonials appear in the essays collected in *Isaiah Berlin: A Celebration*.

[15] By G. A. Cohen, All Souls College, Oxford (conversation, 23 May 1988).

[16] See I. Berlin, 'J. L. Austin and the Early Beginnings of Oxford Philosophy' in *PI*, 101–15. Some of Berlin's essays from this period are included in *CC*. I deal with these debates during the 'golden age' of Oxford philosophy in Ch. 2.

[17] Throughout, I will use 'liberty' and 'freedom' interchangeably.

[18] It is set reading for the University of Oxford B.Phil. and M.Phil. exam papers in political theory. 'Two Concepts of Liberty' was given as an inaugural lecture before that University, on 31 Oct. 1958. For critical reviews of the conceptual debates see William Parent, 'Some Recent Work on the Concept of Liberty' in *American Philosophical Quarterly*, 11 (1974), 149–67, who is unsympathetic to Berlin; and John Gray, 'On Negative and Positive Liberty' in Gray's *Liberalisms: Essays in Political Philosophy* (London, 1989) 45–68, who is quite sympathetic to Berlin.

the publication of his early book *Karl Marx: His Life and Environment*, in 1939; and by the end of the 1940s he was committed to the history of ideas.[19]

None the less, he always preserved a philosophical sense for conceptual analysis, as the 'Two Concepts' lecture demonstrates. The same is true of his methodological essays in the field of historiography. His criticisms of scientific history are major contributions to the philosophy of history, and have sparked many responses and interchanges, most notably with the Marxist historian, E. H. Carr.[20] Along with Arthur O. Lovejoy, Edmund Wilson, Arnaldo Momigliano, and John Plamenatz, he stands as a giant, and pioneer, in the field of the history of ideas. His studies on the Russian intelligentsia of the nineteenth century, his penetrating essays on Sorel, Machiavelli, Churchill, and the early book on Marx, all exhibit standards by which others are judged but rarely match. So do such achievements as having helped to resurrect the work of Giambattista Vico in the English-speaking world. And as a frequent guest lecturer, interview subject, and radio broadcaster, his passion for ideas and his belief that ideas shape all our lives, have been disseminated beyond academic circles.[21]

Given all these intellectual and academic achievements, one wonders why his work has not elicited more systematic attention. Surprisingly, two current reference books on political thought lack entries on his work, even though one of them cites his work in the bibliography for a number of subject headings.[22] Three doctoral dissertations have been written on his thought, one in the United

[19] I. Berlin, 'Author's Preface' in *CC*, pp. vii–viii.

[20] For the polemic with E. H. Carr, see the latter's *What is History?* (London, 1962). Berlin's initial criticisms are in the *Listener* (18 May and 15 June 1961), 877 and 1048–9. For Carr's defence, see his letter in the *Listener* (1 June 1961), 973–4. Berlin's review of Carr's book appeared in the *New Statesman* (5 Jan. 1962), 15–16. His last response to Carr occurs in the 'Introduction' to *FE*, pp. xxv–xxxi.

[21] Many of Sir Isaiah's essays began as lectures. This is evident in his style, which is vigorous and sinuous, like one side of a lively conversation. Moreover, he dictates virtually all his work, thus preserving much of his conversational style on the printed page. He has given numerous interviews on various subjects, from the sources of Romanticism to the nature of philosophy. Many of these interviews and lectures are preserved on tape in the National Sound Archive (The British Library), London.

[22] See Roger Scruton, *A Dictionary of Political Thought* (London, 1982), and David Miller, *et al.* (eds.), *The Blackwell Encyclopaedia of Political Thought* (Oxford, 1987), which often cites his work but grants him no entry. But see Alan Bullock and R. B. Woodings (eds.), *The Fontana Biographical Companion to Modern Thought* (London, 1983), where Berlin is granted an entry.

States, a second in Poland, and a third in Canada. Sir Isaiah has responded in print, although rather unfavourably, to the first attempt to deal thematically with his political thought.[23] Apart from a few overview essays, however, the full range of his work has not received comprehensive and systematic commentary.[24]

One reason may be a common view of Berlin: namely, that although a great conversationalist, he has actually written very little. This view began to change once Henry Hardy started editing Sir Isaiah's work in the late 1970s. Hardy has been the force behind the publication, so far, of five volumes of Sir Isaiah's writings. Moreover, he has also compiled an extensive and useful bibliography, running to over two hundred items, and including entries which the author does not even remember producing![25] Most of these items are scattered in journals of varying accessibility published throughout the world, but mainly in Britain, the United States, and Israel, and cover more than 60 years of publication. To date, no one has dealt with all or even most of these sources; from the earliest works of literary and music criticism to the most recent items about the collapse of Soviet Communism. John Gray, one of Berlin's sympathetic critics and admirers, still believes that his work is 'insufficiently appreciated'.[26] A former student, Larry Siedentop, is clear on the need for a study which will link together

---

[23] The third is my own dissertation: Claude Jean Galipeau, 'Isaiah Berlin's Liberalism: An Exposition and Defense', unpublished Ph.D. dissertation, University of Toronto, 1990. Cf. Robert Kocis, 'Rationalism and Romanticism Redux: The Political Philosophy of Sir Isaiah Berlin' (University of Pittsburgh Ph.D. dissertation, 1978. Published in a revised version as *A Critical Appraisal of Sir Isaiah Berlin's Political Philosophy* (Lewiston, NY, 1989)). See also Kocis, 'Reason, Development, and the Conflicts of Human Ends: Sir Isaiah Berlin's Vision of Politics' in *American Political Science Review*, 74 (1980), 38–52; and his 'Toward a Coherent Theory of Human Moral Development: Beyond Sir Isaiah Berlin's Vision of Human Nature' in *Political Studies*, 31 (1983), 370–87. Berlin rebuts Kocis's thesis in 'Reply to Kocis' in *Political Studies*, 31 (1983), 388–93. Berlin has not responded to Polanowska's dissertation (which is written in Polish); for an English version of her sympathetic views, see Beata Polanowska-Sygulska, 'One Voice More on Berlin's Doctrine of Liberty' in *Political Studies*, 37 (1989), 123–7.

[24] Some notable attempts are the relatively short articles by Lieberson and Morgenbesser for the *New York Review of Books*, now reprinted in *Isaiah Berlin: A Celebration*; Roger Hausheer's 'Introduction' to *AC*, pp. xiii–liii and his 'Berlin and the Emergence of Liberal Pluralism' in Pierre Manent, *et al.*, *European Liberty* (The Hague, 1983), 49–80; and Bernard Williams's 'Introduction' to *CC*, pp. xi–xviii.

[25] On the task of compiling Sir Isaiah's bibliography see Henry Hardy, 'Editing Isaiah Berlin's Writings' in *British Book News* (Jan. 1978), 3, 5.

[26] J. Gray, Jesus College, Oxford (correspondence, 14 Mar. 1988).

Berlin's work in the history of ideas, his understanding of human nature, his reflections on the philosophy of history and modern society, with his defence of negative liberty.[27] Richard Wollheim echoes this need.[28] The fact that two *Festschriften* have been published in his lifetime is further evidence to the need for systematic treatment.[29]

This book aims to meet this demand. In what follows, I present a systematic, and virtually exhaustive, survey of his work. However, I focus principally on Berlin's defence of political liberalism. I am less concerned with the veracity of Berlin's studies in the history of ideas, in whether he understands Turgenev or Machiavelli adequately, still less in whether his judgements about Verdi and Wagner as composers are defensible; but more with what his studies lead him to conclude about the importance of liberal principles to modern civil society, and how these can be defended. It is the purpose of this book to link together most, if not all, of the strands which form Berlin's defence of political liberalism. The emerging complexity of this defence will not only correct a number of misinterpretations, but will point to a way to approach political theory and justify liberal practice, to which an increasing number of theorists are returning for enlightenment and guidance.

Overview of the Chapters and Arguments

Chapter 2 begins the reconstruction of Berlin's work with a discussion of his understanding of the history of ideas, philosophy, and moral and political theory. The chapter is methodological; it shows that Berlin's studies in the humanities have focused on supporting his fundamental intuitions about individual liberty. For example, he is an ardent critic of scientific history and of determinism in historical studies. He is also critical of attempts to assimilate philosophy in general, and moral and political theory in

[27] Conversations, Keble College, Oxford (27 May and 3 June 1988).
[28] R. Wollheim, 'The Idea of a Common Human Nature' in Edna and Avishai Margalit, *Isaiah Berlin: A Celebration* (1991), 64–79; 64.
[29] The first came at the start of Hardy's publication project (see Alan Ryan (ed.), *The Idea of Freedom: Essays in Honour of Isaiah Berlin* (Oxford, 1979)). The second came within a year of the fifth volume of Hardy's edited series (see *Isaiah Berlin: A Celebration* (1991)).

particular, to either the natural or formal sciences. He takes political theory to be irreducible to either empirical or analytical proposi- tions; it is a hybrid discourse that includes conceptual, empirical, and normative propositions and arguments. This chapter prepares my claim that Berlin's defence of political liberalism, in particular as presented in the 'Two Concepts' essay, does not rest solely on conceptual arguments about the use of the term 'liberty'. It is no accident that one encounters conceptual, empirical, and normative arguments in his defence of political liberalism; Berlin follows his own prescribed method.

Chapter 3 uncovers Berlin's model of human nature and society. Here I have followed his own interpretative dictum, which holds that every moral or political philosophy rests on a particular model or vision of human nature and society. Consequently, I reconstruct the model of human nature and society that sustains Berlin's political liberalism, and discuss his view that freedom is part of human nature as much as moral action is; in fact, for Berlin, moral action presupposes free will. I also present what is perhaps Berlin's most distinctive contribution to moral theory: his view that our moral life is pluralistic, and hence that not all goods are compatible or commensurable. This not only defines the ambit of theory in ethics, at least as a guide to correct action, it undermines all perfectibilist theory in political and social thought. In addition, I show that Berlin's theory of moral pluralism does not result in ethical relativism. This is because he abides by a minimum content and empirical theory of natural law; this point is taken up again and developed in Chapter 5, where the linkages between pluralism and liberalism in Berlin's thought are presented.

Chapter 4 deals with the conceptual side of Berlin's defence of political liberalism, in particular his famous distinction between negative and positive liberty. I show that Berlin's distinction between freedom *from* (negative liberty) and freedom *to* (positive liberty) rests on a reading of the history of ideas, and of the political consequences of holding to particular conceptions of liberty. On the one hand, he points out two important conceptual uses of the word liberty in the history of Western thought and political affairs. On the other, he is concerned with exposing the consequences of political movements, ideologies, and polities that emphasize one use to the exclusion of the other. In his conceptual analysis, Berlin does not so much argue that negative liberty is true freedom;

rather, he is arguing that negative liberty is 'basic' to all coherent and plausible understandings of liberty. According to Berlin, it is senseless to speak of liberty without including claims about non-interference, and opportunities for action, which is what negative liberty is about. This is true no matter what one may do with one's liberty, or how one may express oneself with it. Opportunities and freedom from interference are at play (at least, if one wishes to act freely) regardless of the propriety of one's free acts, or whether one acts individually or collectively. For freedom to exist, one or one's group must be able to act without interference. In this sense, the concept of negative liberty is 'basic' to all types of freedom.

But these distinctions do not carry us very far. They do help us avoid the abuses of language, and protect us from being swayed by tyrants who speak untruthfully, or by the cant of ideologies; but more is needed to defend political liberalism, to defend civil polities. Berlin furnishes some additional arguments. Because he takes political theory to be a hybrid discourse, one that needs to apply normative and empirical arguments, and not just conceptual ones, and because he is a historian of ideas, Berlin naturally conducts his defence on more than a conceptual front. His defence works at a high order of abstraction as well as on the concrete level of history and politics. This distinguishes him from the analytical philosophers of his day and continues to distinguish him from much Anglo-American political thought. None the less, it is these empirical, historical, prudential, and normative facets of his defence that are so often missed by critics of the distinction between negative and positive liberty. The result is that his defence of liberalism has been reduced to his analysis of *that distinction alone*; when in fact, much more is involved in the case he makes.

Hence it is important to explore these additional facets, organize them, and present them in the best possible order. I have done this in Chapters 5 to 7, where his model of human nature and society is analysed and linked to the defence of liberal institutions. His debt to nineteenth-century French liberalism is noted in Chapter 6, and I show how he updates arguments first used against Robespierre and Napoleon in his attempt to deal with twentieth-century enemies of liberty, such as Hitler and Stalin.

Chapter 7 offers another little-known facet of Berlin's work that again distinguishes him among twentieth-century liberals: the importance he attaches to the need to belong. While he tells us that he chooses to live in Britain and feels at home there, he claims to being 'formed by three traditions—Russian, British, Jewish'. His liberalism and empiricism are clearly British in origin; his Russian roots figure in his love of ideas, and are expressed in his studies of Russian writers, and his love of Turgenev in particular; but he states that his Jewish roots have shown him the importance of belonging, of the human need for a home.[30] I present in Chapter 7 Berlin's Zionist writings, dealing with this need to belong, and his studies of the founding of Israel. While he criticizes the policies of right-wing governments in Israel, Berlin demonstrates sensitivity to community, and the hope and tragedy that communal attachments engender in politics.

In this sense, Berlin cannot be accused of being unsympathetic to communal sentiment. But he is not so easily brought into a camp that would justify authority on the basis of community values or tradition, let alone unlimited authority based on such sentiments. Although sensitive to context and community, to a majority tradition, he is aware of the need to limit authority, especially given the resources of the modern state. It is a sense of history that preserves him from being carried away with concern for locality, community, nation. This is part of his British-bred scepticism, and even-keeled moral sense.

In Chapter 8 I conclude that there are many advantages to Berlin's defence of political liberalism. It is based on a theory of human nature, of human needs and interests, as well as on an empirical and historical interpretation of cultures. Little is abstract here. He does not claim that we would all accept liberal principles if we had an impartial moral viewpoint, or would decide what is best for everyone while ignoring our own particular status in society. His tack is different: it is to present human beings as he knows them, and to argue about what political arrangements are needed if we wish to give ourselves decent lives, without excessive misery, without tyranny, and by meeting a variety of our needs and interests. Given that most people today live under abhorrently unjust and unfree conditions, pointing out what is best for modern conditions remains no small task; to convince others, no small achievement.

[30] 'The Three Strands in My Life', 5–7.

2

INTERPRETATION AND ENLIGHTENMENT

The goal of philosophy is always the same, to assist men to understand themselves and thus operate in the open, and not wildly, in the dark.

(Isaiah Berlin, 'The Purpose of Philosophy')

In this chapter I present Isaiah Berlin's views of the nature and purpose of historical and philosophical studies. My aim is to show how Berlin's interest in these fields is not incidental, or peripheral, to his liberalism; rather, these studies support his defence of liberal political morality. He, however, is hesitant to link together his studies in the history of ideas, his understanding of the role of philosophy, and his defence of negative liberty. He will admit that, in some ways, the history of ideas underlies his defence of political liberalism. Unfortunately, he wishes to go no further.[1] The full reason is unknown; his antipathy for grand systems may perhaps explain the reticence.

None the less the links are present in his writings. It is clear to any reader that Berlin's understanding of moral pluralism owes much to a study of the history of cultures and ideas. Equally clear is that moral pluralism is a pillar of his defence of liberal institutions. Less well known is the fact that he accepts the Enlightenment notion that progress is possible in our knowledge of human nature and institutions; this is how we can know that certain ideologies have a tendency to entail tyranny, regardless of their pretensions to the contrary, while other ideologies guard against such perversions.[2] Although he hesitates to point them out, there are obvious

---

[1] Athenaeum interview.
[2] This seems to me to be an important presupposition of the argument in 'Two Concepts of Liberty' (1958).

ties between Berlin's historiography, his understanding of the role of philosophy, and his moral and political beliefs.

The most famous of his books, *Four Essays on Liberty* (1969), contains many of these ties. There one finds a fine interweaving of conceptual analysis, the history of particular ideas, such as liberty and tyranny, as well as a presentation of the argument that moral goods are plural. And for Berlin, if moral goods are plural, then they cannot all be combined without loss; thus choice and loss are both unavoidable in moral life. Because certain liberals, including himself, recognize this fact about moral life, they are truer to the human condition than all the moral philosophers who deny either the centrality of choice or the plurality of values.

The linking of these interests and beliefs began early in Berlin's academic career. In 1929, as a first-year undergraduate in Classics at Corpus Christi College, Oxford, Berlin wrote an essay entitled, 'Pelican s'en va-t-en guerre: A Tale of War and Peace'. This essay exhibits an early passion for enlightenment and personal liberty.[3] The essay is a moral fable, similar to those of Aesop and La Fontaine, telling the story of a pelican, who, with his 'feathered minions', decides one day to descend on a nearby quad populated by magpies and a robin. The pelicans annex the quad and put the magpies under the charge of a pelican governor, Sinistrari. Notwithstanding his brusque exterior, this governor has a soft heart. The magpies remain placid subjects, and, whenever perplexed, they seek guidance from a 'sacred kettle' located in the middle of the quad. The robin cannot understand such idolatry and decides one day to put the kettle to a test. The robin asks: 'Kettle, surely the time for rebellion has come?' The kettle responds merely by giving 'forty gurgling reasons why it was better to submit'.

Pugnacious by nature, and unsatisfied with the answer, the robin begins abusing the kettle, first with words, and then by overturning it. The magpies retreat to their rooms, fearful of the consequences of this act of vandalism and sacrilege. Hearing the ruckus, the governor presents himself. Even the robin fears this manifestation; yet, unlike the magpies, his fear quickly turns to courage. The robin stands steadfast and audaciously addresses the pelican thus: 'Good evening, Sinistrari, I feel sure that you have never heard of what the navvy said to the bishop's wife when she asked him what

[3] I. Berlin, 'Pelican s'en va-t-en guerre: A Tale of War and Peace' in the *Pelican Record* (magazine of Corpus Christi College), 11 (Mar. 1929), 34–6.

he was doing. "What are you doing my man," says she; "nothing particular," says he, "only . . ." ' The magpies are terrified, but the pelican governor is impressed and amused by such courageous insolence. Sinistrari and the robin exchange amusing words and eventually, laughter and merriment break out. The magpies sense that the old order is no more. They 'fear their lord no more, they have now found a sure way to his heart, which they have discovered to be softer than honey. Prosperity and happiness have succeeded the Reign of Terror in Magpieland, and, as its citizens loudly boast, it is now little short of being an Earthly Paradise.'

Berlin concludes that while '[t]here is obviously some highly interesting moral to be drawn from so long a story', he does not know or propose one. An interpreter familiar with the city plan and symbols of Oxford knows that a pelican is the symbol of Corpus Christi College, that Magpie Lane is near the College, and so on. This fable may refer to some particular incident in the College, but the tale of despotism and liberation might have had a wider target. The 'Reign of Terror in Magpieland' could have referred at the time to the Soviet Union, which Berlin left at the age of 9. But for my purposes I wish to explore other meanings.

The story is one of courageous defiance in the face of illegitimate authority and social conformity. All liberals agree that the right of conquest is unjustifiable. In liberal theory, consent, not force, is the basis of a legitimate order. When faced with invaders, or native usurpers of power, liberal theory, at least since La Boétie, Locke, and Diderot, has argued for the legitimacy, even the duty, of revolt. Since Benjamin Constant and J. S. Mill, liberals have argued that freedom is needed to avoid the tyranny of majority opinion, to allow for individual and social variety. Berlin's fable exhibits this concern with the bases of legitimate authority, and a distaste for uniformity. Furthermore, the tale speaks of the importance of critical attention to public symbols of power. After questioning the kettle, the robin becomes convinced of the illegitimacy, stupidity, and conformist aspects of the pelican order. This oracle befuddled the magpies; it made them accept their domination against their best interests. The robin is driven to find enlightenment. It cannot accept idolatry or slavish conformity and, as a free thinker, it demands good reasons for accepting a particular political order. When none are given, both the source of the confusion and the order itself are overturned.

Like the robin, Berlin's work is driven by the twin goals of enlightenment and liberty. The history of ideas is one part of contemporary self-knowledge and knowledge of society. But it is a crucial part because it enables one to know 'from the inside' what motivates people to be free or enslaved. It also allows us to grasp the sense of past moral beliefs, the lineages of present norms, so that we may more adequately question their validity today. For Berlin, such self-knowledge prepares the way to a critical review of the ideologies of this century, from liberalism and socialism to fascism and communism.

What does Berlin mean by the history of ideas? What is its purpose? How does this study relate to philosophy in general, and moral and political philosophy in particular? What are their purposes?

The History of Ideas: Vico and the Birth of Historicism

History has not always been well regarded. Certainly the ancients had their great historians, Herodotus, Thucydides, Tacitus, and Livy. History was the tale of great deeds and offered, to all who were interested, ennobling stories of courage and weakness, glory and shame, wisdom and folly, splendour and decay. But philosophical movements have often dismissed history as bunk. This view was strongly expressed at the beginning of the modern age, and is no doubt related to the birth of modern science.[4]

For many early modern philosophers the model of perfect knowledge was mathematics or mechanics. Such models offered clear, distinct, self-evident knowledge. The knowledge one could derive from the study of man, his behaviour and institutions, was viewed as comparatively untidy, unclear, vague, and less than self-evident. Hence, from the birth of modern science throughout the age of Enlightenment, mathematics and the natural sciences became the rod to measure all other forms of knowledge. The study of history was correspondingly degraded, at least as the source of true and immutable knowledge. As a result, countless attempts were made to turn history and ethics into a branch of science, the goal being systematic knowledge. If there could be a

---

[4] See *VH*, 9–12.

science of nature, there could surely be one of man, for he was part of nature.[5]

Throughout his academic career, Berlin has sought to resist this assimilation of the study of human nature to the study of natural processes and formal systems, such as mathematics and logic. This project began early in his career, while he was still an analytical philosopher, and in the thick of neo-positivist debates. In two essays from this period, 'Verification' (1939) and 'Empirical Propositions and Hypothetical Statements' (1950), Berlin criticized the view, then one of the cornerstones of logical positivism, that the meaning of statements about the world is equivalent to the procedures we use to verify such statements. Berlin also attacked the phenomenalist tenets expounded by his friend and Oxford philosopher, A. J. Ayer. The latter argued that statements about the external world could be reduced to statements about our actual sense perceptions. Against the neo-positivist theory of verification, Berlin argued that many of our beliefs about the world, such as its independent existence, are valid regardless of the procedures used to verify existential propositions. Against Ayer's phenomenalism, Berlin stated that many forms of knowledge, such as our intuitions about the independent existence of the world and other selves, and our knowledge of history, are irreducible to actual or possible sense-data and the procedures to verify the correctness of such data.[6]

Berlin therefore criticized the logical positivists and A. J. Ayer for reducing all provinces of human experience to one standard of analysis. He found them guilty of reductionist designs and in a later essay, 'Logical Translation' (1950), Berlin expanded his critique of methodological monism. He argued against the tendency of logicians and epistemologists to classify propositions and judgements into various types, and seek to extract from them simple, or atomic, or basic parts. While many of his contemporaries were targets of criticism, such as Ayer and Bertrand Russell, Berlin was making a general claim about the history of philosophical analysis. He stated that the search for basic and fundamental propositions, or an underlying set of formal or empirical rules of verification of

[5] See I. Berlin, *The Age of the Enlightenment* (Boston, Mass., 1956), 11–29.

[6] See 'Verification' and 'Empirical Propositions and Hypothetical Statements', in *CC*, 12–31 and 32–55, respectively. See also Bernard Williams's comments in the 'Introduction' to *CC* pp. xii–xiii.

knowledge of all things, is as old as Western philosophy; early modern scientific theory was not unique in this regard.

Methodological monism can be traced to the ancient Ionian physicists who asked such questions as 'What is everything made of?' and answered that 'Everything is made of water, fire, air, and earth; but that water, or fire, or air, or earth is primary'. To such views, Berlin counters with the claims that no methodological translation can occur without loss of meaning; that the natural and human worlds are not reducible one to the other; and that no set of atomic impressions underlies all known phenomena. In 'Logical Translation', he points to our use of language, its metaphorical development, our unverifiable intuitions about the world, and our knowledge of history, to show the irreducibility of certain types of knowledge either to basic formal or empirical propositions. Because of such irreducibility, and pluralism of phenomena, Berlin concludes that it is futile to search for basic propositions or impressions. Berlin calls this the 'Ionian fallacy' after the originators of this method. In the same essay, he attributes its force in the history of philosophy to a psychological desire for certainty and metaphysical security. Unfortunately, belief in methodological monism forces one to think like Procrustes: one must cut off (or stretch) those experiences, those statements, which do not fit one's particular bed of formal or empirical rules.[7]

In his early writings, Berlin had already argued the case for methodological pluralism, at least with regard to literary criticism.[8] But it was not until the 1950s that he began to study in detail the methods particular to the humanities. In his Auguste Comte Lecture 'Historical Inevitability' (1953) and his essay 'The Concept of Scientific History' (1960), he argues that historical knowledge is not a species of scientific knowledge.[9] Historical knowledge is about human agency, or collective and individual behaviour, or the meaning of acts and institutions; and because of this, intentions, motives, and purposes are essential to understanding and explaining history. Yet such phenomena are not studied by the natural

[7] 'Logical Translation' in *CC*, 56–80. For details on the philosophical atmosphere of Oxford during this period, in particular the anti-historical bias of his colleagues, see 'Giambattista Vico', in the *Listener*, 88 (28 Sept. 1972), 391–8.

[8] I. Berlin, 'Some Procrustations', in *Oxford Outlook*, 10 (1930), 491–502.

[9] 'Historical Inevitability', repr. in *FE*, 41–117; and 'The Concept of Scientific History', repr. in *CC*, 103–42.

sciences, for they are not needed: one cannot know the intentions of rocks, for they have none. We observe non-human phenomena from the outside; it is only human phenomena that we come to know 'from the inside'. The point is that one needs to know the intentions of historical actors to comprehend and explain their actions. Berlin argues that this knowledge is different from that acquired by the methods of the natural sciences. This is how he relates the differences:

The contrast I mean is one between different types of knowledge. When the Jews are enjoined in the Bible to protect strangers, 'for ye know the heart of a stranger, seeing ye were strangers in the land of Egypt', this knowledge is neither deductive, nor inductive, nor founded on direct inspection, but akin to the 'I know' of 'I know what it is to be hungry and poor', or 'I know how political bodies function', or 'I know what it is to be a Brahmin'. This is neither (to make use of Gilbert Ryle's useful classification) the 'knowing that' which the sciences provide, nor the 'knowing how' which is the possession of a disposition or skill, nor the knowledge of direct perception, acquaintance, memory, but the type of knowledge that an administrator or politician must possess of the men with whom he deals. . . .

It might be that the deepest chasm which divides historical from scientific studies lies between the outlook of the external observer and of the actor. It is this that was brought out by the contrast between 'inner' and 'outer' which Vico initiated, and after him the Germans, and is so suspect to modern positivists; between questions 'How?' or 'What?' or 'When?' on one side, and the questions 'Why?', 'Following what rule?', 'Towards what goal?', 'Springing from what motive?' on the other. It lies in the difference between the category of mere togetherness or succession (the correlations to which all sciences can in the end be reduced), and that of coherence and interpretation; between factual knowledge and understanding.[10]

Berlin credits the seventeenth-century Neapolitan jurist and philosopher Giambattista Vico with the discovery of this new type of knowledge.[11] Vico had uncovered this new type of knowledge by accepting the view that mathematics gives us clear and

[10] 'The Concept of Scientific History', in *CC*, 136, 137. Notice that Berlin himself is guilty of reducing science to one kind of enterprise, that is, the search for empirical correlations. Philosophers of science, such as Karl Popper, Thomas Kuhn, and Paul Feyerabend, have shown that the methods of science are varied and complex (see Morgenbesser and Lieberson, 'Isaiah Berlin', 7–15, esp. 14).
[11] See I. Berlin, 'One of the Boldest Innovators in the History of Human Thought', in Ben B. Seligman (ed.), *Molders of Modern Thought* (Chicago, 1970), 41–56; and *VH*, 11–41.

indubitable knowledge. But this is not because mathematics mirrors the structure of nature. Vico claimed that mathematical knowledge is pure and certain because we have made it *ex nihilo* from axioms devised in our minds. We have certain knowledge of mathematical principles because we have created them, and not because they may help us organize our perceptions of the world. This insight Vico stated in the principle that *Verum et factum convertuntur*—'the true (*verum*) and the made (*factum*) are convertible'.[12]

This principle had its roots in medieval scholastic thought, in the belief that only a creator knows fully what he creates. Thus God knows all of nature because he is its creator. Since we have not created nature, natural processes and natural purposes are opaque to us. The boldness of Vico, according to Berlin, was to apply the *verum/factum* principle to the possibility of knowledge that men have of themselves, their institutions, their histories. If the principle is correct, then we have an 'inside' view of all our creations, including art, morals, institutions, the economy, and so on. Moreover, we understand history in a more direct sense than we do nature. God is the sole creator of nature, and thus only God can know nature fully. We observe nature at a disadvantage, from the outside, with no understanding of the first and final causes of nature.[13]

On the other hand, we are not just spectators of historical phenomena, but also participants in it—actors—and thus creators of historical deeds and artefacts. We can know history fully because history is a human creation; as a result, historical knowledge is a form of self-knowledge—it concerns human actions and human institutions. Vico concluded that human self-knowledge, including historical knowledge, could be as perfect as that found in mathematics, if only the principles or laws of historical development were fully apprehended.[14]

The *verum/factum* principle was a revolutionary discovery; Vico made it legitimate to say that we, as historians, can reconstruct in

---

[12] *VH*, 15–16.

[13] Ibid. 99–142; 'Giambattista Vico,' in the *Listener*, 88 (28 Sept. 1972), 391–8. See Vico's 'On the Ancient Wisdom of the Italians Taken from the Origins of the Latin Language', in L. Pompa (ed. and trans.), *Vico: Selected Writings* (Cambridge, 1982), 50–2.

[14] *VH*, 64–7. See also 'Vico's Concept of Knowledge' in *AC*, 111–19.

our imaginations the purposes and goals that motivated past actors. We can do this because, we, like our historical subjects, have goals and purposes which motivate us to action. By grasping hold of these intentions we give full, rounded, and realistic representation of past cultures and historical events. Vico called this capacity of sympathetic understanding *fantasia*.[15] Its revolutionary character resides in the fact that it leads to knowledge different in kind from that acquired by scientific method. By discovering the *verum/factum* principle, Vico became the founder of the humanities.

Berlin follows Vico in believing that proper history and human self-understanding are impossible without some form of re-constructive imagination.[16] Historical writing and historical explanation cannot do without 'speaking of agents, their motives, their purposes, fears, hopes, feelings, ideas, acts: not only those of individual human beings, but those of groups or classes or movements or institutions or entire societies'. In other words, proper historical writing and explanation evoke the 'concrete texture of a society' and present 'the reader with a picture of human life—the complete experience of a society as a possible form of life, something which could have occurred, and which the evidence available makes sufficiently probable'. This is what gives 'depth' to, or what one means by 'deep', historical writing.[17]

To achieve such depth, historical writing must avoid dealing with historical facts as experimental data, as facts to confirm or disprove some general law of human behaviour. A history written solely according to putative laws of behaviour does not give meaning to acts. Scientific history is too shallow to give relevant explanations. It does not evoke the living fabric of an age, a person's character, the meaning of a symbol or ritual in the context of a whole cultural formation.[18] For this one needs understanding based on the grasp of human qualities; something which abstract models cannot provide. Thus to understand the meaning of

---

[15] *VH*, 30–2 and 107–12. See Vico's 'On the Ancient Wisdom of the Italians Taken from the Origins of the Latin Language' and his *The [First] New Science*, in Pompa (ed.), *Vico: Selected Writings*, 69; 120–1.

[16] Athenaeum interview. See also Berlin's essay 'Giambattista Vico and Cultural History', in *CTH*, 49–69, esp. 65–6.

[17] I. Berlin, 'Is a Philosophy of History Possible?, in Yirmiahu Yovel (ed.), *Philosophy of History and Action* (Dordrecht, 1978), 219–25 at 223–4.

[18] 'The Concept of Scientific History', in *CC*, 131–4.

historical action, more needs to be known than behaviour patterns.
Motives, purposes, ends, evaluations, have to be grasped, compre-
hended, or related to institutions, laws, and familiar conduct. Only
in this fashion can a meaningful rendition and explanation of
historical action be provided. Hence the ends of historical research
are to produce, by Berlin's account, an 'inside view' of events: what
it could have been like to want to win a battle, to worship a sun
god, to act with fellow citizens and wage war against one's enemy;
or to live in another age with different ideals and practices from
one's own. The ability to evoke such historical facts calls upon
imagination, aesthetic talent, moral discrimination, the abilities of
the novelist or playwright. Hence historical explanation exhibits
'depth of insight' when it paints a picture of the living and vibrant
texture of a society.[19] To elaborate, Berlin tells us that,

historical explanation is related to moral and aesthetic analysis, in so far as
it presupposes conceiving of human beings not merely as organisms in
space, the regularities of whose behaviour can be described and locked in
labour-saving formulas, but as active beings, pursuing ends, shaping their
own and other's lives, feeling, reflecting, imagining, creating, in constant
interaction and intercommunication with other human beings; in short,
engaged in all the forms of experience that we understand because we share
in them, and do not view them purely as external observers. This is what is
called the inside view: and it renders possible and indeed inescapable
explanation whose primary function is not to predict or extrapolate, or
even control, but fit the loose and fleeting objects of sense, imagination,

---

[19] 'The Concept of Scientific History', 140–2. This understanding of explanation
in the humanities owes much to Berlin's theory of artistic interpretation. It may pre-
date his reading of Vico. As early as 1930 Berlin wrote that great artistic expression
in music is typified by the self-effacement of the interpreter, of his or her ability to
evoke the intentions of the composer. He credits the twentieth-century pianist,
Arthur Schnabel, as one of the greatest of these interpreters (see Albert Alfred
Apricot [Berlin's *nom de guerre*], 'Music Chronicle', in *Oxford Outlook*, 53 (Nov.
1930), 616–27; and 'Lament for Lipatti', in *House and Garden*, 7 (1952), 91, 98). Much
the same standard of authenticity is applied by Berlin in his judgement of
composers. For instance, he considers Verdi to be the last great humanist composer:
'He was the last great voice of humanism not at war with itself, at any rate in music.'
His operas express 'major human emotions'. As a composer Verdi 'expressed
permanent states of consciousness in the most direct terms: as Homer, Shakespeare,
Ibsen, and Tolstoy have done.' Accordingly, Verdi's operatic art is more authentic
than that of composers who seek to use their art to convey personal messages or
favoured ideologies, such as Wagner for example ('The "*Naïveté*" of Verdi' in *AC*,
287–95 at 294–5). For a discussion of Berlin's views on opera, see Bernard Williams,
'Naive and Sentimental Opera Lovers' in Edna and Avishai Margalit (eds.), *Isaiah
Berlin: A Celebration*, 180–92.

intellect, into the central succession of patterns that we call normal, and which is the ultimate criterion of reality as against illusion, incoherence, fiction. History is merely the mental projection into the past of this activity of selection and adjustment, the search for coherence and unity, together with the attempt to refine it with all the self-consciousness of which we are capable, by bringing to its aid everything that we conceive to be useful—all the sciences, all the knowledge and skills, and all the theories that we have acquired, from whatever quarter.[20]

To reiterate, Berlin credits Vico with discovering and defending historical knowledge. Although he did not directly influence them, Vico's *verum/factum* principle was reborn as the centrepiece of the German Historical School, starting with J. G. von Herder. According to Berlin, the whole German historicist tradition, and later the interpretative sociology of Max Weber, reproduced Vico's original insights. Dilthey's distinction between the *Geistes-wissenschaften* (humanities) and the *Naturwissenschaften* (natural sciences) was presaged by Vico's bold new principle which claimed that, what man could make, including history, he could know better than what he did not make, such as nature.[21] This elevation and defence of historical knowledge not only undermined the imperialist pretensions of scientific rationalism, but ushered in a 'divorce between the sciences and the humanities'; a divorce that contemporary academic culture, for good and ill, still accepts as binding.[22]

[20] 'The Concept of Scientific History', 132–3.
[21] Berlin tells a detailed story of Vico's reception in 'Corsi e Ricorsi' in *Journal of Modern History*, 50 (1978), 480–9. See also 'The Divorce between the Sciences and the Humanities' in *AC*, 80–110; and Berlin's 'Foreword' to the J. E. Anderson translation of Friedrich Meinecke's *Historism: The Rise of a New Historical Outlook* (London, 1972) pp. ix–xvi. For a list of Vico's discoveries, see *VH*, pp. xvi–xix; 'Giambattista Vico', in *Listener*, 88 (1972), 492; and 'One of the Boldest Innovators in the History of Human Thought', in Seligman (ed.), *Molders of Modern Thought*, 41–56. Berlin has been criticized for exaggerating Vico's originality. See Hans Aarsleff, 'Vico and Berlin', in *London Review of Books*, 3 (5–18 Nov. 1981), 6–7. Berlin replies to these criticisms in the same issue, 7–8. See also Arthur H. Scouten's review of *Vico and Herder*, in *Comparative Literature Studies*, 15 (1978), 336–40. Berlin's reply to this review was published as 'Professor Scouten on Herder and Vico' in *Comparative Literature Studies*, 16 (1979), 141–5. Finally, Peter Burke has criticized Berlin and others for creating a myth about the originality of Vico's ideas (see Peter Burke, *Vico* (Past Masters Series; Oxford, 1985), 1–9. Even if it is myth making, the point remains that historical and scientific knowledge differ, and that Berlin is a proponent of the uniqueness and advocate of the validity of the former.
[22] Unlike Vico, Berlin does not believe that historical knowledge is better than scientific knowledge—they are just different kinds of knowledge (see his 'On Vico'

But this is not all that Vico initiated. Berlin claims that Vico discovered the modern 'concept of culture'. From his study of Vico, Berlin concludes that cultures exhibit their own internal unity, or 'a pervasive pattern which characterizes all the activities of any given society: a common style reflected in the thought, the arts, the social institutions, the language, the ways of life and action, of an entire society'.[23] Therefore, the context of human creation becomes essential to understanding the meaning of historical artefacts and events. Accordingly, the business of the cultural historian is to grasp this totality of a past age, of the full context of action and artefacts. In effect, 'the creations of man—laws, institutions, religions, rituals, works of art, language, song, rules of conduct and the like—. . .' cannot be understood except within their specific cultural context.[24]

Moreover, what began in the Renaissance as an attempt to recover the timeless wisdom of the ancients, paradoxically ended with a creeping suspicion of the historical specificity of customs, mores, laws, institutions, and the conceptions of human nature and society that support them. This was because the reading of actual documents for their authentic meaning eventually led to the view that there exists a plurality of cultures.[25]

Hence Renaissance studies, and later cultural historical studies, unwittingly shook one of the foundations of Western thought, namely, the belief in natural law and a fixed order to human nature.[26] I will deal with the substantive implications for moral theory of cultural pluralism in Chapters 3 and 5. What is important here are the methodological implications of the historicist tenet that cultures are unique and varied in composition.

If cultures are understandable mainly in their own terms, then the student of cultural manifestations—mores, artistic styles, even the history of scientific theories—has to guard against errors of

in *Philosophical Quarterly*, 35 (1985), 281–90). Nor does Berlin accept the view that there are 'two cultures', one for the humanities and one for the sciences. Rather, he sees at work two different forms of judgement, two types of cognitive skills (see 'The Divorce between the Sciences and the Humanities' in *AC*, 80–110; and 'The Concept of Scientific History' in *CC*, 140–2). In his essay, 'General Education' in *Oxford Review of Education*, 1 (1975), 287–92, Berlin argues that a rapprochement between these divorcees can only be achieved by a comprehensive curriculum, that is, a combined liberal-arts and science education.

[23] *VH*, p. xvii.
[24] Ibid., p. xviii.
[25] Ibid. 125–42.
[26] Ibid., p. xvi, 133–42.

anachronism and parochialism when interpreting such manifestations. And if cultural manifestations have to be understood in context, then it is a gross distortion of the facts of history to apply contemporary standards to past ages.

The problems of anachronism and parochialism are clearest in aesthetics. Vico teaches us the importance of taking into account the specificity of social and historical eras, 'of the inexorable succession of the stages of development'. One must know the order of things before one can understand the meaning of artistic expression, otherwise, it would be impossible to understand why *Hamlet*, for example, could not have been written at the court of Genghis Khan.[27] Knowing *what fits when* is an essential attribute of aesthetics no less than historical judgement. There is no transitivity in artistic styles: the joke behind Marcel Duchamp's exposition of a urinal as an art-object could not have occurred in the eighteenth century. If we were to suspend our disbelief for a minute, and imagine its presentation, such a work would certainly fall flat; it no doubt would have been vilified by someone like Sir Joshua Reynolds. The twentieth-century critique of eternal aesthetic standards, the impetus behind exhibiting *un objet trouvé*, would have made little sense to a firm believer, like Reynolds, in eternal forms in the art of portraiture. Nor, to take another example, could Aristotle or Polybius have held to modern notions of progress; they believed in a cyclical theory of time, of the rise and inevitable decline of civilizations. Today, the nineteenth-century belief in unchecked progress is beyond the ken of our cynical and hypersceptical age, which some call postmodern.

Once again, Berlin credits Vico with discovering this truth. Vico used the example of Homer, and said that his heroic poetry could only have been written in a mythopoetic age.[28] The metaphors used in Homeric poems, the role of the gods, and the focus on heroes all come from an enchanted age. In order to understand the meaning of the metaphors used in the poems, and understand a people who could name the sky 'Jove', one has to recreate in one's imagination an age and culture that had animistic beliefs.[29] And to

---

[27] 'The Concept of Scientific History' in *CC*, 134–5.

[28] See Vico, *The [Third] New Science* in Pompa (ed.), *Vico: Selected Writings*, 209–14.

[29] *VH*, 42–55. See Berlin's essay, 'Vico and the Ideal of the Enlightenment' in *AC*, 120–9.

do this one must be able to know *what fits when*; that is, to exhibit the

kind of awareness (the historical sense) that is said to enable us to perceive that a certain type of legal structure is 'intimately connected' with, or is part of the same complex as, an economic activity, a moral outlook, a style of writing or of dancing or of worship; it is by means of this gift (whatever may be its nature) that we recognise various manifestations of the human spirit as 'belonging to' this or that culture or nation or historical period, although these manifestations may be as different from one another as the way in which men form letters on paper from their system of land tenure. Without this faculty we should attach no sense to such social-historical notions as 'the typical', or 'the normal', or 'the discordant', or 'the anachronistic', and consequently we should be unable to conceive the history of an institution as an intelligible pattern, or to attribute a work of art to its time and civilisation and milieu, or indeed to understand or explain how one phase of civilisation 'generates' or 'determines' another. This sense of what remains identical or unitary in differences and in change (of which idealist philosophers have made altogether too much) is also a dominant factor in giving us our sense of unalterable trends, of the 'one-directional' flow of history.[30]

Historical interpretation combines a measure of imagination with historical evidence. We have to grasp the essentials of a cultural formation in order to compare it with our own, to judge its advantages and disadvantages, as well as our successes and failings in light of past moral ideals. A cultural formation rarely, if ever, eclipses another. This is presupposed by the *verum/factum* principle. We understand what we have made. Yet all civilizations seek to meet basic human needs. As long as we live and act in societies and express ourselves in cultural works, a sufficient amount of universality exists for one age to understand the ideals and ways of life of another age. The same is true of the plurality of existing cultures. We may be self-transformative beings, exhibiting many life forms, but we are not gods who can transfigure themselves into any shape, nor are we animals with fixed dispositions and immutable needs. Human beings lie in the middle: human nature is manifold; dispositions and capacities are revealed over time, but not so radically as to preclude understanding between ages and cultures. This is an important point, for as I will show in later

---

[30] 'The Concept of Scientific History' in *CC*, 109–10.

chapters, it is a part of Berlin's argument against ethical relativism.[31]

Berlin develops this point by deducing that certain basic 'concepts and categories' must exist for our knowledge of human affairs.[32] Berlin is not speaking about the Kantian categories of time and space, which Kant saw as the condition for the possibility of our knowledge of the physical world. What Berlin means by 'concepts and categories' of human experience refers to the various basic notions that must be presupposed if we are to have any knowledge of cultural life. These notions are, for example, those we assume when we speak of the human will as free, or when we attribute intentions, hopes and fears, loves and hates, to human actions.[33] Berlin argues that historical narrative makes sense, and historical explanations are plausible only if they include such basic 'concepts and categories' of human existence. He elaborates:

The categories and concepts in terms of which situations and events and processes are described and explained in such accounts are, to a large extent, imprecise; they have a so-called 'open texture'. They are the everyday notions common to mankind at large, related to the permanent interests of men as such. They may be modified at particular periods, in particular countries, by particular circumstances, but all of them are species of basic human attitudes, outlooks, goals, beliefs. Without some degree of understanding—indeed, sharing of—these concepts, it would not be possible to understand either men or history at all.

If this were not so, we should scarcely be able to understand Homer or Herodotus as, at least to some extent, we claim to be able to do, in spite of the fact that they wrote about societies widely different from our own. If you ask, for example, such a question as why some historical figure acted as he did, the explanation of his behaviour is likely to rest upon the use of concepts, categories and beliefs about human nature, which we take for granted in our everyday lives, and upon the assumption that much, if not all, of these similarly entered the outlook of our predecessors from the beginnings of recorded history.[34]

---

[31] Athenaeum interview. See 'Giambattista Vico and Cultural History' in *CTH*, 59–62; I. Berlin, 'Note on Alleged Relativism in Eighteenth-Century European Thought' in *CTH*, 70–90; and his 'Reply to Kocis' in *Political Studies*, 31 (1983), 388–93.

[32] See 'The Purpose of Philosophy' in *CC*, 7–8; 'Does Political Theory Still Exist?' in *CC* 162–6 at 165; and *VH*, 73–89, 196.

[33] 'The Concept of Scientific History' in *CC*, 129 ff; and 'Does Political Theory Still Exist?' in *CC*, 166.

[34] 'Is a Philosophy of History Possible?' in Yovel (ed.), *Philosophy of History and Action*, 221–2.

These basic concepts and categories organize our experience of historical phenomena. They are neither exclusively empirical, nor exclusively formal; neither solely a priori nor solely a posteriori. Yet 'fundamental categories of human experience' are presupposed in any plausible recording and retelling of human action.[35] Historical explanations would not be intelligible otherwise. Berlin speaks of a need to grasp the 'social *Gestalt*' of human experience; or, in another formulation, to apprehend the '*Wirkungszusammenhang*, the general structure or pattern of experience'.[36]

Different mixtures of these categories and concepts, however, are present in history. Peoples have different sets of experiences, praise different things, and praise the same things differently. There are limits, to reiterate, to such permutations.[37] Yet different mixtures exist. Each civilization has what Herder called a specific 'physiognomy' or 'centre of gravity'.[38] Civilizations are characterized according to what R. G. Collingwood called 'absolute presuppositions'.[39] The cultural historian needs to keep this background of cultural norms in mind when explaining historical phenomena. This is what gives credence and veracity to historical explanation. For these reasons, Berlin concludes that a proper understanding of the 'absolute presuppositions' of civilizations makes the difference between *thick* and *thin* historical narratives, *deep* or *shallow* explanations of action. We need to know the context of actions and sentiments before fully explaining or properly judging them.[40]

Berlin believes that all historical writing, in fact all study of human behaviour, presuppose and deal with various models of human nature and society.[41] Much of his writing in the history of ideas focuses on the plurality of world-views exhibited by Western civilizations and great thinkers in Western thought. But Berlin does

---

[35] 'The Concept of Scientific History' in *CC*, 134–5.

[36] Ibid. 139.

[37] See Ibid. 135 where Berlin explains the limits to such permutations.

[38] See *VH*, pp. xxi–xxvii, 145–216.

[39] See 'Is a Philosophy of History Possible?' in Yovel (ed.), *Philosophy of History and Action*, 222–3.

[40] 'The Concept of Scientific History' in *CC*, 139; and 'Is a Philosophy of History Possible?' in Yovel (ed.), *Philosophy of History and Action*, 224. See also the discussion of the criteria to determine whether a historical writing is 'rounded' or 'flat', 'living' or 'lifeless', in *VH*, pp. xxv–xxvii.

[41] See 'The Purpose of Philosophy' in *CC*, 1–11.

not stop there. The study of the history of ideas is not just for amusement or for antiquarian interest; there are other goals at work. One of them is to come to terms with and to understand the plurality of world-views possible in Western civilization. Another is to understand how we moderns have become what we are from an analysis of our evolution. A third is to judge the worth of various models of human nature and society. All these didactic enterprises are useful in that they check the wildest fantasies about human nature and society. This is especially important with regard to utopian aspirations, the critique of which is a motive force of Berlin's work.[42]

Berlin argues that the adequacy of historical writing is determined by two things. One is how well the narrative 'fits' with our sense of what was possible at a particular time: the point here is to avoid anachronism. As Berlin says: 'What is meant by historical sense is the knowledge not of what happened, but of what did not happen.'[43] The second test of adequacy is how well the model of human nature and society used to explain action 'fits' with our sense 'of what human beings, as we understand the term, could have felt or thought or done'.[44] This second test is fundamental; beyond the problems of anachronism and parochialism, it tests what could and could not happen in any possible world of experience. Once a narrative has passed these tests, we can accept it because it gives us a plausible rendition of a possible historical event, as well as an adequate 'account of reality'.[45]

There are accounts of history which fail both tests. Scientific history, which imitates the methods of the sciences and reduces human action to general covering laws, fails the second test. Because it excludes a discussion of intentions and motives, scientific history is too 'thin' or 'flat' to be plausible. It gives an X-ray view of history, a skeletal representation, and not a vivid portrait.[46] Such an account also fails the first test because it assumes a great similarity in human conduct, and thus remains oblivious to

---

[42] See Ch. 3.
[43] 'The Concept of Scientific History' in *CC*, 140. For the Vichian discovery of the fallacy of anachronism, see *VH*, 67–73. For its development with Herder, see *VH*, 186–9.
[44] 'The Concept of Scientific History' in *CC*, 139–40.
[45] Ibid. 139.
[46] *VH*, 89; 'The Concept of Scientific History' in *CC*, 124–6.

changes in the purpose and meaning of human action across time. Oblivious to context, such a historical picture will be flat and anachronistic.

These tests of adequacy rest on our sense of what human nature is and what it has become. There are no hard-and-fast rules for their application, yet we know when a historical account fails these tests. Berlin often points out that Marx's analyses of modern society usually failed both tests. The belief that the mode of production is the determining factor in social and political affairs is simplistic. Economic determinism occludes the relevance and persistent importance of other motivations for human action. One major omission is the sense of belonging, which Herder found so crucial to human nature,[47] and which is the basis of nationalism. Marx, in contrast, argued that nationalism is epiphenomenal, linked to the bourgeois mode of production, and that it would in time, after a socialist revolution, fade away. According to Berlin, Marx's economic understanding of human nature and society impeded his vision about the importance of national sentiments in modern politics. Nationalist sentiments are not mere epiphenomena of the economy, but autonomous, and constitutive of much modern politics. Not only was Marx wrong about human nature on this account, his understanding of modern society lacked explanatory potential as well. As a result, it quickly became dated and less than useful: Marx's historical materialist theory of society could not account for the importance of nationalism in nineteenth- and twentieth-century world politics. In this case, Berlin has all the empirical evidence on his side. The withering away of nationalism, which Marx and Engels prophesied in the *Communist Manifesto*, has not occurred. In fact, state-sponsored nationalism and sub-state nationalism have become widespread. Virtually every twentieth-century political movement has used or exploited nationalist sentiment. The civil wars which have followed the collapse of communist regimes in central Europe further attest to the strength and persistence of ethnic sentiments and nationalist ideologies.[48]

The case of Marx is not unique. Berlin argues that much writing about human nature and society, in particular path-breaking

[47] *VH*, 153–65, 180–99.
[48] See I. Berlin, *Karl Max* 4th edn. (Oxford, 1978), 22; 'Benjamin Disraeli, Karl Marx and the Search for Identity' in *AC*, 280; 'The Bent Twig: On the Rise of Nationalism' in *CTH*, 238–61 at 239–40.

statements in philosophy, political theory, and sociology, often risk simplification of the human condition. Their boldness often renders them wildly exaggerated. This is perhaps the only way creative and innovative visions can make their mark.[49] Great thinkers propose new conceptions, radical models of human nature and society.

In fact, the history of ideas presents to us various examples of great visions that are purblind to some facets of human nature and certain kinds of social-historical experience. In this sense, the history of ideas presents us with moral tales of intellectual excess.[50] Part of the utility of the history of ideas is that it enlightens us about the limits of human practice and understanding. Great writing about human nature and society, grandiose systems of political thought, are often *démesuré*. They may be unreasonable because they lack a sense of proportion; their visions can lack proper perspective, as is the case with Marx's or Freud's. The history of ideas, of cultures, is often a study of such extremes. It can be a study of contrasts and, as such, further our self-understanding by showing what can be, is, and has been thought about human nature and society.

In this sense, cultural history and the history of ideas are cultivating exercises, showing us how we became who we are and what we have become. Studying history develops our sense of ourselves and our fellows. However, Berlin never fails to warn us of the limits of plausibility of thoughts about human nature and society. This is particularly true of utopian visions, or visions of what we could become if only we reordered the totality of social, economic, cultural, and political relations. Berlin's style in the history of ideas prepares one for a balanced and moderate view of what is possible. Regardless of the facts of cultural pluralism, Berlin believes that there are limits to human mutability. As he says, 'arrangements and goals, . . . given the limitations of men's natures, cannot be infinite in number, but must be recognizable as human ends in all their rich but not endless variety'.[51] With working limits in mind, Berlin is concerned with how well a particular vision of human nature and society coheres with a common sense view; one which people have held for uncounted

[49] See *VH*, p. xxiv.
[50] 'Benjamin Disraeli, Karl Marx and the Search for Identity' in *AC*, 284–6.
[51] 'Reply to Kocis', 390.

ages, and which forms the foundations of what we recognize and call human.[52] Cultural pluralism and a plurality of views of human nature and society notwithstanding, Berlin believes that there is a *just measure* to things.

Balanced and discriminating judgements are concerned with the validity of models of human nature and society and as such they are philosophical questions. The transition in Berlin's thought from the history of ideas to philosophy rests on this unavoidable question of validity, of truth.

The Purpose of Philosophy: Beyond Positivism

The history of ideas is a species of self-knowledge. Philosophy is another. Political theory is yet another, although it is a sub-species of philosophical enquiry. All three fields of knowledge have suffered attempts to assimilate their methods to those found in the natural or formal sciences. The Enlightenment thinkers believed in the possibility of a science of man, with laws of behaviour as solid as those in the natural sciences. Auguste Comte, Thomas Buckle, Herbert Spencer, Karl Marx, and many socialists in the nineteenth century, believed in the possibility of a science of history. As is evident from the preceding section, Berlin has sought to undermine these attempts at assimilation. The methods found in the humanities, particularly in historical studies, are *sui generis*: the object-domain and the methods of the historical studies are irreducible to the object-domain and methods of the natural or formal sciences.

The drive to colonize the humanities did not stop at the island of historical studies; other places came unde fire. In the twentieth century, Berlin came face-to-face with arguments against the autonomy of philosophy and political theory. The logical positivists tried to reduce all philosophical enquiry to either formal or empirical fields of enquiry. A new field of analytical study, the philosophy of language, sought to cleanse philosophical language of its muddles (which were seen to be due to the existence of misleading metaphysical terms in epistemology and moral theory).

---

[52] Athenaeum interview. See also 'The Concept of Scientific History' in *CC*, 132–4, 139–40; 'Is a Philosophy of History Possible?' in Yovel (ed.) *Philosophy of History and Action*, 219–25; and 'Reply to Kocis', 388–93.

The hope was that most problems would evaporate after these had been expunged. In political studies, American behaviouralist political scientists proclaimed the demise of normative political theory. In the immediate post-war period, the end of ideological debates was announced. Politics was now to be an empirical science and a matter of administration, for all ultimate ends had been agreed upon.[53]

Convinced that these beliefs were as wrong about philosophy and political theory as the 'concept of scientific history' was about history, Berlin made various counter-attacks. In 'The Purpose of Philosophy' (1962) and 'Does Political Theory Still Exist?' (1962; first published in French in 1961), Berlin made a series of ripostes to the positivist and analytical attacks on philosophy and to the analytical and behaviouralist views of political theory.[54] In this section, I will focus on Berlin's defence of philosophy. The following section will deal with his defence of political theory.

On the attempts to colonize philosophy, Berlin was most ironic. 'The Purpose of Philosophy' begins with the well-known positivist separation of knowledge into two fields, the empirical and the formal. What is typical about both types is that questions which are either empirical or formal immediately imply the methods appropriate to answer them. If I ask 'Where is my jacket?' or 'At what temperature does water boil?', I immediately know how to go about finding an answer: I look in the room for my jacket; I measure the temperature of boiling water with a thermometer. The same is true of formal questions. If I ask 'How many sides has a triangle?', there is a definition which tells me this automatically. With all axiomatic systems one knows where to find the answers to one's questions of definition and rules of operation. This is the case with chess and heraldry and geometry. Berlin agrees that most questions fall into either of these two 'baskets', the empirical or the formal. When they do, there is virtually universal agreement on the methods of answering these questions, on where and how to proceed and on what is a valid answer. Hence these two kinds of

---

[53] For good surveys of these debates see Richard Bernstein, *The Restructuring of Social and Political Theory* (Philadelphia, 1978), Parts I–II; and John G. Gunnell, *Between Philosophy and Politics: The Alienation of Political Theory* (Amherst, Mass., 1986), esp. 1–90.

[54] The two essays are reprinted in *CC*, 1–11 and 143–72, respectively.

questions 'carry within their own structure clear indications of the techniques of their own solution'.[55]

But this is not the case with all questions. If I ask, 'What is the nature of Time?, or 'Is my perception of colour due to the nature of objects or my own senses?', or 'Are all people equal?', there are no universally agreed-upon answers. Furthermore, there is no agreement on the correct methods, the appropriate paradigm of research, that will produce answers that everyone could call valid. In short, such questions are perennially contestable. From this, Berlin concludes that some questions cannot be thrown into the 'baskets' designed by the positivists. There is a type of question that 'does not seem to contain a pointer to the way in which the answer to it is to be found'.[56] We can call this the basket of 'philosophical' questions and problems. To cite Berlin in full:

> This shows that between the two original baskets, the empirical and the formal, there is at least one intermediate basket, in which all those questions live which cannot easily be fitted into the other two. These questions are of the most diverse nature; some appear to be questions of fact, others of value; some are questions about words and a few symbols; others are about methods pursued by those who use them: scientists, artists, critics, common men in the ordinary affairs of life; still others are about the relations between various provinces of knowledge; some deal with presuppositions of thinking, some with the nature and ends of moral or social or political action.
>
> The only common characteristic which all these questions appear to have is that they cannot be answered either by observation or calculation, either by inductive methods or deductive; and, as a crucial corollary of this, that those who ask them are faced with a perplexity from the very beginning— they do not know where to look for the answers; there are no dictionaries, encyclopedias, compendia of knowledge, no experts, no orthodoxies, which can be referred to with confidence as possessing unquestionable authority or knowledge in these matters. Moreover some of these questions are distinguished by being general and by dealing with matters of principle; and others, while not themselves general, very readily raise or lead to questions of principle.[57]

However, we continue searching for answers to such questions,

---

[55] 'The Purpose of Philosophy' in *CC*, 5. For more examples, see 'An Introduction to Philosophy: Dialogue with Isaiah Berlin', in Bryan Magee (ed.), *Men of Ideas: Some Creators of Contemporary Philosophy* (Oxford, 1982), 2–27 at 8–10 and *passim*.

[56] 'The Purpose of Philosophy', in *CC*, 3.   [57] Ibid. 3–4.

regardless of their indefinite nature and unanswerable status. This is because they are interesting in themselves.[58] Those who seek to answer them are properly called philosophers: they are driven solely by a love of knowledge, regardless of the success rate. Of course, the history of thought can be told around the imperial conquests by the formal and positive sciences. Many areas of study started as philosophical problems, only to become conquered by the sciences. The subject matter of these disciplines could be reduced to either empirical or formal questions: such is the history of astronomy, much psychology, cosmology, even logic.[59]

Yet despite the imperial designs of modern thinkers, from Descartes and Hobbes onward: 'The realm of philosophy was not partitioned into a series of scientific successor states'.[60] Not only do the sciences contain second-order problems which are baffling, such as epistemological questions; not all the provinces of human knowledge can be dealt with solely with empirical or formal tools. This is true of questions of moral and political affairs, as well as questions about the ultimate meaning of the universe, God's existence, and so on. Modern logic, the analytical philosophy of language, and contemporary science have failed to conquer all these questions, these provinces of human thought.[61]

Berlin develops this insight further. He gives reasons why philosophy will continue to deal with certain types of questions. His reasons stem from Kant, and the Kantian view of philosophy as critical philosophy. The Kantian revolution in modern philosophy was to distinguish between the data of experience and the concepts and categories through which we sense, imagine, and reflect upon experience. These concepts and categories do not stem from experience; nor are they formal; they organize our perceptions of the world, and are the conditions for the possibility of our knowledge of phenomena. Thus 'patterns or categories or forms of experience' underlie all thought about the world. These 'patterns' are the objects of philosophical reflection.[62] Kant was concerned with giving firm foundations to our scientific knowledge of the world. It quickly became evident to others that there might exist

---

[58] 'An Introduction to Philosophy: Dialogue with Isaiah Berlin' in Magee (ed.), *Men of Ideas*, 2.   [59] 'The Purpose of Philosophy' in *CC*, 4–6.
[60] Ibid. 7.   [61] Ibid. 4–7. And see the Magee interview in *Men of Ideas*.
[62] See 'The Purpose of Philosophy' in *CC*, 7–9; and I. Berlin, *The Age of Enlightenment* (Boston, 1956), 23–7.

categories in addition to space and time; perhaps ones that order the cultural world. Berlin relates that,

> Kant, in his doctrine of our knowledge of the external world, taught that the categories through which we saw it were identical for all sentient beings, permanent and unalterable; indeed this is what made our world one, and communication possible. But some of those who thought about history, morals, aesthetics, did see change and difference; what differed was not so much the empirical content of what these successive civilizations saw or heard or thought as the basic patterns in which they perceived them, the models in terms of which they conceived them, the category-spectacles through which they viewed them.[63]

He argues that Kantian critical philosophy opened new terrain for philosophical reflection: the study 'not [of] the items of experience, but [of] the ways in which they are viewed, the permanent or semi-permanent categories in terms of which experience is conceived and classified'.[64] From this point on, the nature of philosophical reflection became more dynamic. It began to look through and analyse the different 'category-spectacles' worn throughout the ages. The study of human nature and society became linked to historical study. The highest expressions of this type of philosophy were those of Vico, Herder, and Hegel.

To reiterate, development is discernible in human self-understanding. For example, the concept of 'purpose', the notion of teleology, is part of human self-understanding. But moral life is understood in one way if it is held that all things in nature, including human beings, have divinely ordained purposes; and it is understood differently if the notion of purpose is secularized and humanized, and we come to believe that we, and not God, are the creator of purposes. The concept of 'purpose' remains in both a theocratic and a secular humanist world, but it is differently identified and has a different place in the general world-view of persons in society.[65] Hence models of concepts and categories conflict in the history of ideas. Plato and Aristotle exhibit patterns of thought different from those of Hobbes. Because they each use the category of purpose differently, their views of human nature and society conflict. Indeed, such contrasts are most apparent in moral and political philosophy. With respect to the latter, Berlin cites some examples:

[63] 'The Purpose of Philosophy' in *CC*, 8.   [64] Ibid. 9.
[65] See ibid. 8–10; 'Does Political Theory Still Exist?' in *CC*, 153–66.

In politics, for example, men tried to conceive of their social existence by analogy with various models: Plato at one stage, perhaps following Pythagoras, tried to frame his system of human nature, its attributes and goals, following a geometrical pattern, since he thought it would explain all there was. There followed the biological pattern of Aristotle; the many Christian images with which the writings of the Fathers as well as the Old and New Testaments abound; the analogy of the family, which casts light upon human relations not provided by a mechanical model (say that of Hobbes); the notion of an army on the march with its emphasis on such virtues as loyalty, dedication, obedience, needed to overtake and crush the enemy (with which so much play has been made in the Soviet Union); the notion of the state as a traffic policeman and night watchman preventing collisions and looking after property, which is at the back of much individualist and liberal thought; the notion of the state as much more than this—as a great cooperative endeavour of individuals seeking to fulfil a common end, and therefore as entitled to enter into every nook and cranny of human experience, that animates much of the 'organic' thought of the nineteenth century; the systems borrowed from psychology, or from theories of games, that are in vogue at present [1962]—all these are models in terms of which human beings, groups and societies and cultures, have conceived their experience.[66]

But regardless of the historical succession of models, the question of validity remains salient. For example, many argue that Aristotle's teleological view of human nature is superior to Hobbes's mechanistic view. Given the perennial existence of such questions, Berlin argues that philosophy has three tasks to meet. One is to uncover 'the hidden categories and models in terms of which human beings think'.[67] This goal is one of clarification. The second is to determine the adequacy of these models. This concerns, on the one hand, the internal consistency of models, and on the other, their *fit* with human experience. This test of adequacy is both formal and empirical. It asks whether the model is logically coherent and founded on a reasonable description of human experience. The aim here is to produce 'less internally contradictory, and (though this can never be fully attained) less pervertible metaphors, images, symbols and systems of categories'.[68] The third task is meta–theoretical. It is 'to examine the nature of this activity itself (epistemology, philosophical logic, linguistic analysis), and to bring to light the concealed models that operate in

[66] 'The Purpose of Philosophy' in *CC*, 9–10.
[67] Ibid. 8–11 at 10.   [68] Ibid. 10–11 at 11.

this second-order, philosophical, activity itself'.[69] The purpose here
is greater comprehension of the limits of fields of enquiry; of
finding out that, for example, the humanities cannot be—without
great distortion or perversion—assimilated to the natural or formal
sciences. This indeed is the main conclusion of Berlin's short essay
'The Purpose of Philosophy'.

In the end, the goal of philosophy is illumination, enlightenment,
and critical self-knowledge. This is achieved by reflection upon the
concepts, categories, and principles that order our experience of the
natural and human worlds, or have been devised to order such
experience. The aim is more than historical, it is philosophical,
concerned with questions of validity no less than matters of fact.
For Berlin, it is crucial that persons 'understand themselves and
thus operate in the open, and not wildly, in the dark'.[70] The
importance of this goal is immediately apparent when one
considers moral and political affairs. And as the examples cited
above attest, Berlin is of the opinion that what model is accepted as
adequate for moral life is important. Such philosophical judgements
have practical ramifications for good and ill.[71] Philosophy enables
one to clarify these issues, in order to make more informed and
reasonable, and possibly more prudent choices, about the ends of
life.[72]

The Nature of Political Philosophy:
Beyond the End of Ideology

The post-war era was a bleak one for political theory. Various
branches of analytical philosophy and empirical social science were
united in their claims that normative political theory was becoming
extinct. Berlin answered these claims in his 1961 essay 'Does
Political Theory Still Exist?'[73] He answered this question in the
affirmative, and took upon himself the task of showing how
political theory was an indestructible kind of thinking.[74] In the

---

[69] 'The Purpose of Philosophy' in *CC*, 10.   [70] Ibid. 11.
[71] See e.g. 'Does Political Theory Still Exist?' in *CC*, 148–50.
[72] The aim is to avoid being duped by charlatans in political and social affairs.
Philosophy basically is good for one thing: it helps us to know when people 'are
talking rot' (see the Jahanbegloo interview, 29).   [73] Included in *CC*, 143–72.
[74] Berlin did not act alone in this battle. For a critique of the attempt to assimilate
political philosophy, or practical philosophy, to a branch of analytical philosophy of
language, see the article by one of Berlin's contemporaries, John Plamenatz, 'The
Use of Political Theory' in *Political Studies*, 8 (1960), 37–47.

essay, Berlin relates that the project of reducing ethics and political theory to an objective science, whether intuitive, metaphysical, formal or empirical, is as old as Plato. This tendency runs through the history of Western thought. In modern times Enlightenment thinkers hoped to reduce ethics to a branch of a natural science of man. Attempts by political scientists in the 1950s and 1960s to assimilate normative problems to the empirical study of political behaviour amounted to the same thing. Yet this desire for a rational science of ethics presupposes that there can be a consensus over both method as well as the answers given as solutions to moral dilemmas. Berlin concludes that this goal is impossible, and for two interrelated reasons: the pluralism of the subjectmatter itself and the contestability of the methods used to focus on the field of ethics.

Berlin's preferred counter-example to a science of ethics turned out to be political theory; a domain which at the time was under attack by proponents of scientism. Berlin argued that in political theory, as in ethics in general, final and universally agreed-upon answers are not just unavailable, they cannot be achieved. This is due to the plurality of goods which constitute the subject-matter itself; determined by the fact that for any number of moral questions, more than one reasonable answer is possible. This is true 'inasmuch as men can pursue many distinct ends, none of them means to, or parts of, one another . . . nor is there any reason to suppose that all of them must, even in principle, be compatible with one another'.[75]

Berlin did not pursue a justification for moral pluralism in this essay—he did so later; at this point he was satisfied to draw out the implications for political theory of his thesis. One implication was that moral pluralism constitutes the condition for the possibility (and continuity) of normative thought, and political thought in particular. As he puts it:

If we ask the Kantian question 'In what kind of world is political philosophy—the kind of discussion and argument in which it consists—in principle possible?' the answer must be 'Only in a world where ends collide'. In a society dominated by a single goal there could in principle only be arguments about the best means to attain this end—and arguments about means are technical, that is, scientific and empirical in character: they

[75] 'Does Political Theory Still Exist?' in *CC*, 150.

can be settled by experience and observation or whatever other methods are used to discover causes and correlations; they can, at least in principle, be reduced to positive sciences. . . . It follows that the only society in which political philosophy in its traditional sense, that is, an inquiry concerned not solely with elucidation of concepts, but with the critical examination of presuppositions and assumptions, and the questioning of the order of priorities and ultimate ends, is possible, is a society in which there is no total acceptance of any single end.[76]

Hence in 'Does Political Theory Still Exist?' Berlin offers a second-order analysis of political philosophy—of the nature of political thought—and concludes that only in a fully administered society would a pure politics of formal and empirical rules be possible. But given the fact that pluralism constitutes moral life, such an eventuality is unlikely; or if it occurs, it is the result of force, as Berlin notes is the case in totalitarian societies at the time of writing. Ordinarily, and essentially, monism, or governance by a 'single goal', is impossible. This is due to the conflict of ends that is constitutive of moral life.[77] And given that ends are plural, and often incompatible, reflection on the best course of action remains constitutive of any life touched by philosophy. As Berlin writes:

To suppose, . . . that there have been or could be ages without political philosophy is like supposing that as there are ages of faith, so there are or could be ages of total disbelief. But this is an absurd notion: there is no human activity without some kind of general outlook: scepticism, cynicism, refusal to dabble in abstract issues or to question values, hard boiled opportunism, contempt for theorising, all the varieties of nihilism, are, of course, themselves metaphysical and ethical positions, committal attitudes. Whatever else the existentialists have taught us, they have made this fact plain. The idea of a completely *wertfrei* theory (or model) of human action (as constrasted, say, with animal behaviour) rests on a naïve misconception of what objectivity or neutrality in the social studies must be.[78]

Political thought is thus philosophical in Berlin's sense of the term. Its operations and conclusions conform neither to formal rules nor to empirically verified laws. Political thought is non-scientific, but none the less remains essential to human thought for it deals with fundamental attitudes towards existence and dilemmas posed by social life. It concerns what we all do: question the ordering of our

[76] 'Does Political Theory Still Exist?' in *CC*, 149–50.
[77] Ibid.   [78] Ibid. 158.

fundamental purposes and values. Yet Berlin goes further than discussing the reasons for the existence of ethics and political thought and their nature. He presents what he considers to be the best ways of doing political philosophy.

In the same essay, Berlin states that political philosophers must be able to intuit, to sympathize with the position of others.[79] As with historical explanation, one must be able to evoke the world-view behind particular political judgements. Socrates' pursuit of an answer to the question of justice in *The Republic* would have failed if, at the outset, he had been unable to understand the views of his opponents. His quest would have been vain, perhaps fruitless, if in Book 1 he did not understand what Cephalus meant by tradition and the rule of elders or what Thrasymachus meant by force and the rule of mighty kings. This is only a starting point, however. Having a wide imagination at one's disposal is not enough, political philosophers need to do more. As with philosophy in general, they need to assess political doctrines for logical coherence, or 'internal consistency'. Yet political thought is also about human affairs; it is about practical things. Empirical knowledge comes into play, therefore. Political philosophers must be concerned with the 'explanatory force' of political doctrines, otherwise their thought misses the mark of actual human experience.[80] Political theory is thus only partly formal; it must also be informed by accurate knowledge of experience.

Here is one link, unexposed by Berlin, between his historical and cultural studies and his political theory. If knowledge of experience is crucial to doing political theory well, then historical and cultural knowledge offer the widest perspective and bank of information upon which to found one's normative arguments and conclusions. This is indeed how Berlin operates; in his work, normative arguments are peppered with historical references, no less than logical points. This link between empirical and normative thought is made, however obliquely, when Berlin argues that political theory deals with fundamental models of human nature and society. He argues that in the end the validity of political doctrines depends on the plausibility of those models of human nature and society which they presuppose and to which they explicitly refer. These models in turn contain identifiable concepts and categories,

[79] Ibid. 168.   [80] Ibid. 167–8.

ones which have been present in thought for millennia. Ultimately the political thinker, if at all critical, asks if the foundational model in question is adequate to our understanding of what human nature is and what persons have judged to be good.[81] Hence, foundational claims are partly normative and partly empirical. They deal with what is good no less than what human beings normally call good. As Berlin puts it, foundational claims are made up of

> networks of categories, descriptive, evaluative, and hybrids compounded of the two, in which the two functions cannot be disentangled even in thought—categories which, if not eternal and universal, are far more stable and widespread than those of the sciences; sufficiently continuous, indeed, to constitute a common world which we share with medieval and classical thinkers.[82]

What is indicative of failed and inadequate political doctrines and the models that support them, is their distortion of our fundamental categories, of what we believe to be true about human experience. This is the empirical dimension to political theory. Moreover, political doctrines and models may be judged inadequate if they lack what we judge to be good in human life. This is the evaluative dimension of the discipline.

   Unfortunately, Berlin does not tell us explicitly what makes up the good, or what are valid arguments for what is 'good'. Instead, he focuses on the ways in which past political doctrines have worked with improper models of human nature and society, distorting both in the process of description and prescription. For example, Berlin tells us that the Hobbesian use of mechanical models of human behaviour distorts much human behaviour. It excludes explanations based on human purposes and intentions. Or, if it accepts these, reduces them to the effects of motion on the senses. What strikes the critical reader of Hobbes is the exaggerated aspects of his assumptions, such as the fundamentally egocentric nature of people. Regardless of the fact that the Hobbesian model may illuminate certain facets of human nature in our historical situation—bourgeois life, perhaps, in this case—it fails as a plausible model in its entirety. With Hobbes we encounter no people in communities, no history, and certainly no free will. Hobbes sketches a distorted picture of people in society. His

[81] 'Does Political Theory Still Exist?' in *CC*, 158–60, 166–71.
[82] Ibid. 169.

mechanical model is 'inadequate' because it fails to 'understand what we mean by motive, purpose, value, personality and the like'.[83] His model offers no insights into the inwardness of human life. And his paranoiac emphasis on personal security can be judged morally impoverished. Indeed, his vision cannot be reasonably accepted holus-bolus; it must be complemented with a fuller vision.

In this fashion, Berlin considers it the job of political philosophers to expose distortions and exclusions in political doctrines, 'in the name of our own view of what men are, have been, could be'.[84] Therefore, an adequate understanding of human nature must support the arguments of political philosophers. Such an understanding will be guided by an adequate empirical sense of what experience is like, and what people value.[85] If we take Berlin's historicism seriously, this means that political theory must be concerned with the actual development of people in history. Ahistorical models of human nature and society are ruled out from the beginning. Political philosophy must be informed by history, as well as the values held by people across and within cultures.

An adequate understanding of human nature and society will necessarily contain our evaluations of what we believe to be good and right. Hence Berlin contests the premiss, central to modern positivism, that there can be an axiologically neutral study of human behaviour: a person without belief, like an age without faith, is absurd. For this reason the hope for the possibility of a society without ideology, of the end of ideology, is wrong-headed. Normative questions and conflicts over the evaluations of ends and models of human nature and society are constitutive of political life. The plurality of political theories, today and throughout the ages, is a proof of this, and not evidence of the muddle-headedness of contemporary and past thinkers. This pluralism cannot be thought away. A society with universal agreement about ends is just as implausible as one in which only empirical questions of means fill the public agenda. In matters of both ends and means, disagreements and conflict are common. We cannot reasonably infer moral and political life to be otherwise.[86]

Berlin's answer to the positivist attack on political theory is that a

---

[83] See ibid. 164. [84] Ibid. 160.
[85] Ibid. 165–6. [86] See ibid. 157–8, 172.

science of morals is unreasonable. Indeed, a person operating according to formal rules or empirical laws is outside our knowledge of human experience. Only robots would operate that way. Human beings are too complicated, morally torn, unpredictable, to be assessed according to the rules of formal logic or empirical science. Much of what is unquantifiable and cannot be formalized belongs to moral and political life. Without a complex and irreducible moral life human beings would be radically different from what they are now, and unrecognizable as such.[87]

Nevertheless, political argumentation is not so marred by different normative and empirical perspectives that universal judgements are impossible. Moral judgements and political doctrines, notwithstanding their differences, often refer to a common human experience.[88] The objectivity of judgements demands no less; their reference to human beings requires a core set of universal principles. For this reason, we can dismiss or alter those views that we consider inadequate or distorting of our knowledge of human nature and society, and of what persons fundamentally value. It is important to cite Berlin in full on the mixture of normative and empirical categories which form the barometer of validity for political theories:

The basic categories (with their corresponding concepts) in terms of which we define men—such notions as society, freedom, sense of time and change, suffering, happiness, productivity, good and bad, right and wrong, choice, effort, truth, illusion (to take them wholly at random)—are not matters of induction and hypothesis. To think of someone as a human being is *ipso facto* to bring all these notions into play: so that to say of someone that he is a man, but that choice, or the notion of truth, means nothing to him, would be eccentric: it would clash with what we mean by 'man' not as a matter of verbal definition (which is alterable at will), but as intrinsic to the way in which we think, and (as a matter of 'brute' fact) evidently cannot but think.

This will hold of values too (among them political ones) in terms of which men are defined. Thus, if I say of someone that he is kind or cruel, loves truth or is indifferent to it, he remains human in either case. But if I find a man to whom it literally makes no difference whether he kicks a pebble or kills his family, since either would be an antidote to *ennui* or

[87] 'Does Political Theory Still Exist?' in *CC*, 165–6. As Berlin states (p. 186): 'Political categories (and values) are a part of this all but inescapable web of ways of living, acting and thinking, a network liable to change only as a result of radical changes in reality, or through dissociation from reality on the part of individuals, that is to say, madness.'   [88] Athenaeum interview.

inactivity, I shall not be disposed, like consistent relativists, to attribute to
him merely a different code of morality from my own or that of most men,
or declare that we disagree on essentials, but shall begin to speak of insanity
and inhumanity; I shall be inclined to consider him mad, as a man who
thinks he is Napoleon is mad; which is a way of saying that I do not regard
such a being as being fully a man at all. It is cases of this kind, which seem
to make it clear that ability to recognise universal—or almost universal—
values enters into our analysis of such fundamental concepts as 'man',
'rational', 'sane', 'natural' etc.—which are usually thought of as descriptive
and not evaluative—that lie at the basis of modern translations into
empirical terms of the kernel of truth in the old *a priori* natural law
doctrines. It is considerations such as these, urged by neo-Aristotelians and
the followers of the later doctrines of Wittgenstein, that have shaken the
faith of some devoted empiricists in the complete logical gulf between
descriptive statements and statements of value, and have cast doubt on the
celebrated distinction derived from Hume.[89]

Hence there are limits to the pluralism of values. Moreover, Berlin
believes in the existence of a common core of values, the 'empirical
. . . kernel of truth in the old *a priori* natural doctrines'. As will
become evident in the next chapter, this common core of values is
Berlin's touchstone, the one that stops his doctrine of moral
pluralism from slipping into relativism and nihilism. Indeed, just as
much as historical study exposes the pluralism of values and
cultures, it also, upon philosophical reflection, allows one to see a
common set of human aspirations, a core of categories and
concepts, that, if thought away, would so radically alter our sense
of ourselves and society that we would enter a wholly foreign and
implausible realm of existence.

Conclusion

In this chapter I have presented Berlin's views on the nature and
purpose of historical and philosophical studies. My aim has been to
highlight the Enlightenment ideals within his work. One reason for
doing this is to avoid any implication that his historicism commits
him to relativism and that he is thus unable to speak of progress in
our knowledge of human nature and society.[90] I do not think that

[89] 'Does Political Theory Still Exist?' in *CC*, 166.
[90] Berlin believes that historical studies can deepen and advance our self-
knowledge (see Berlin's 'On Vico', 288–9). And see below, Chs. 3 and 5, for my
treatment of these charges of relativism.

these conclusions are borne out by the evidence, nor are they in line with the fundamental drive of his thinking.[91] Moreover, the charge of relativism, if correct, would render his defence of political liberalism empty; it would amount to little more than a personal attachment, rather than something in keeping with basic human needs. Like the robin, Berlin's work is driven by the twin goals of enlightenment and liberty. I am not claiming that Berlin is a rationalist who believes that all virtues can be harmonized by reason; but his view of the purpose of philosophy is that by practising it one clarifies and reviews the validity of moral ideals. Moreover, that branch of philosophy concerned with the application of morals to society, political theory, is concerned with the validity of models of human nature and society. And the history of ideas offers a panoply of models of human nature and society. It is up to the political philosopher to question the worth, or validity, of those models which underlie all claims of rightful authority, justice, equality, liberty, and so on.

In sum, the history of ideas offers the student contrasting views of human nature and society. The goal is self-understanding, something Berlin has called 'man's highest requirement'.[92] Political philosophy furthers this goal by seeking to arrive at a reasonable understanding of human nature and society, and by questioning the validity of normative statements. As a historian of ideas, Berlin argues that the study of human nature and society must be interpretive. Yet an argument about proper method entails that some models of human nature and society, some kinds of explanation of human behaviour are inadequate and thus wrong, while others are better because they are closer to the truth.[93] For example, historical and genetic models of human nature and society are superior to static and ahistorical ones. The former grasp the reality of human self-development and the variety of customs, mores, institutions, and practices; the latter do not. Similarly,

---

[91] In his essay on John Stuart Mill, Berlin makes a rhetorical case for enlightenment and humanist learning: 'Yet what solutions have we found, with all our new technological and psychological knowledge and great new powers, save the ancient prescription advocated by the creators of humanism—Erasmus and Spinoza, Locke and Montesquieu, Lessing and Diderot—reason, education, self-knowledge, responsibility—above all, self-knowledge? What other hope is there for men, or has there ever been?' ('John Stuart Mill and the Ends of Life' in *FE*, 198–9).

[92] 'Benjamin Disraeli, Karl Marx and the Search for Identity' in *AC*, 252–86 at 286.   [93] See Bernard Williams, 'Introduction' to *CC*, p. xv.

contextual and imaginative explanations of many kinds of social behaviour are superior to ones founded on statistical laws. A statistical analysis may work in explaining the fluctuation in currency rates, but it fails in explaining all the policies of a central bank. For this we need to delve into the goals of its managers, their motives and purposes, in short, the self-understanding of their role and mission as central bankers. In making such points, one has to believe that some progress in our knowledge of ourselves and society is possible. Otherwise, we would have no reason to dispense with outdated models or consider some superior to others. Indeed, Berlin tells us that the history of human thought can be traced by this search for adequacy and truth in empirical and normative matters.[94] With respect to political theory, Berlin argues that doctrines must be tested against experience in the widest sense of the term. That is, our standards must include universal and particular ones about human nature and society. Certain statements will prove to be false; that is, experience will show them to be in error. Progress in self-understanding results from such testing.

This is what has happened, for instance, to the ancient notion that some persons are born to be slaves. Unlike the ancients, we have come to know that slavery is a social and not, as Aristotle believed, a natural category. Slavery denotes a juridical relation between persons; it cannot issue from natural attributes. To believe that slavery is natural is to make an empirical mistake about human nature. Put another way: to argue for a natural basis for slavery is to commit a category mistake, to render natural what is thoroughly social. Because we find such a mistake in ancient political thought, Berlin concludes that the ancients lacked 'sufficient self-understanding' of human nature and society. We moderns, on the other hand, have a greater grasp of psychology, sociology, and history. This enables us to forgo naturalistic explanations where we know that psychological, social, and historical ones are better, or more adequate for the subject-matter at hand. For this reason, Berlin believes that there is 'progress' in 'the objective knowledge of what men are'.[95]

[94] 'Does Political Theory Still Exist?' in *CC*, 159–60.
[95] Correspondence (17 Nov. 1988). This does not imply that regression, or wrong turns, in the development of human self-knowledge are not also possible. Indeed, such a possibility is presumed by Berlin's focus on counter-Enlightenment thinkers: they captured some of what was lost, or expelled, by Enlightenment

Inasmuch as there is progress in our knowledge, there can be progress in our moral development.[96] Since ancient thought was corporatist and organic, Berlin considers modern norms which grant liberty to individuals an advance over the past. Ostracism, slavery, and torture for ordinary forensic purposes are no longer tolerated in Western societies, and this for reasons of natural or human rights. That these notions of natural and human rights arose historically does not render them any less valid.[97] It is a virtue of Berlin's political thought that it recognizes the historical genesis of norms, while maintaining that universal statements about human nature and society are possible. As I will show in the following chapters, Berlin's defence of political liberalism is founded on a theory of human nature and society. He makes universal statements about persons, about the human need for freedom, for example; and about our moral condition, about its pluralistic constitution.

Moreover, Berlin draws from the history of Western culture in order to show the prudence and adequacy of liberal constitutional principles. This historical element in his argument is an essential characteristic of his defence of political liberalism. It is the explanatory and contextual side of his defence. With it, Berlin gives us a narrative of Western cultural history with the development of liberty as one of its central themes. Following from his own philosophical criteria, the adequacy of this defence is based on two things. First, on the fit his model of human nature and society has with our knowledge of experience. Secondly, on how political liberalism fits modern social and cultural conditions. In seeking such adequacy, Berlin tells us that liberalism respects the universal characteristics of persons, such as free will and the pluralism of our moral condition; and also that political liberalism is the best way we know to order and limit the vast powers of the modern nation-state. As he argues himself, political doctrines must respect our understanding of human nature, as well as avoid the pitfalls of anachronism and parochialism. In short, political doctrines must be both true to human nature and fitting for the times.

The ultimate test of a political principle for Berlin is whether we

thought, and, Berlin finds it important to point this out, put to rights the picture of human nature distorted by the scientific models used by Helvétius, Condillac, and others.

[96] Once again, progress of some norms does not entail that regression in others is not possible as well.   [97] Athenaeum interview.

can operate without it and still make sense of human nature and society. In his view, if we were to think away free will, or the pluralism of our moral constitution, the remaining picture of the world would be highly distorted, if not unrecognizable. None the less, our self-knowledge as well as the validity of our political principles are conditional on the available evidence. We progress intellectually by questioning our fundamental beliefs. If we have no reason to question these beliefs, we proceed 'as if' they were true.[98] It is knowledge of human needs and historical development that secures our moral and political judgements. Self-knowledge and self-understanding should guide our action; that is, if we wish to act prudently and 'not wildly, in the dark' to cite the epigraph at the head of this chapter. Together, these universal and particular statements about human nature and society are the bases for an interpretative defence of political liberalism.[99] It is one of my theses that Berlin is a good representative of interpretative political theory. His defence is contextual and historical, full and deep. However, before developing his historical and sociological arguments, I need to discuss his theory of human nature and description of our moral condition.

[98] Athenaeum interview.

[99] Stuart Hampshire calls this the 'two faces of morality' and moral reason. For his defence of moral reasoning which incorporates both universal and particularistic arguments, see his *Morality and Conflict*, 1–9, 129–43, 158–69.

3

PLURALISM, FREEDOM, AND HUMAN NATURE

> Single-minded monists, ruthless fanatics, men possessed by an all-embracing coherent vision, do not know the doubts and agonies of those who cannot wholly blind themselves to reality. But even those who are aware of the complex texture of experience, of what is not reducible to generalization or capable of computation, can, in the end, justify their decisions only by their coherence with some over-all pattern of a desirable form of personal or social life, of which they may become fully conscious only, it may be, when faced with the need to resolve conflicts . . .
>
> (Isaiah Berlin, 'Introduction' to *Four Essays on Liberty*)

In this chapter, I sketch Berlin's model of human nature and society, with particular emphasis on his theory of moral pluralism and freedom of will. The point is to show that regardless of his critique of fixed theories of human nature, Berlin's political liberalism is supported by a model of human nature. His aim has been to criticize the tenets within the Western tradition and models of human nature and society which he believes have lent support to authoritarian rule not only in this century, but since ancient times.

The central antagonists in Berlin's work are the 'single-minded monists' mentioned in the quotation above, as well as their political minions. He has consistently sought to undermine the ideologies of those 'ruthless fanatics', all too common in this century, who seek perfection in politics because they believe in a vision of a perfect, wholly harmonious, moral order. Like the robin in the fable, Berlin is a maverick. His critique of monism in moral and political thought in effect gives the rationalist thought-kettle one swift kick. In this thought-kettle are brewed at least two principles. The first holds that the cosmos, including human nature and moral life, exhibits a fixed structure throughout time which reason can apprehend. The second refers to the just political regime and holds that a fixed structure of moral ends is rationally intelligible, and thus the best political regime is one that is ordered according to the timeless strictures discovered by rational thought. Both principles are present, for instance, in the natural law tradition; they are also present throughout the canon of political theory. According to Berlin, both principles commit what he calls the Ionian fallacy, that is, that for all genuine questions one answer can be found; that one method exists to find these answers; and that all such answers are necessarily compatible.[1] Berlin responds to both principles with a critique inspired by a reading of Machiavelli, Vico, and Herder. This leads him to posit the existence of a moral universe with plural ends, which are not always compatible and often incommensurable when measured against the same yardstick.

Yet, as was discussed in Chapter 2, Berlin believes that every philosophy, especially every political philosophy, is founded on a model of human nature and society, which *ex hypothesi*, must hold for his own political thought as well. This presents an immediate and thorny problem. For if Berlin subscribes to the critique of natural law, of fixed theories of human nature and eternal moral orders, then how can he still have a model of man and society upon which to found his political tenets? Are his positions on human nature and society compatible with this critique of rationalist ethics, in particular natural law? This paradox is not so unresolvable as it seems at first.

While Berlin criticizes the rationalist version of human nature, he does believe in the existence of human nature, of a set of shared characteristics amongst people. Berlin replaces a static view of human nature with a dynamic one; a model that he believes is better suited to our sense of human beings as free agents living within unique cultures and historical societies. For the belief that human ends are eternally fixed and ranked, Berlin substitutes the understanding that human ends are multiple, plural, often in conflict, developing, changing, and at times incommensurable. Moreover, he claims that his theory of moral pluralism is superior to monist theories, in that it fits with both our knowledge of historical development and our present understanding of moral life and the cultural differences amongst civilizations. With this model in mind,

---

[1] See 'The Pursuit of the Ideal' in *CTH*, 5–7.

Berlin claims that no final and timeless answer to moral and political dilemmas can be envisioned. This in effect strikes at the centre of Western thought, undermining all thought, both religious and secular, which seeks final answers to questions of moral and political order.

A Note on the Ionian Fallacy

According to Berlin, the Ionian fallacy marks much of the Western tradition of ethical reflection. The tradition from Plato to Kant, from Descartes to Marx and beyond, holds that final and eternal answers to questions about the genuine ends of man can be discovered. This belief is monistic in both method and substance. The tradition assumes that one correct method exists which can be used to discover the set of genuine moral ends for all people. Indeed, from Plato onwards, the discovery of immutable truths has been taken to be a function of correct method. If only we had the right logic, method of reasoning, verification procedures, and the like, we would arrive at immutably correct, final answers to moral dilemmas. Moreover, the tradition has held that these answers must all entail one another, for no truths are incompatible a priori. Yet there is no reason to conclude that one set of final answers can be found to questions of human import. Nor is it certain that one, and only one, method exists to arrive at solutions to moral problems. Indeed, it is counter-intuitive to hold that all reasonable answers to human moral dilemmas are necessarily compatible. On both empirical and logical grounds, Berlin finds the methodological assumptions and conclusions of rationalist thought to be wanting and in need of critical revision.

Much of Berlin's work in historiography and moral theory has been directed at exposing what he considers to be the fallacious assumptions of Western philosophy. He first mentions the Ionian fallacy in the 1950 article, 'Logical Translation'. Here the point was to show that not all philosophical questions are open to one set of answers, arrived at with one methodology. Questions such as 'What is everything made of?', must presuppose a fundamental substratum to all reality and one way of apprehending it.[2] But what

---

[2] 'Logical Translation' in *CC*, 76–7.

if, Berlin asked, the assumption of a unity to all things is questioned? Then the whole project of finding one set of answers to all genuine questions is put in doubt.

While Berlin first began to write about the Ionian fallacy in the 1950s, the principles which he used to identify it were discovered by him much earlier. In his intellectual testament, 'The Pursuit of the Ideal' (1988), Berlin relates how it dawned on him as an undergraduate that most Western moral and political theory is united by a common search for a set of final and certain answers to normative questions. He soon realized that this search is driven by the assumption that the whole universe, including human existence, is rationally structured and intelligible. Whether he was reading in the Christian or Hebraic tradition, or studying the philosophies of Plato and Aristotle, the Stoics, the Scholastics, the Natural Law theorists, the Empiricists, or the Enlightenment thinkers and their heirs, such as the Utilitarians, or Hegel and Marx, Berlin detected a set of common methodological and metaphysical assumptions.[3] He says:

At some point I realized that what all these views had in common was a Platonic ideal: in the first place that, as in the sciences, all genuine questions must have one true answer and one only, all the rest being necessarily errors; in the second place, that there must be a dependable path towards the discovery of these truths; in the third place, that the true answers, when found, must necessarily be compatible with one another and form a single whole, for one truth cannot be incompatible with another—that we knew *a priori*. This kind of omniscience was the solution of the cosmic jigsaw puzzle. In the case of morals, we could then conceive what the perfect life must be, founded as it would be on correct understanding of the rules that governed the universe.

True, we might never get to this condition of perfect knowledge—we may be too feeble-witted, or too weak or corrupt or sinful, to achieve this. The obstacles, both intellectual and those of external nature, may be too many. Moreover, opinions . . . had widely differed about the right path to pursue—some found it in churches, some in laboratories; some believed in intuition, others in experiment, or in mystical visions, or in mathematical calculation. But even if we could not ourselves reach these true answers, or indeed, the final system that interweaves them all, the answers must exist—else the questions were not real. The answers must be known to someone: perhaps Adam in Paradise knew; perhaps we shall only reach

---

[3] 'The Pursuit of the Ideal' in *CTH*, 2–9.

them at the end of our days; if men cannot know them, perhaps the angels know; and if not the angels, then God knows. These timeless truths must in principle be knowable.[4]

So the Ionian fallacy stems from the 'Platonic ideal'; it extends into the search for knowledge of the True, the Good and the Beautiful. Philosophical reflection alone does not lead to the fallacy. What leads to it is the belief that one can discover final, eternal, compatible, harmoniously ordered answers to moral or metaphysical questions. This belief itself is related to the crucial assumption that behind the phenomena of life, natural and moral, there is an order to be uncovered. The problem is how to fit the jigsaw pieces of life and thought together. The assumption is that there is a master plan, that all the pieces must fit together. Thus this form of thinking is monistic because it believes in the existence of a timeless and eternal model to life present somewhere behind or underneath or above the manifold appearances of ordinary experience. Proper philosophical method seeks to apprehend and comprehend this plan, and philosophical theory is correct once it identifies the eternal order of things.

The Ionian fallacy is a frequent topic in Berlin's writings; its formulation appearing often and in several variations.[5] Berlin's intent has remained constant: to identify the chief characteristics of the rationalist tradition and then to present a counter-argument, one that was submerged by the intellectual hegemony of rationalism; a parallel tradition that swims 'against the current' of classical and modern rationalism, of monistic thinking in general. He points to the ancient sceptical tradition, the thought of Sextus Empiricus, sceptics like Carneades, and relativists like Protagoras. Such thinkers contested the principle of the rational intelligibility of the universe. Some, such as Carneades, argued that conflicts between

---

[4] 'The Pursuit of the Ideal' in *CTH*, 5–6.

[5] These various versions do not differ significantly. For a few of them, see Berlin's 'European Unity and its Vicissitudes' in *CTH*, 183–6; Berlin's 'Preface' to H. G. Schenk, *The Mind of the European Romantics* (London, 1966), pp. xiv–xv; his 'The Originality of Machiavelli' and 'The Divorce between the Sciences and the Humanities' both in *AC*, 66–8 and 80–1 respectively; 'Does Political Theory Still Exist? and 'From Hope and Fear Set Free' both in *CC*, 150–4 and 198 respectively; 'The Decline of Utopian Ideas in the West' in *CTH*, 23–5; 'Two Concepts of Liberty' in *FE*, 145–54, 167–71; and 'The Apotheosis of the Romantic Will' in *CTH*, 209.

moral ends may be inevitable and irresolvable on rational grounds.[6] But these sceptical thinkers had little influence on the subsequent development of Western thought: in this intellectual battle, the rationalism of Plato and Aristotle won the day.[7]

It was not until the Renaissance that rationalism and monistic assumptions came once again under strong critical scrutiny. One turning-point was the critique of natural law begun by Renaissance jurists. In the latter part of the 16th-century students of Roman law, in particular the Protestant Reformers, began to realize that the principles, codes, and ways of life of the Romans did not fit modern conditions. Yet the universal claims of natural law, along with the assumption of the superior wisdom of the ancients, implied that what was right for the ancients must be so for the moderns. These assumptions and conclusions were soon contested. For example, a problem arose in understanding the ancient laws regarding slavery and manumission. The laws and social structure that supported such acts were clearly at odds with Christian precepts of human dignity. For most modern political thought, persons are understood to be free by nature: none are born slaves. In this case, it is possible that the ancients were not as wise as the moderns. In how many other cases are the ancients equally wrong?

Berlin tells that such questioning eventually led to the realization that ancient law could be flawed in regard to persons and society. Thus the Renaissance attempt to revive ancient principles ended, paradoxically, in undermining the belief in their eternal worth as moral standards. Indeed, the content of natural law could change. However, past errors can be rectified; and thus some progress in moral development is possible. But if this is the case, then our understandings of human nature and natural law are tentative, open to revision. According to Berlin, it was this realization that led to the first kick at the thought-kettle of rationalism in modern times.[8]

---

[6] See *VH*, 207; 'The Decline of Utopian Ideas in the West' in *CTH*, 30–1; 'The Originality of Machiavelli' and 'TE Divorce between the Sciences and the Humanities' both in *AC*, 72 and 80–8 respectively. See also Philip de Lacy, 'Skepticism in Antiquity' in Philip P. Wiener (ed.), *Dictionary of the History of Ideas* iv (New York, 1973), 234–40; A. A. Long, *Hellenistic Philosophy: Stoics, Epicureans, Skeptics*, 2nd edn. (London, 1974), 75–106; and G. B. Kerferd, *The Sophistic Movement* (Cambridge, 1981), 83–110.

[7] All Souls interview and 'The Apotheosis of the Romantic Will' in *CTH*, 207–37.

[8] I. Berlin, 'Comments' in Yirmiahu Yovel (ed.), *Philosophy of History and Action*, 38–40. See also *VH*, 125–40.

Berlin accepts and closely identifies with both the historicist and empirical critiques of natural-law theories.[9] He does not believe in such a thing as 'a fixed and unalterable human nature'. Such a belief commits the Ionian fallacy, for it presupposes that to such questions as 'What is Man?' and 'What are his ends?', conclusive and final answers can be discovered. While Berlin's position is derived from a variety of traditions, including scepticism, empiricism, historicism, cultural pluralism, romanticism, and even, historical materialism, it is consistent in theme:

[T]here is no basic human nature in this sense—in the sense in which, for example, Rousseau believed that if you strip off all the increments, all the modifications, corruption, distortion, etc. (as he thought of it) brought about by society and civilisation—there will be discovered a basic natural man, sometimes identified with, say, Red Indians, who have not had the unfortunate experience of having their natures distorted by European culture . . . [T]here is no central, pure, natural being who emerges after you have scraped off all the artificial beliefs, habits, values, forms of life and behaviour which have been, as it were, superimposed on this pure, natural being. That is what I mean by denying a fixed human nature: I do not believe that all men are in the relevant respects the same 'beneath the skin', i.e., I believe that variety is part of human existence.[10]

As is to be expected, Berlin's belief in variety comes from his study of the history of ideas. Berlin recounts that once natural law and the theory of human nature started to be understood in historical and conventional terms, philosophers and historians became aware of the constitutive differences between ages and cultures. The result of the development of cultural historiography, from the Renaissance jurists, through Vico and up to Meinecke, was to instil in Western consciousness the view that cultural differences are often more important than cultural similarities. The view that cultures are 'organic' social wholes, typified by unique constellations of ideals and practices, is clearly at odds with the view of the unalterable nature of men and women and their morality. This latter view is assumed, uncritically, by all theories of natural law, whether ancient, Christian, or modern. The notions of cultural development

---

[9] See Berlin's discussion of the historical and philosophical criticisms of natural law in the thought of Montesquieu and Hume ('Montesquieu' and 'Hume and the Sources of German Anti-Rationalism' both in *AC*, 130–61 and 162–87 respectively).

[10] Unpublished letter to Beata Polanowska-Sygulska (24 Feb. 1986), 1–2.

and societal uniqueness strike a blow to this tradition; they are a second kick at the thought-kettle of rationalism.

Cultural historiography developed many more critiques. The thesis of cultural pluralism, developed by Hamann, Herder, and others, was especially directed against a view, strongest during the Enlightenment, that all civilizations could be graded on one scale of values, or were variations upon one central theme. These·thinkers argued that cultural history is pluralistic, and that more than one standard exists to judge cultures. This was a blow to the monistic tradition. Historicism and cultural studies thus undermined one of the foundations of Western thought: the belief in 'the great monistic conception of the Universe as a single, unvarying system, intelligible in the light of reason to all men—if only they have eyes to see—at all times, in all conditions, everywhere'.[11]

Of course, Berlin is aware of the horrifying development of historicist tenets into justifications for power politics, chauvinism, and all variants of irrationalism. As usual, he is on guard against distortions, or outlandish views of human nature and society.[12] It is one thing to say that cultures are specific and ways of life differ, but this does not mean that a moral attitude to various practices is impossible. Indeed, we do judge past and foreign practices for being unjust or harmful. A concern with understanding the reasons behind these practices does not entail that we cannot judge them. Even though they are related in discussions of human practices, explanation and justification remain separate theoretical concerns.[13]

Another set of kicks at rationalist thought came from the Romantic movement, which flourished roughly between 1760 and 1830.[14] This movement proved to be a major shift in Western

---

[11] I. Berlin's 'Foreword' to Friedrich Meinecke, *Historism* (London, 1972), p. xii. See also Carlo Antoni, *L'Historisme*, trans. Alain Dufour (Geneva, 1963), 1–10.

[12] See Antoni, *L'Historisme*, where he attempts a balanced assessment of historicism.

[13] On this point, see Stuart Hampshire, *Morality and Conflict* (Cambridge, Mass., 1983), 3–7, 126–39.

[14] See the 'Preface' to Schenk, *The Mind of the European Romantics*; 'The Decline of Utopian Ideas in the West' and 'European Unity and its Vicissitudes' both in *CTH*, 20–48 and 175–206, respectively; 'German Romanticism in Petersburg and Moscow' in *RT*, 136–49; 'The Counter-Enlightenment' in *AC*, 1–24; and 'The Apotheosis of the Romantic Will' in *CTH*, 207–37. There exist tape recordings of lectures by Berlin on Romanticism: two recorded talks with Roy Pascal, 'Romanticism and Liberation' and 'Romanticism and Social Change' (Audio

consciousness—in Berlin's judgement, the greatest transformation in Western consciousness in modern times. This is because Romanticism affected many areas of cultural life, ethical thought, and social and political behaviour, and not just aesthetics. It influenced political movements such as Nazism, as well as philosophical movements, most notably existentialism.[15]

In general, the Romantic movement sought to liberate the creative individual and his group. Romanticism glorifies the purity of heart and sentiment, as well as the ideals of particular communities, especially minorities. Whether one reads the writings of Fichte, Hamann, Herder, Byron, or Baudelaire, the message is the same: it is the (often lonely) individual who creates works of art out of his own inner life, his own genius. The notion of archetypes, of eternal forms which rule artistic expression, of mimesis, is denounced as constraining and enslaving. The Romantics argue that there are no such immutable forms which the artist seeks to approximate. Art and life are the expression of one's inner vision of individual or collective existence, and that alone. Art does not imitate Nature; it does not follow immutable codes: it is creative. Artists may express feelings which others know and experience, but they do so in their own unique way, their own style. Great artists are geniuses because they create new things, develop new themes, establish new styles.[16]

According to Berlin, these Romantic views did much to subvert the long-standing view that an objective structure exists independently of human perception, and that it is the goal of intellection to uncover this structure, this *rerum natura*. Berlin argues that 'the common assumption of the Romantics that runs counter to the *philosophia perennis* is that the answers to the great questions are not to be discovered so much as to be invented'.[17]

This view is sceptical of general laws, of immutable codes. It first

---

Learning Discussion Tape, HUA013 (London, 1974)); and his six Mellon Lectures, 'Some Sources of Romanticism' given at the National Gallery, Washington, DC, in June and July 1965. This last series of lectures is available in the National Sound Archive, The British Library, London. These were rebroadcast on the BBC during June and July 1989 in celebration of Sir Isaiah's 80th birthday.

[15] 'Some Sources of Romanticism' Mellon Lectures (1965), see n. 14, 'In Search of a Definition' and 'The Lasting Effects' 1st and 6th lectures.

[16] See 'The Counter-Enlightenment' in *AC*, 9–10, 17–20.

[17] See 'Preface' to Schenk *The Mind of European Romantics*, p. xvi.

overturned classical aesthetics; it was not long before it attacked moral codes. Given that the various Romantic movements propounded a philosophy of life, it was inevitable that the revolt would proceed beyond the confines of art.

In essence, Romantics find merit not in the perennial, but in the original, and the new. Along with cultural historicist thought, such as that of Herder, Romanticism celebrates individual and cultural variety. Variety itself is good; sameness is a bore. Difference, not uniformity, is the source of life and value.[18] Once again Berlin is on guard against distortions and exaggerations. In this case, he is aware of the disastrous consequences of some Romantic beliefs. He is aware of the dangers in the Romantic cult of the hero, the penchant for grand acts, and the justification of the use of men and women as material for political works. He is conscious of the consequences of such beliefs, in particular the glorification of a superleader, of Napoleon, or worse, a Hitler or Mussolini.[19] Berlin argues that such 'negative' aspects of Romanticism come hand in hand with its 'positive' aspects. Both, undeniably, have had great effects on modern politics. Yet he makes distinctions, and identifies with what he calls the 'positive . . . heritage of Romanticism'.[20] With discernment, he states that the Romantic movement encourages

respect for individuality, for the creative impulse, for the unique, the independent, for freedom to live and act in the light of personal, undictated beliefs and principles, of undistorted emotional needs, for the value of private life, of personal relationships, of the individual conscience, of human rights. The positive and negative heritage of Romanticism—on the one hand contempt for opportunism, regard for individual variety, scepticism of oppressive general formulae and final solutions, and on the other self-prostration before superior beings and the exaltation of arbitrary power, passion and cruelty—these tendencies all at once reflected and promoted by Romantic doctrines have done more to mould both the events of our century and the concepts in terms of which they are viewed

[18] 'European Unity and its Vicissitudes' in *CTH*, 188–95. Berlin says much the same in his talk with Roy Pascal, 'Romanticism and Liberation', as well as in his Mellon Lectures.

[19] In his talk with Roy Pascal, 'Romanticism and Liberation', Berlin claims that Romanticism is appropriate for aesthetics, instructive in moral theory, but disastrous in political practice.

[20] 'Preface' to H. G. Schenk, *The Mind of European Romantics*, p. xvii.

and explained than is commonly recognized in most histories of our time.[21]

It is important to realize that Berlin's historiographical analysis of the various critiques of monistic thought is central to his own view of human nature, of moral and social existence. He agrees with historicists that the ideals of civilizations change over time. He follows cultural critics, such as Herder, in praising the importance of variety in cultural life. With some reservations, he accepts the Romantic critique of morality, and sees much in the view that the individual is a creative fountain, an expressive being, and should be left free to develop. Together, these views lead him to conclude that Ionian principles are false; that there is a plurality of goods; that these often collide; that some of them are incommensurable; and finally, that the freedom of persons and the plurality of ideals preclude the achievement of a final synthesis of cultural ends. Moreover, for Berlin, all these new discoveries about human nature support his belief in political liberalism, in tolerance, diversity, private life, in short, in freedom for individuals and minorities.[22]

Moral Pluralism, Moral Conflict, and Moral Relativism

If there can be said to be anything like a set of central ideas in Berlin's work, then the idea of moral pluralism is among them.[23] As with the critique of Ionian principles, the tenet itself has been worked out in his historiographical studies, in particular in readings of Machiavelli, Vico, Montesquieu, and Herder. Yet Berlin has produced few writings dedicated solely to the notion of moral or value pluralism. Regardless, his references to the subject are numerous; from a survey of them one can gather what are his views

[21] H. G. Schenk, *The Mind of European Romantics*, pp. xvii–xviii.

[22] See the Jahanbegloo interview, 23–48; and 'Two Concepts of Liberty' in *FE*, 167–72. For a general study of Romantic tendencies in liberal thought, with a brief mention of Berlin, see Nancy Rosenblum, *Another Liberalism: Romanticism and the Reconstruction of Liberal Thought* (Cambridge, Mass., 1987), 74–7.

[23] Many scholars have pointed to the centrality of pluralism in Berlin's thought. See John Gray, 'Negative and Positive Liberty' in *Liberalisms: Essays in Political Philosophy* (London, 1989), 45–68 at 64–6; Roger Hausheer, 'Berlin and the Emergence of Liberal Pluralism' in *European Liberty* (The Hague, 1983), 49–80; and Jonathan Lieberson and Sidney Morgenbesser, 'Isaiah Berlin' in *Isaiah Berlin: A Celebration*, 1–30.

of moral pluralism.[24] First, there is a multiplicity of good ends and admirable ways of life. Second, good ends and admirable ways of life may conflict. Third, conflict entails the incompatibility of some ends and ways of life, or that they cannot be combined without loss. Fourth, some ends and ways of life are incommensurable, or cannot be measured according to one universal standard. And fifth, no comprehensive synthesis of moral goods can be revealed by either reason or faith.

The first assertion is unproblematic; though some moral theories, especially utilitarianism, deny this point, or at least its significance. However, we know that justice is different from mercy; love from friendship; moderation from asceticism; liberty from equality; faith from enlightenment; art from knowledge; and so on. We also know that one lives differently if one is a soldier rather than a philosopher; a monk rather than a politician; or a farmer rather than a scholar. Each life has its own characteristic virtues and ideals. Good ends and admirable ways of life can conflict. Liberty and equality may conflict in economic policy. Freedom for the banker may mean poverty for the farmer. Mercy for the accused often clashes with principles of justice. And the artist's dedication to his work may lead to a neglect of his familial obligations.[25] (Both Gauguin and Flaubert sacrificed family life to their art.) Thus to take one path in moral life often restricts another. Moreover, it is often a matter of luck if we achieve our goals: no artist is certain that his quest will be fruitful or successful. Because of moral conflict we cannot achieve an impartial vantage point to calculate the correct and best path. Incompatibility and conflict, choice and luck limit the applicability of abstract moral theories.[26]

---

[24] In addition to essays on Machiavelli, Vico, Montesquieu, and Herder, there are several other places where Berlin is concerned explicitly, though not exclusively, with pluralism. To be noted are his 'Reply to Ronald H. McKinney, "Towards a Postmodern Ethics: Sir Isaiah Berlin and John Caputo" ' in *Journal of Value Inquiry*, 26 (1992) 557–60; 'Note on Alleged Relativism in Eighteenth-Century European Thought' in *CTH*, 70–90; his short statements, 'The Incompatibility of Values' and 'Virtue and Practicality', both in Melvin Kranzberg (ed.), *Ethics in an Age of Pervasive Technology* (Boulder, Colo., 1980), 32–3 and 193; and *VH*, pp. xxii–xxiv, 153, 206–16; his linking of pluralism and liberalism, 'Two Concepts of Liberty' in *FE*, 167–71; and 'The Pursuit of the Ideal' in *CTH*, 1–19.
[25] See 'The Pursuit of the Ideal', 11–14; and Bernard Williams, 'Conflicts of Values' in Alan Ryan (ed.), *The Idea of Freedom*, 221–32.
[26] Stuart Hampshire discusses the case of Flaubert in *Morality and Conflict*, 38–9. On the Gauguin problem, see Bernard Williams, 'Moral Luck' in *Moral Luck:*

For the pluralist, conflict is constitutive of moral life. This is evident in cases where obligations clash. Antigone is torn between her obligation to her brothers and to her city. Competing loyalties force her to make a tragic choice.[27] Another case in point is that of the resistance fighter who must choose between his duty to the nation or his duty to his family. If he chooses the former, he may bring reprisals on his family. If he does not fight, he may protect his family, but only at the cost of the liberty of his nation.[28] This situation is not just one of a conflict of duties within a particular life. It is conflict between 'two different ways of life, which cannot be combined into one' to quote Berlin's lifelong friend, the Oxford philosopher Stuart Hampshire. Either course necessitates the cultivation of particular sets of virtues and dispositions. Some of these virtues are the same, but they may be differently identified. Thus loyalty is a part of either life. But loyalty to one's family and loyalty to *la patrie* are obviously different, and require different subordinate virtues and different rankings of skills. The life of the dutiful son does not usually demand that one be patriotic, or violent and deceitful. The life of the resister does.[29]

To choose between either way of life entails certain losses. To be a resister one may have to kill. One cannot be both a pacifist and a resistance fighter. Less dramatic instances can also be cited. To be a politician requires derogation of some virtues. One cannot be a member of a cabinet and respond openly and fully to all queries put to oneself. A finance minister would be acting inappropriately if she responded openly to questions about a possible change in the currency rate; hence, politics and forthrightness often clash.[30] In short, cultivating one set of virtues leads to the sacrifice of some other virtues or of a whole set of dispositions and skills.

The same holds for cultures. A Christian culture cannot readily sustain civic virtues. A concern with the purity of one's soul is at odds with civic virtue. According to Berlin, this much Machiavelli taught us: that one cannot seek salvation and love one's *patrie* at the same time. One must choose a particular way of life, and derogate or abrogate from other possible lives and virtues. Unlike Machiavelli, Berlin argues that either life *on its own merits* is

Philosophical Papers, 20–39. The moral theories Williams has in mind are utilitarianism and Kantian deontological theories, such as Rawls's.

[27] See 'The Pursuit of the Ideal', 11–14.
[28] Hampshire, *Morality and Conflict*, 32–3.   [29] Ibid. 33.   [30] Ibid. 159.

worthwhile. Machiavelli clearly preferred the civic life, which he considered to be superior to a life lived according to Christian virtues. Regardless of the preference, or debate about the ranking, it remains none the less true, as Machiavelli maintained, that Christian polities cannot be glorious. A polity of Christians cannot exhibit all the virtues of civic-mindness praised by ancient Roman writers.[31]

The claim that cultures and ways of life are multiple and cannot be combined became the centrepiece of much counter-Enlightenment thought, in particular that of Herder. For Herder, each culture is typified by its own unique 'centre of gravity'.[32] Like Vico, Herder explored the differences between cultures. He concluded that not only do we have to interpret cultures on their own terms, but that cultures are valuable because of their differences. Herder concluded that these differences and incompatibilities make it impossible to rank cultures objectively according to one universal standard. Worse is to try to rank another culture according to the standards of one's own civilization.[33] Berlin accepts these views. He argues that pluralism entails the incommensurability of goods and ways of life.[34] If goods are multiple, conflicting, if ways of life or cultures collide, and if a moral decision may necessitate loss, then there can be no 'possibility of some over-arching criterion which objectively determines what, in a given situation, all men at all times in all places are required to pursue'.[35] When conflicts arise, when comparative judgements are needed, there often exists, as Bernard Williams puts it, 'no common currency' to calculate gains and losses.[36] Stuart Hampshire calls this the 'no-shopping principle'. When we deal with whole ways of life, we cannot add up characteristics and dispositions at will. Moral life is not like supermarket shopping. The range of choices is not meaningfully determined by how much free time one may have or the size of one's purse. Sets of dispositions and whole ways of life are exclusionary. To cultivate one admirable way of life has the correlated effect of distancing other no less noble ways of life.[37]

---

[31] 'The Originality of Machiavelli' in *AC*, 58, 66–71.
[32] Cited by Berlin in *VH*, p. xxiii.   [33] Ibid., pp. xxii–xxiv.
[34] Ibid. 210–11.   [35] I. Berlin, 'Reply to Ronald H. McKinney', 557.
[36] Williams, 'Conflict of Values', 226.
[37] Hampshire, *Morality and Conflict*, 146–9.

The experience of incommensurability in moral life restricts in many non-trivial ways the applicability of the two main modern theories of morality, utilitarianism and Kantianism, including John Rawls's theory of justice.[38] The classical theory of ethics also suffers a decisive blow from pluralism.[39] Berlin writes that pluralism leads to the

belief not merely in the multiplicity, but in the incommensurability, of the values of different cultures and societies and, in addition, in the incompatibility of equally valid ideals, together with the implied revolutionary corollary that the classical notions of an ideal man and of an ideal society are intrinsically incoherent and meaningless.[40]

For Berlin, the incompatibility and incommensurability of goods and cultures make it impossible to think of realizing a perfect synthesis of virtues. An ideal unity of all virtues is nonsensical. This is true of individuals and of societies. Utopia is 'nowhere' not because conditions will never allow for it; the fault, according to Berlin, is intrinsic and conceptual. He tells us that if goods are multiple and cannot be combined without loss, then a perfect polity is in principle incoherent. It is not by accident that we cannot have a utopia. Utopian schemes for a harmony of goods are wrong in theory, because goods are intrinsically competitive and incompatible.[41]

Yet Berlin insists that moral pluralism does not amount to moral relativism, to a Babel of moral codes, without the possibility of comparative judgement.[42] While cultural studies do indeed enable us to understand that 'our values are ours, and theirs are theirs'. None the less, '[w]e are free to criticise the values of other cultures, to condemn them' if we so wish.[43] But if our values are culturally specific, on what grounds can we judge other cultures, or past ways of life? Further, if we live with our values, how can we begin to understand other foreign dispositions, habits, and mores?

To solve this problem, Berlin draws on his theory of imaginative

[38] Hampshire, *Morality and Conflict*, 143–9, 151, 161–2; and Williams, 'Moral Luck', 24–5, 33–9.

[39] See Hampshire, *Morality and Conflict*, 150–6.

[40] *VH*, 153.

[41] See 'The Pursuit of the Ideal' and 'The Decline of Utopian Ideas in the West' both in *CTH*, 11–19 and 20–48.

[42] See 'The Pursuit of the Ideal' in *CTH*, 10–14; and 'Introduction' to *FE*, pp. l–lii. See also Hampshire, *Morality and Conflict*, 154–8.

[43] 'The Pursuit of the Ideal' in *CTH*, 11.

interpretation, discussed in Chapter 2. He argues that the possibility of empathy, of understanding other cultures, presupposes a certain unity of the species. If we did not exhibit similarities in our dispositions and habits, then we could not begin to enter into and comprehend different ways of life and foreign cultures. Because we can understand the past and foreign cultures, there must be commonality between people in different civilizations.[44] His views do not entail relativism, nor did those of Vico and Herder:

Members of one culture can, by the force of imaginative insight, understand (what Vico called *entrare*) the values, the ideals, the forms of life of another culture or society, even those remote in time and space. They may find these values inacceptable, but if they open their minds sufficiently they can grasp how one might be a full human being, with whom one could communicate, and at the same time live in the light of values widely different from one's own, but which nevertheless one can see to be values, ends of life, by the realisation of which men could be fulfilled.

'I prefer coffee, you prefer champagne. We have different tastes. There is no more to be said.' That is relativism.[45]

Unfortunately, this will not do. What this defence asserts is that cultures are intelligible. We do not inhabit cultural monads, or live in windowless boxes.[46] Habits are not so many and so different that we cannot understand other ways of life. But here Berlin confuses issues. He confuses epistemological relativism with moral relativism, and asserts that if the former is untrue so is the latter.[47] But the claim of moral relativism is distinct from the epistemological claim, even though moral unity would entail common intelligibility.

The cultural relativist will assert that we cannot judge foreign or past practices *because* they are different. Intelligibility may or may not be a factor. One can understand an ancient practice—say, slavery—and still hold that we cannot pass judgement on such a practice. Or, if we do, then we impose our standards on those of past eras and foreign lands. To take another example: it is not our

[44] See 'Introduction' to *FE*, pp. xxx–xxxiii, liii.
[45] 'The Pursuit of the Ideal', 10–11. On this score, Berlin states that the criticism of his views by Arnaldo Momigliano is wrong. See Arnaldo Momigliano, 'On the Pioneer Trail' (review article of *Vico and Herder*), in the *New York Review of Books* (11 Nov. 1976), 33–8 at 34 ff.; and Berlin's 'Note on Alleged Relativism in Eighteenth-Century European Thought' in *CTH*, 70–90, esp. 76–8.
[46] 'Note on Alleged Relativism in Eighteenth-Century European Thought' in *CTH*, 85.
[47] Ibid. 85–9; and the Jahanbegloo interview, 36–40.

place to judge the practice of female circumcision. This ritual is part of a whole way of life, indeed it is a crucial ritual of initiation for some cultures, and as such we have no business judging it. An honest interpreter will resist judgemental attitudes. To denounce such rituals, from outside the cultures that practise them, is to delude oneself and fail to tolerate norms and attitudes specific to foreign cultures.[48]

It is a commonplace point in moral theory that relativism is incoherent. This is because the injunctions neither to judge nor to interfere with foreign practices presuppose a non-relative moral standard. Relativists prescribe tolerance, yet such a universal norm cannot be allowed on relativist grounds. The same holds for any proscription or injunction which a relativist may make: according to the theory one cannot make such assertions, and thus one is inconsistent and self-contradictory in holding and invoking them.[49]

In places, Berlin seems to accept this critique.[50] He also tentatively asserts that some 'universal and "basic" human values' must exist. But he is uncertain what they are.[51] He believes that the malleability of the human species in moral matters is limited. Pluralism has its limits. We know that men have many similar needs and dispositions; that they need food and shelter, liberty, justice, a sense of belonging, and make moral judgements with the use of concepts like good and evil, decent and vile, just and unjust, beneficial and harmful. Human beings are recognizable as human beings only if they are moral beings, only if they make worthy moral judgements.[52] But this continues to beg the question. What we need to know is whether moral judgements can be valid apart from the context of their enunciation; that is, that moral judgements can in principle exceed the bounds of a given culture, that they can be valid universally.

Berlin's argument concludes that the intelligibility of past

---

[48] For a survey of relativist thought, see D. H. Monro, 'Relativism in Ethics' in Philip P. Wiener (ed.), *Dictionary of the History of Ideas*, iv. 70–3.

[49] See Bernard Williams, *Morality: An Introduction to Ethics* (Cambridge, 1972), 34–9.

[50] See his 'Introduction' to *FE*, pp. li–lii; and 'Note on Alleged Relativism in Eighteenth-Century European Thought' in *CTH*, 87–8, n. 1.

[51] 'Introduction' to *FE*, pp. lii–liii; and the Jahanbegloo interview, 37–40.

[52] Letter to Beata Polanowska-Sygulska (24 Feb. 1988), 3. See also his 'Introduction' to *FE*, pp. xxxi–xxxii; 'Reply to Kocis', 389–90; 'Rationality of Value Judgments' in Carl J. Friedrich (ed.), *Nomos 7, Rational Decision* (New York, 1964), 221–3; 'European Unity and its Vicissitudes' in *CTH*, 202–6.

practices implies the possibility of trans-cultural and trans-historical judgements. This is because whenever we judge others (be they dead or alive) we do so with some understanding of what they have done. Understanding allows for moral judgement. Berlin explicitly states that this occurs in historical writing. A principal thesis of his essay 'Historical Inevitability' is that there can be no axiologically neutral rendition of past events; that historical writing contains moral judgement.[53] But on what grounds can we assert the validity of our moral judgements? Berlin answers that we must bring to bear all that we know about human interests and cultures. We must then apply informed moral standards to human practices. Regardless of cultural pluralism, he is convinced that 'there is a great deal of broad agreement among people in different societies over long stretches of time about what is right and wrong, good and evil'. Thus 'we must not dramatize the incompatibility of values . . .'. We know that fundamental justice cannot allow for torture, slavery, and pogroms. Even though past cultures may have engaged in such practices, and justified them by various arguments, we know the practices and justifications to be wrong (as many at the time and place of their occurrence knew as well). In this sense, it is up to the sceptics to show how society can be just, good, and decent, and still allow, let alone condone, such practices.[54]

Berlin believes that we make moral judgements under the assumption that they are true. We proceed 'as if' our injunctions and sanctions are correct.[55] Moral judgements are assertions about what is true and good for persons in society, as we have come to understand human needs and social and cultural situations. We can reason about moral affairs, even upon this tentative basis.[56] Yet what happens when goods and judgements about them conflict? Berlin offers little more than an ancient invocation of balanced assessments and moderation.[57] In 'The Pursuit of the Ideal' he puts

---

[53] See 'Historical Inevitability' in *FE*, 41–117. This article led to a series of polemical exchanges with the British historian E. H. Carr. See the latter's, *What is History?* Berlin's initial criticisms are in the *Listener* (18 May and 15 June 1961), 877 and 1048–9. For Carr's defence, see his letter in the *Listener* (1 June 1961), 973–4. Berlin's review of Carr's book appeared in the *New Statesman* (5 Jan. 1962), 15–16. And his last response to Carr occurs in the 'Introduction' to *FE*, pp. xxv–xxxi.

[54] 'The Pursuit of the Ideal' in *CTH*, 17–19; 'Reply to Ronald H. McKinney', 557–60; and the Jahanbegloo interview, 37–9.

[55] Athenaeum interview.   [56] 'Reply to Ronald H. McKinney', 559–60.

[57] See his treatment of equality in 'Equality' in *CC*, 81–102 at 96–102.

the problem this way:

How do we choose between possibilities? What and how much must we sacrifice to what? There is, it seems to me, no clear reply. But the collisions, even if they cannot be avoided, can be softened. Claims can be balanced, compromises can be reached: in concrete situations not every claim is of equal force—so much liberty and so much equality; so much for sharp moral condemnation, and so much for understanding a given human situation; so much for the full force of the law, and so much for the prerogative of mercy; for feeding the hungry, clothing the naked, healing the sick, sheltering the homeless. Priorities, never final and absolute, must be established.[58]

This is a call for moderation, for *sophrosyne*, and for balanced and prudent judgement, for *phronesis*. Berlin tells us that these two latter virtues assure 'morally acceptable behavior', and a decent and just life.[59] He also adds the modern virtue of toleration, for avoiding the occurrence of intolerable choices.[60] These are Berlin's minimal moral invocations. They presuppose conflict between goods, tragic losses and yet they search for an integration of fundamental human interests and good ends. Unfortunately, this designates little that is specific about the best political order.[61]

   This is no serious failing, however. It should be remembered that Berlin's critique of monism is only directed against some kinds of moral theory. What he rejects is 'the traditional belief in the necessary harmony of values in a rational universe, whether as the reality beneath the appearances, or as the ideal presupposed both by reason and faith'.[62] Such a vision commits the Ionian fallacy. It presupposes that because we rank ends, prescribe some acts, and censure others, that there must be an ideal order *of all goods* lying behind the phenomena of moral life. But if goods conflict, and there exist a multiplicity of admirable ways of life, none of which can be combined without some loss, then there is no ideal political order that can contain all goods and all admirable ways of life.

   The target of Berlin's critique is this monistic model, not moral

---

[58] 'The Pursuit of the Ideal' in *CTH*, 17. See also 'Introduction' to *FE*, pp. lv–lvi.
[59] 'The Pursuit of the Ideal' in *CTH*, 17–19. See also 'The Three Strands in My Life' 5–7.
[60] 'Reply to Ronald H. McKinney', 558–9; and the Jahanbegloo interview, 43–8, 142–4.
[61] I give a full treatment of Berlin's arguments for a liberal political order in Chs. 5–8.   [62] *VH*, p. xii.

judgement in general. As Berlin, and other scholars indicate, a monistic model runs throughout the ethical tradition, from Plato and Aristotle to Hegel and Marx, and from Kant to, possibly, Rawls. This whole tradition takes conflict of goods to be a sign of pathology, as a disease that only clear and ordered thinking can, should, and will overcome.[63] Historicists and pluralists, such as Vico and Herder, have done much to undermine this vision.[64] This counter-Enlightenment movement is anti-rationalist, but its teachings are not for that irrational. It is possible to argue, on the one hand, that no rational theory of morality will specify a right order for any particular culture, and on the other, still hold that we can reasonably speak of essential virtues, universal values, common goods, and superior political orders.[65] Berlin's stand is quite reasonable. His preference for moderation, prudence, and toleration lead him easily to claim that the best political order is one that accommodates numerous virtues, a plurality of values, or most of the dispositions which specific cultures, peoples, individuals will hold to be valuable.[66] Nor does his position preclude morality, or entail relativism. A pluralist can still make moral judgements. Pluralism does not preclude us from having a universal or common human moral attitude toward specific cultures and particular practices. We can say that ancient Greek society was unjust because it dealt unfairly with women and slaves. We can call female circumcision a violation of fundamental justice because it impinges on the security of the person. We can also say, as many within and outside such cultures now do, that the damage done by clitorectomies far outweighs its functional worth in maintaining tribal customs and social unity. The practice can be eliminated without significant damage to the traditional culture. The same holds true for the Indian custom calling widows to throw themselves on their husband's funeral pyre, which was banned by British imperial order.[67] In these cases, the loss is borne by men as a

[63] See Hampshire, *Morality and Conflict*, 1–3, 140–69; and Williams, 'Conflicts of Values', 221–6, 230–1.

[64] See *VH*, pp. xiii–xxvii; 'Vico and the Ideal of the Enlightenment'. in *AC*, 120–9; and Hampshire, *Morality and Conflict*, 164–9.

[65] See 'Introduction' to *FE*, pp. lv–lvi; and 'Reply to Ronald H. McKinney', 557–60. On this point, also see Hampshire, *Morality and Conflict*, 36–42.

[66] This is of course a liberal political order. See the Jahanbegloo interview, 40–8.

[67] Correspondence (15 Apr. and 16 May 1991).

loss of control over women; which, upon reflection may be judged improper even according to the codes of such a culture.[68]

What this ideal of balance and toleration dismisses are moral theories that seek to order goods and ways of life according to one single criterion.[69] The moral pluralist considers it wrong to order cultures, as the Enlightenment did, according to a single criterion, such as scientific enlightenment. More, much more, must be understood and come into any judgement of cultures, their ends and their ways of life. Such a theory none the less still accepts that we proceed with a set of moral values and ideals, with what is considered good for persons in general. Moral debate always involves such models of humanity and society. These models always include hierarchies, priorities, and conceptions of the best and perfect life.[70] What Berlin argues is that any such model can at best be a sketch, and not a full picture of the best ethical life. For example, if human rights exist and are based on common human values (such as the prohibition of murder), their promotion does not cover the full extent of ordinary moral life. Rather, they deal with a minimal moral order, what can be accepted by all human beings as good, just, and the basis for a decent form of life.[71]

Stuart Hampshire, for one, supports this view and develops the implications of Berlin's thesis about moral pluralism. Hampshire argues that moralities are like natural languages. We can speak of their grammar and syntax, but a moral Esperanto or an Adamantine language are limited in their capacity to capture customs and mores. Moralities, conventions, manners, and institutions are like idioms and dialects. Differences and variations of moral codes and customs are constitutive of human life. To abstract from these differences, and consider this abstraction the essence of moral life, is to operate with a limited moral vision, not a full or accurate one. Of course we may speak of consistent and essential values and virtues, such as justice, courage, friendship, temperance, and intellectual acumen. But these virtues may be identified and

---

[68] For contemporary African cases, see Dominique Vernier, 'La blessure de l'excision', in *Le Monde diplomatique* (Oct. 1988), 10.

[69] Thus utilitarianism is a deficient theory because it cannot deal with the complexity of moral life. On this case, see 'Equality' in *CC*, 81–102 at 81, 88, 101–2; 'Does Political Theory Still Exist?' in *CC*, 150–4. See also Hampshire, *Morality and Conflict*, 18–31.   [70] See 'Reply to Kocis', 390–1.

[71] 'Reply to Ronald H. McKinney', 558–60; the Jahanbegloo interview, 39–40, 113–15; and correspondence (16 May 1991).

ordered differently in different societies. The forms they take are specific to historically developed cultures. The error in ancient theory, even with so reasonable a thinker as Aristotle, was to identify one particular form of life as the final and best actualization of human virtues. A dominant error in the tradition is to believe in and search for an Adamantine moral language, a kind of moral Esperanto.[72] Of course we may add to a list of essential values and virtues. Thus we may include charity and forgiveness, Christian values, as possible candidates for common values; and add them to some of those put forward on a systematic basis by ancient Greek theorists. What this pluralist and developmental model presumes is that we can make moral judgements, but allows for the fact that we accumulate knowledge, find new values and virtues, order old ones differently, even dispense with some dispositions and practices, which, upon reflection, can be considered less worthy than they once appeared to be or perhaps are now judged to be false.[73] Indeed, as Berlin states, such moral progress is often the result of conflict and the accommodation between cultures and visions of the good life.[74]

Thus it is one thing to say that the particular form and ranking that virtues will take is relative to history and specific cultures, and another to say that we can neither reason about these differences nor judge various practices across time and space. Or, the claim that no ideal culture exists or that cultures are incommensurable in the light of abstract theory does not imply that we cannot judge particular cultural traits to be either praiseworthy or blameworthy. As Stuart Hampshire says, 'the "no shopping" principle in its application is . . . a matter of degree'.[75] If we could not judge our practices against other ways of life, nor reform them, moral life would be quite senseless and unintelligible. Thus it is one thing to agree with Berlin and deny that there is a 'necessary harmony of

---

[72] See Hampshire, *Morality and Conflict*, 36–43, 134–5, 140–54, 156, 160, 166–7.

[73] See Hampshire, *Morality and Conflict*, 35. In the latter instance, torture could be cited as an example. The ancients and early moderns considered torture to be a justifiable device of forensic investigation. Only during the 16th century, starting with Montesquieu, did arguments against the utility and morality of this practice emerge and gain credence. Today, the human right not to be tortured is part of national and international legal cultures.

[74] 'Note on Alleged Relativism in Eighteenth-Century European Thought' in *CTH*, 90.

[75] Hampshire, *Morality and Conflict*, 149. See Williams, 'Conflicts of Values', 229–32.

values in a rational universe', and another to assert that this means that all moral judgements are non-cognitive, spurious, or relativistic.

What is good for us? What is best for us? What polity best fulfils our fundamental interests? These are all questions which can be put and answered regardless of the thesis of moral and cultural pluralism. We can accept moral pluralism and still hold to the claim that regardless of culture and history there exists a 'horizon of common human values'.[76] It is not a contradiction to do so. In short, notions of the human good and conceptions of the ideal life survive the historicist critique of ethics; while the notion of one, and only one, ideal life for all, does not.[77]

In sum, Berlin's version of moral pluralism does not imply moral relativism. On the contrary, relativism is false because pluralism is a fact of moral life. The very experience of conflict exposes how objective ethics can be. If morality were a matter of preference or subjective desire, then conflicts would not be experienced in the pathetic and tragic ways we know that they are in fact experienced.[78] Michael Walzer put this best when he wrote that pluralism

can indeed be borne, can even be celebrated as the necessary outcome of human freedom and creativity. But this celebration does not entail relativism—for two reasons: first, because the discovery of a pluralist universe is a real discovery; there really are many visions and many ways, self-validating and uncombinable; and second, because the freedom that gives rise to these visions and ways is genuinely valuable.[79]

As with anyone else's, Berlin's political theory would make no sense if he were a relativist. If he were a relativist, he could not sustain a meaningful or coherent defence of liberty and liberalism. In Chapter 5 I will return to the charge that his liberalism is founded on relativist assumptions, and thus is incoherent. At this point, I wish only to assert that Berlin takes moral pluralism to be a

[76] 'Introduction' to *FE*, p. xxxii; and 'Reply to Ronald H. McKinney', 56.

[77] Thus Hampshire argues for the continuing relevance of Aristotelian ethics (see *Morality and Conflict*, 37–42).

[78] 'Two Concepts of Liberty' in *FE*, 169. Williams ('Conflicts of Values', 225) puts the point this way: '[I]n so far as we are drawn towards the objectivity of ethics by an impression which is borne in on us in moral experience, the experience of ultimate moral conflict is precisely one which brings most irremovably with it the impression of objectivity: that there is nothing one decently, honourably, adequately, *can* do in a certain situation seems a kind of truth as firmly independent of the will or inclination as any truth of morality seems.'

[79] Michael Walzer, 'Introduction' to Isaiah Berlin's *The Hedgehog and the Fox* (New York, 1986), [p. x].

strong argument for liberal institutions. Liberal states give individuals and minorities room to realize their capacities and seek their own ends, and thus recognize pluralism as a constitutive characteristic of moral life. Yet this giving of liberty would be absurd if men were not free. Moral pluralism implies the need to make choices, but it does not entail that we choose freely. For this point about freedom we have to turn to a discussion of Berlin's critique of determinism.

Freedom and Morality

The fact of pluralism entails a central place for liberty in moral life. If goods are multiple, often conflicting, and incommensurable, then we must choose our path in life. In other words, liberty has a 'privileged status' in moral life once the fact of pluralism is taken into account.[80] But the perennial questions remain: Are persons free? Do they have free will?

Berlin does not so much argue that freedom is a permanent characteristic of human nature, as claim that determinism is counter-intuitive. He starts with the question: If all human actions were determined, then what would follow? He believes that the consequences of such a position, if consistently held, run counter to what we take to be true about persons and society, in particular, our moral experiences. On Berlin's grounds, the determinist model is inadequate to our general understanding of people: it distorts much of what we know to be true of our behaviour, and discounts much of what we need in order to act as moral beings. This argument needs to be unpacked.

In general, determinists claim that the cause of any human action can be attributed to conditions antecedent to any particular action. These conditions may be social, psychological, natural, or a composite of such causes. To understand an action is to know these antecedent causes. Once known, we can predict human action and explain it by pointing to its causes. As in scientific explanation, the test of any determinist theory is its power of prediction. And most, if not all, determinists believe that human action is potentially fully predictable.

[80] John Gray, 'On Negative and Positive Liberty' in *Liberalisms*, 47–8; and his *Liberalism* (Minneapolis, 1986), 38–9.

Free actions, on the other hand, are neither so conditioned, nor necessary. I am said to be free, if and only if, in doing *X*, I could just as well have chosen to do *Y*, or *Z*, or *A*, or *B*, and so on. Free acts concern the choice of two or more alternative paths. It will not do to say that I am free but can only choose one path. Furthermore, free acts are commonly taken to mean acts that are unconstrained by physical or psychological impediments. According to Berlin 'freedom is to do with the absence of obstacles to action'.[81] Freedom is a function of the lack (or removal) of any 'obstacles to action', whether they be external ones, such as the police, or internal ones, such as neuroses. To be free, therefore, is to make an unconditioned and uncoerced choice between two or more possible unimpeded avenues of action.[82]

In his 1964 article, 'From Hope and Fear Set Free', Berlin discusses the twin theses of freedom and determinism. He writes that,

> The central assumption of common thought and speech seems to me to be that freedom is the principal characteristic that distinguishes man from all that is non-human; that there are degrees of freedom, degrees constituted by the absence of obstacles to the exercise of choice; the choice being regarded as not itself determined by antecedent conditions, at least not as being wholly so determined. It may be that common sense is mistaken in this matter, as in others; but the onus of refutation is on those who disagree.[83]

In supporting his claim, Berlin finds little to question in the common-sense view of freedom.[84] He does grant that some acts may well be determined; this is confirmed by advances in science. Increases in our knowledge of human behaviour have eliminated much action from the category of free activity.[85] But advances in psychology or economics do not demonstrate full determinism; some human acts may well be determined, this is quite plausible. What is implausible is a claim that most if not all human acts are

---

[81] 'From Hope and Fear Set Free' in *CC*, 190.

[82] Ibid. 182–4, 190–1. Berlin does not accept the version of self-determination which claims that one is free to act according to one's character, but that one's character is determined by antecedent causes. Such a theory is at variance with our normal understanding of freedom and moral worth (see 179–89; and 'Historical Inevitability' in *FE*, 64–5, n. 1).

[83] 'From Hope and Fear Set Free' in *CC*, 190.   [84] Ibid.

[85] See 'Historical Inevitability' in *FE*, 70–5; and 'From Hope and Fear Set Free' in *CC*, 182, 188–9.

ineluctably the result of antecedent causes, whether these be sociological or psychological or physiological, or a combination of all these factors. On this issue, on the validity of strong determinism, the burden of proof, as Berlin states above, falls on the determinists.[86]

Berlin, however, wants to make the determinist's job harder. His hope is that by showing the absurd consequences of the determinist claim, the plausibility of the idea of human freedom will be strengthened. One senses of course that Berlin hopes that determinism is false (and freedom true). Yet his exercise is negative and critical, in the sense that he wonders about the conditions which would make the determinist's claim true. Once these conditions are shown to be absurd and untenable, this thesis is half-defeated, or at least kept at bay. By showing the limits of the determinist's thesis, Berlin makes room for the position of freedom. He does not establish the thesis of free will. Nor does he argue that determinism is false. He only finds that without free will, a good deal of what is human, and what we do, makes no sense at all.[87] To argue his case, Berlin conducts a thought experiment. He asks us to think of a world in which all human acts are determined by antecedent causes.[88] Second, he asks us to assume that we know these causes. What would happen if one knew all causes of human behaviour? What would change if human actions were not only caused, but known to be caused? Berlin tells us that,

Knowledge of the causes and conditions that determine my choice—knowledge, indeed, that there are such conditions and causes, knowledge that choice is not free (without analysis of this proposition), knowledge that shows that the notion of moral responsibility is wholly compatible with rigorous determinism, and exposes libertarianism as a confusion due to ignorance or error—that kind of knowledge would assimilate our moral views to aesthetic ones, and would lead us to look on heroism or honesty or justice as we now do on beauty or kindness or strength or genius: we praise or congratulate the possessors of the latter qualities with no implication that they could have chosen to own a different set of

---

[86] See Berlin's 'Introduction' to *FE*, pp. x–xxxvii, where he responds to criticisms of his position on determinism.

[87] Berlin had to repeat these points several times, especially in response to E. H. Carr's criticisms of 'Historical Inevitability' (see Berlin's two letters to the editor of the *Listener* (18 May and 15 June 1961), 877 and 1048–9; and Berlin's 'Introduction' to *FE*, pp. x–xiv).

[88] See 'From Hope and Fear Set Free' in *CC* 188–9, for one such exercise.

characteristics. This world view, if it became generally accepted, woul
mark a radical shift of categories. If this ever occurs, it will tend to make u
think of much of our present moral and our legal outlook, and of a grea
deal of our penal legislation, as so much barbarism founded on ignoranc
it will enlarge the scope and depth of our sympathy; it will substitut
knowledge and understanding for attribution of responsibility; it wi
render indignation, and the kind of admiration that is its opposit
irrational and obsolete; it will expose notions as desert, merit, responsibility
remorse, and perhaps right and wrong too, as incoherent or, at the ver
least, inapplicable; it will turn praise and blame into purely corrective o
educational instruments, or confine them to aesthetic approval c
disapproval.[89]

In other words, once we imagine such a 'radical shift in categories'
human action no longer is recognizably moral. Nor is it recogniz
ably human without being moral.[90] Full determinism is incompat
ible with our sense of persons as moral agents. In this regard, Berli
is an incompatibilist. He holds that determinism is incompatibl
with moral talk, which is supported by our sense that people ca
act freely. Only free acts can be morally praised or censured, fo
only free persons can be held to be responsible for their actions
Thus Berlin points out that without the concept of free will, th
dependent notions of individual responsibility and moral valu
make no sense. And without moral talk, we can make little sense c
human action.[91]

Of course, we could and eventually may find moral talk to b
nonsense. People may in fact be shown to be un-free, and neve
actually responsible for their acts. Berlin admits that this i
possible. Yet the 'radical shift' in our sense of the world which thi
would entail makes the claim of the determinist suspicious. Th
position is counter-intuitive. For this reason, Berlin believes tha
the onus of proof is on the determinists. It is they who must argu
for determinism; the incompatibilist, like the common person, ha
no reason to change common moral talk, or to dismiss commoi
intuitions about the moral status of people.

Literary examples illustrate these points well. Oedipus' destiny i
fated: his tragedy is determined by antecedent causes, by th
machinations of gods. The same is true of Agamemnon's destiny

[89] 'From Hope and Fear Set Free' in *CC*, 183–4.
[90] Athenaeum interview.
[91] See 'Introduction' to *FE*, p. xviii; 'From Hope and Fear Set Free' in *CC*, 180;
and 'Historical Inevitability' in *FE*, 63–8.

Both are victims of the curse on the House of Atreus. Most of the action in the *Iliad*, to take another example, is the result of the gods fighting amongst themselves. The heroes of the epic are the instruments of the gods. In epic literature we are spectators; somewhat like gods contemplating our own handiwork. In epic literature the world of human action approaches the outward motion of billiard balls; or of atoms moving in space, sometimes colliding, sometimes not, but always acting in accordance with predetermined conditions. Like gods or scientists, we may change the conditions of interaction; but in both instances we are not dealing with what we ordinarily would take to be free interaction on the part of those being acted upon and determined. Indeed, we have an aesthetic attitude towards Oedipus, or Achilles, or Priam. It is out of place to attribute choice to these fictional characters, no less than to all determined agents. It is for this reason that Greek tragedy and Greek epic have no interior plan. The characters in these works are archetypes; their assigned roles determine their acts; their acts do not determine their roles. For this reason it is absurd to praise or blame them for their acts. If we do so, we do it only in the sense that they are archetypes of behaviour which a particular culture considers good and noble, or evil and base. We cannot praise or blame them personally, for they do not act on their own.

A pertinent representation of a radical shift in moral categories occurs in the novel by Anthony Burgess, *A Clockwork Orange*. Here, the vicious and antisocial hero, Alex, goes through a transformation after his treatment by psychologists. He is trained (like Pavlov's dog) to react with disgust to both sex and music. Unfortunately, after his conditioning Alex no longer appears fully human. Certainly his viciousness is subdued, but his capacity to act freely has evaporated. The treatment is successful at one level. Yet we cannot praise him for his newly conditioned good behaviour. Burgess presents us with a pathetic shell of a man, which was his intent. As a Catholic thinker, Burgess's point is very clear: without free will, the notions of sin, guilt, and morality make no sense. Not only is Alex amoral, he is no longer recognizably human. At best the portrayal evokes pity, but no praise for the acts of the conditioned Alex.

Berlin is not a Catholic thinker, like Burgess; yet his point is the same. If one thinks of human beings as fully determined, if one imagines clockwork people, then it is not possible to use moral categories when talking of their acts. Indeed, if full determinism is valid, we cannot be moral beings. As Berlin puts it:

[I]f I literally cannot make my character or behaviour other than it is by an act of choice (or a whole pattern of such acts) which is itself not fully determined by causal antecedents, then I do not see in what normal sense a rational person could hold me morally responsible either for my character or for my conduct. Indeed the notion of a morally responsible being becomes, at best, mythological; this fabulous creature joins the ranks of nymphs and centaurs.[92]

If strong determinism is valid, then action must be archetypical and plastic, as in ancient literature; or human agents must be other than we know and take them to be; they must actually be the deformed half-human beings who inhabit dystopic novels, or the fabulous creatures of myth. But reality is otherwise. For this reason, Berlin holds that determinism and morality are incompatible. Strong determinism may make sense in the plots of some playwrights, novelists, and ancient epics; yet it is only sensible in these works. As a hypothesis about lived human action, full determinism is quite implausible given our ordinary understanding of experience. If it were valid, then the shift in our categories of experience would indeed be radical, and perhaps beyond the ken of our best fiction writers to represent fully.

Berlin also approaches the problem from the opposite end, from the perspective of freedom. He argues that moral talk needs the concept of freedom. Like Kant, he argues that the free will is constitutive of human beings *qua* moral agents.[93] Without the presumption of free will, it is senseless to attribute responsibility to actors for their acts; and without responsibility, moral terms are meaningless. Furthermore, this is not an empirical but rather a 'conceptual' truth. Not only is freedom a concept we use and apply (correctly or incorrectly) when we describe human action, it is also essential to any moral judgements about man. Thus,

The supposition that, if determinism were shown to be valid, ethical language would have to be drastically revised is not a psychological or a physiological, still less an ethical, hypothesis. It is an assertion about what

---

[92] 'Introduction' to *FE*, p. xvii.

[93] See Immanuel Kant, *The Moral Law [Groundwork of the Metaphysic of Morals]*, trans. H. J. Paton (London, 1948), 107–8; and cf. 'Reply to Kocis', 388–9.

any system of thought that employs the basic concepts of our normal morality would permit or exclude. The proposition that it is unreasonable to condemn men whose choices are not free rests not on a particular set of moral values (which another culture might reject) but on the particular nexus between descriptive and evaluative concepts which governs the language we use and the thoughts we think. To say that you might as well morally blame a table as an ignorant barbarian or an incurable addict is not an ethical proposition, but one which emphasizes the conceptual truth that this kind of praise and blame makes sense only among persons capable of free choice. This is what Kant appeals to; it is this fact that puzzled the early Stoics; before them freedom of choice seems to have been taken for granted; it is presupposed equally in Aristotle's discussion of voluntary and involuntary acts and in the thinking of unphilosophical persons to this day.[94]

In short, Berlin considers the determinist thesis to be incoherent conceptually, and also too radical given our common-sense notions of moral life. Moreover, Berlin believes that in fact few people act as if determinism were valid. He agrees with the Oxford philosopher J. L. Austin on this point. Austin liked to say that he never encountered a determinist who really owns up to the consequences of the thesis. Notwithstanding the position taken by determinists, whether they be scientists or historians, such persons continue to use moral categories.[95] In ordinary life, people in fact do not make the 'radical shift of categories' demanded by the determinist's position. Rather, they act as if moral categories made sense to them. And persons live and die by these categories. Our whole world is inconceivable without them. Few people, if any, be they philosophers or not, think and act, when pressed, as if determinism were true.[96]

Armed with this critique of determinism, Berlin attacks all species of historical determinism. In his 1953 lecture, 'Historical Inevitability', he denounced the tendency in post-Enlightenment historiography to mimic the methods of the natural sciences. Many of these arguments against scientific history are discussed in Chapter 2, above. Berlin's major claim is that the hypothesis that

[94] 'Introduction' to *FE*, pp. xxii–xxiii.
[95] See 'J. L. Austin and the Early Beginnings of Oxford Philosophy' in *PI*, 114; and 'Historical Inevitability' in *FE*, 96–101.
[96] See 'From Hope and Fear Set Free' in *CC*, 188–9. Of course these claims are the object of persistent philosophical debate. I have chosen not to cover this terrain, but merely to survey Berlin's position. For criticisms of Berlin's position, see Morton White, 'Oughts and Cans' in Alan Ryan (ed.), *The Idea of Freedom*, 211–19.

some acts are undetermined must be kept in mind whenever history is written. This is because history would be implausible if things could not have been other than what they were, if counterfactuals, or alternative scenarios, could not be imagined in reference to some events. Moreover, if all acts are in fact predetermined by character, or social forces, or climate, or diet, then it would be impossible to apply moral categories to past events. History would be unlike present experience, in that freedom and moral life would be non-existent.

Berlin finds much evidence in historical writing of the use of concepts such as choice, free will, and their moral correlates, praise, blame, and the attribution of responsibility to individual actors. Historical writing, no less than ordinary discourse, is replete with such concepts; and this is presumably because history could not be radically different from contemporary experience. If it were, we would have difficulty imagining the historical field of activity, or reconstructing accurately and understanding past events. Hence, for Berlin, to think away moral categories would lead to flat historical narratives; one that would miss much of what we hold true of human agency: its interior aspects, its openness, its freedom and morality.[97] Because Berlin takes freedom to be a kind of regulative principle for historical writing, he is sceptical of all types of historical evolutionism, whether the liberal–capitalist brand, such as Saint-Simon's and Comte's, or the scientific-socialist variety, such as Marx's or Stalin's, or that of cultural pessimists, such as Oswald Spengler. These types of evolutionism (or models of decline) are historical variants of the Ionian fallacy, for they hold that human history has but one end, is fixed on one course, such as happiness, or the end of class warfare, or industry and commerce, or universal peace, or the decline of civilization, or whatever.[98] Berlin, in contrast, subscribes to the 'conception of man as an actor, a purposive being, moved by his own conscious aims as well as causal laws, capable of unpredictable flights of thought and imagination'.[99] If this model of human nature and society were not true, Berlin believes that historical change would be meaningless.[100] His view of persons, society and history is dynamic and open-

[97] See 'Introduction' and 'Historical Inevitability' both in *FE*, pp. x–xxxviii and 42–117, respectively.
[98] See 'Historical Inevitability', 41–61, 106–17; and the Jahanbegloo interview, 34–7.   [99] 'Giambattista Vico and Cultural History' in *CTH*, 68–9.
[100] 'Reply to Kocis', 391–3.

ended. He accepts the view that great figures often rise above the tide of history and change it.[101] He does not, however, reduce history to biography and noble deeds. The truth lies somewhere in between the history of social forces and the freedom of individuals to change the course of events.[102] Civilizations develop due to the self-transformation of people and their goals—many people and many goals, not just the great and mighty. In responding to one of his sympathetic critics, Berlin explains that,

One of my deepest beliefs is that one of the causes of continuous change in human history is the fact that it is precisely the fulfilment (or partial fulfilment) of some human aspiration that itself transforms the aspirant, and breeds, in time, new needs, new goals, new outlooks, that are *ex hypothesi* unpredictable; and that this is one of the main objections to the view that it is possible to discover rigorous laws of social change, and its corollary, a knowable causal determinism. Indeed, the novel situations that are created by the very fulfilment of men's original ideals (or their frustrations), and the new outlooks that spring from this, refute the doctrine of a single, final, unalterable, universal goal for mankind . . . The belief in an open future itself rests on anticipation of change, and indeed, development, although not necessarily in a wholly predictable direction.[103]

Thus the freedom and historicity of human agency precludes a determined course to events. History is not necessarily tending toward a final goal, proceeding along a straight, linear, uni-directional course, be it for good or ill. It can take a number of courses, some progressive, others regressive.[104]

Like any other philosopher of history, Berlin relies on a particular view of human nature to support his argument.[105] In the case of the nature of history and social development, he holds the view of persons as free agents capable of developing in numerous directions. Human capacities and ends are multiple; not all of them are harmonious. Some ends are lost and some interests are forgotten along the way. Therefore, it is false to believe that a final and comprehensive end to social and political development is unfolding in history.

[101] See 'Historical Inevitability' in *FE*, 95; and 'Zionist Politics in Wartime Washington: A Fragment of Personal Reminiscence', a Yaacov Herzog Memorial Lecture (Jerusalem, 1972), 8–9.
[102] See 'Introduction' to *FE*, pp. xxvi–xxviii, xxxiii; and the Jahanbegloo interview, 35–7.   [103] 'Reply to Kocis', 392.
[104] The Jahanbegloo interview, 33–7; and see 'European Unity and its Vicissitudes' in *CTH*, 202–6.   [105] See 'Introduction' to *FE*, p. xxviii.

It is the hypothesis of freedom of the will which allows one to attribute responsibility for past acts. It is something which Berlin defends adamantly. For without free choice, it would be senseless to attribute blame (and seek justice for) past crimes. Berlin tells us that if 'we reduce history to a kind of physics', then we might 'as well blame the galaxy or gamma-rays as Genghis Khan or Hitler' for their deeds.[106] In reading 'Historical Inevitability' one feels that Berlin wants to resist those forms of historiography which would explain away horrific historical events. For if historical acts were fully determined, and if we knew all the causes, then it would be out of place to blame persons for horrible acts, including those of this century, possibly the most horrific of all. This Berlin will not accept, and is clear in attacking the view that *Tout comprendre, c'est tout pardonner*.[107] Hence Berlin is not only concerned with exposing the absurd consequences of historical determinism. His goal is moral as well. His critique of historical determinism seeks to preserve the possibility of moral censure (and praise). He considers moral categories crucial to historical writing no less than to ordinary life and thought.[108]

Of course this defence is negative and tentative. In spite of this, the move does at least point out the crux of the issue; it puts the burden of proof on the determinists, and identifies the stakes involved in defending both liberty and a liberal political order. On this score, a regime that seeks to eradicate liberty, or considers it inconsequential to human existence, in effect represses a fundamental characteristic of human nature. As a judgement against political regimes, this one goes far and wide, both into the past and for the present.

Conclusion

Berlin has a theory of human nature. He holds that human nature and the human condition are typified by certain basic characteristics. These include the use of language and reason, and life within unique and different cultures and societies. He believes that persons

---

[106] 'Historical Inevitability' in *FE*, 81.   [107] Ibid. 76.

[108] See ibid. 63–8, 81, 113–17. None of this means that historical writing need be censorious. It only means that historical writing is queer if it excludes a sense of individual responsibility for acts (see 'Introduction' to *FE*, pp. xviii–xxxvii).

cannot be thought of except as free agents, and thus as moral agents. Yet our moral condition is pluralistic and complex and therefore not amenable to eternal and final ordering. We are not only moral but historical agents as well. We are purposive beings who develop in history, and thus are self-transformative, never complete. Berlin considers this model to be an advance over the one prevalent within the dominant tradition of political thought. Classical political theory seeks to discover a fixed order beneath the appearance of ordinary moral and political life. It presupposes a fixed hierarchy of needs and ends for human nature. A polity is said to be ideally ordered and truly good if and only if it conforms to the eternal forms of morality discovered by well-disciplined thought. Similarly, many Enlightenment thinkers believed in the possibility of a science of man and society, in the discovery of fixed laws of human nature and social development. The goal was clear: Man would be authentically free and secure once scientific laws ordered a polity.

With the aid of thinkers in a counter-tradition, Berlin criticizes the model of human nature and society presupposed by this dominant tradition. He argues that neither classical nor modern rationalism is suited to our sense of moral conflict and the open-ended nature of historical development. Each distorts these facts in order to achieve a vision of a harmonious moral order. Each commits the Ionian fallacy by holding, in one version, that a fixed and perfect moral universe exists above the fleeting images of ordinary life; or in another, that such an order can be found innate in human nature with the use of proper scientific technique; or, in still another, that order is emerging as a result of historical development, and is discernible with the correct, 'scientific' method.

Berlin stands apart from this rationalist tradition in political theory, which runs from Plato to Marx. He states that perfectibilist moral theory is conceptually incoherent, as well as founded on an inadequate empirical understanding of moral life. Yet his pluralism does not amount to relativism. With this theory of pluralism, one can still speak of common values, and essential needs of individuals and also of growth in our knowledge of human nature and society.[109] We know of and have experienced moral progress in

---

[109] Correspondence (17 Nov. 1988).

social and political organization.[110] Yet we must accept an empirical rider. We have to state that our knowledge and judgement are subject to modification; that they are true only in the light of experience. Even though he is aware of the dogmatism and narrowness of some Enlightenment thinkers, Berlin still remains with this tradition: he will not jump ship and side with Romantics, cultural pessimists, relativists, or nihilists. He learns from the counter-enlightenment, but remains unconverted. As he put it in a 1989 interview:

Fundamentally, I am a liberal rationalist. The values of the Enlightenment, what people like Voltaire, Helvétius, Holbach, Condorcet, preached are deeply sympathetic to me. Maybe they were too narrow, and often wrong about the facts of human experience, but these people were great liberators. They liberated people from horrors, obscurantism, fanaticism, monstrous views. They were against cruelty, they were against oppression, they fought the good fight against superstition and ignorance and against a great many things which ruined people's lives. So I am on their side.[111]

As will become evident in the following chapters, Berlin is a distinguished thinker in the liberal tradition because he recognizes two sides to moral life. He uses universal moral language, in the form of human rights or human values, to justify some aspects of liberal–democratic polities; but he also knows that these are too thin to support all the legitimate practices of these polities. From the perspective of abstract reason or nature we cannot adequately justify all of our complex moral life (nor, conversely, adequately condemn certain practices). That is why Berlin complements his discussion of universal moral categories with appeals to conventions, customs, traditions, and the history of workable institutional

---

[110] 'European Unity and its Vicissitudes' in *CTH*, 206.

[111] The Jahanbegloo interview, 68–76, at 70. Berlin continues and states why he is interested in the counter-enlightenment (70–1): 'But they [the *philosophes*] are dogmatic and too simplistic. I am interested in the views of the opposition because I think that understanding it can sharpen one's own vision, clever and gifted enemies often pinpoint fallacies or shallow analyses in the thought of the Enlightenment. I am more interested in critical attacks which lead to knowledge than simply in repeating and defending the commonplaces of and about the Enlightenment . . . If you believe in liberal principles and rational analysis, as I do, then you must take account of what the objections are, and where the cracks in your structures are, where your side went wrong: hostile criticism, even bigoted opposition, can reveal truth. Hatred can sharpen vision as much as love. I do not share, or even greatly admire, the views of the enemies of enlightenment, but I have learnt a good deal from them; some of the central concepts, and the age of reason, and, above all, of their political implications, are exposed as inadequate, and, at times, disastrous.'

arrangements. He never fails to remain empirical and interpretative. By working on two fronts, the universal and the particular or historical, he develops a rich and complex defence of political liberalism. The strength of his defence comes from the way he draws from the twin facets of moral existence, the natural or universal and the conventional or historical.[112]

It is my contention that the famous essay, 'Two Concepts of Liberty', can only be properly understood by keeping Berlin's other works in mind, especially the twin facets of moral experience about which he writes. In that essay one finds conceptual arguments and naturalist ones about the universal presence of liberty in moral life. This is one side of his defence of political liberalism. But there is also a historical *tableau*, one that portrays the fate of individuals and minorities throughout the ages, in particular in contemporary times. It is this *tableau* that gives life to his defence of political liberalism; yet its importance has been generally overlooked by the critics. This is the reason for linking his theory of interpretation, his theory of moral pluralism, his model of human nature and society, his belief in the liberty of persons, to his defence of political liberalism. The purpose is to present a full exposition of his defence, and also to correct an overemphasis in the literature on its conceptual aspects. The next chapter begins the presentation of this defence.

[112] On the importance of double-sided moral justifications, see Hampshire, *Morality and Conflict*, 164–9.

4

TWO CONCEPTS OF LIBERTY

It was, I think, Bertrand Russell—Mill's godson—who
remarked somewhere that the deepest convictions of philosophers are seldom contained in their formal arguments:
fundamental beliefs, comprehensive views of life, are like
citadels which must be guarded against the enemy. Philosophers expend their intellectual power in arguments and
although the reasons they find, and the logic that they use,
may be complex, ingenious, and formidable, they are
defensive weapons; the inner fortress itself—the vision of life
for the sake of which the war is being waged—will, as a rule,
turn out to be relatively simple and unsophisticated.

(Isaiah Berlin, 'John Stuart Mill and the Ends of Life')

Bertrand Russell's dictum applies fittingly to Berlin's work. The
thoughts and beliefs protected by his own 'inner fortress' are
'simple and unsophisticated'. His is a clear and consistent 'vision of
life'. Simply put, it is that of a classical liberal, with romantic
tinges. This is apparent in his essay, 'Two Concepts of Liberty'.
Critics, however, have dwelt less on the aspects of the vision than
on the analytical coherence of the distinction he makes between
negative and positive freedom.[1] I think that this misses much that is

---

[1] For surveys of the analytical debates, see John Gray, 'On Negative and Positive
Liberty' in *Liberalisms*, 45–68; Robert Kocis, 'Reason, Development and the
Conflicts of Human Ends: Sir Isaiah Berlin's Vision of Politics', in *American Political
Science Review*, 74 (1980), 38–52; 'Introduction' by David Miller (ed.), *Liberty*
(Oxford, 1991), 1–20; William Parent, 'Some Recent Work on the Concept of
Liberty', in *American Philosophical Quarterly*, 11 (1974), 149–67; Beata Polanowska-
Sygulska, 'One Voice More on Berlin's Doctrine of Liberty' in *Political Studies*, 37
(1989), 123–7; and Quentin Skinner, 'The Idea of Negative Liberty: Philosophical
and Historical Perspectives' in Richard Rorty, J. B. Schneewind, and Quentin
Skinner (eds.), *Philosophy in History* (Cambridge, 1984), 193–221.

worthwhile in the article, and may have resulted in more than a few misinterpretations of his message and intent.[2] Of course, Berlin did not help matters. The title of the article itself points to the fact that he will make conceptual distinctions, which he does, and then his response to critics continued to explore formal points.[3] Much of this can be attributed to the analytical style of Anglo–British philosophy in the 1950s and 1960s, and Berlin's willingness to follow it. But clearly the article contains more than logic chopping. It has a distinct polemical force, arguing vehemently against distortions of the positive concept of liberty. In fact, Berlin dedicates almost three times as much space to his critique of positive liberty as he does to an analysis and argument for the negative concept.[4] His main thesis is historical, for he argues that negative liberty in practice has been less often perverted into a justification for authority than the positive concept.[5] The times set the focus: Berlin was arguing to protect a liberal conception of freedom, which he dubs 'negative liberty', against contemporary communist, socialist, and Marxist thought.[6]

Another reason for the imbalance in treatment by the critics has to do with ignorance of Berlin's other work. Once this work is surveyed, and related to his famous article, more complex goals than conceptual clarification can be discerned in the essay. It is my contention that Berlin's essay works on several levels, conceptual, normative, historical, and sociological. The essay is a defence of political liberalism which relies on a model of human nature and society, and a narrative about the fate of conceptions of liberty in Western history. The following chapters deal with all the levels of his defence, starting, in the next section, with the conceptual level.

---

[2] A few sympathetic critics have pointed to this imbalance in the literature about the distinction. See Gray, 'On Negative and Positive Liberty' in *Liberalisms*, 48–56; Kocis, 'Reason, Development, and the Conflicts of Human Ends', 42–4; and Polanowska-Sygulska, 'One Voice More on Berlin's Doctrine of Liberty', 123–7.

[3] See 'Introduction' to *FE*, pp. xxxvii–lxiii.

[4] Polanowska-Sygulska, 'One Voice More on Berlin's Doctrine of Liberty', 123.

[5] Athenaeum interview; and 'Introduction' to *FE*, pp. xliii–xlvii.

[6] All Souls and Athenaeum interviews. See 'Two Concepts of Liberty' in *FE*, 166. On the 'liberal' conception of freedom, see Miller, 'Introduction' to *Liberty*, 3–4, 7–8.

Concepual Distinctions

Berlin has recently refined his conceptual analysis of 'liberty'. In interviews conducted in 1988, he speaks of ' "basic" liberty', by which he means the capacity for free choice and the exercise of free will. It is what Kant designates as *Willkuer*, or the determining ground of practical reason.[7] Berlin takes this 'basic' sense of liberty to be prior to concerns about the extent and distribution of social and political liberty. The power of free choice is thus 'basic' to all forms of liberty, negative and positive. In making this claim, Berlin brought his moral and political theory closer to his theory of human nature, discussed in Chapter 2.[8] Yet it is the social and political senses which are the primary focus of his 'Two Concepts of Liberty'.[9]

At one level the essay is an exercise in the clarification of concepts and values.[10] Berlin considers this necessary because liberty *per se* is often conflated with its conditions, or with other goods, like equality, virtuous conduct, a stable political regime, and the like. In order to analyse the concept 'liberty', it must first be separated from its conditions and the ends often sought with it. This exercise fulfils one of the functions that Berlin ascribes to philosophy: to clarify our thinking about terms. It also prepares one to make coherent and responsible decisions about the ends to be sought in particular circumstances, be they related to a kind of liberty, a use of liberty, or some other good.[11] Nevertheless, apprehending

[7] See Immanuel Kant, *The Metaphysical Elements of Justice*, trans. Alan Ladd (Indianapolis, 1965), 12. In his 'Reply to Kocis' (388, 391) Berlin points to Kant's concept of choice as the grounds for morality itself.

[8] All Souls and Athenaeum interviews. Berlin has also written (correspondence, 17 Nov. 1988) that his 'Two Concepts' essay was insufficiently clear on natural liberty. He did not distinguish it from what 19th-century liberals, like Benjamin Constant and Henry Michel, called civil liberty. Thus he writes that 'Perhaps I ought to have said in my piece, in a sense, there are two kinds of [liberty]: (*a*) basic liberty of choice between x and not x. Creatures who cannot do this can scarcely be described as human—such wholly conditioned robots cannot be called fully human. (*b*) There is the liberty that Constant, Michel etc. value, i.e., no interference within certain limits, capacity for choosing between values, forms of life, pluralism, etc. The root of both (*a*) and (*b*) is the same, but the basic liberty (*a*) underlies everything. (*b*) can be expanded or curtailed.'

[9] In his 'Reply to Kocis' (391), Berlin writes of two 'distinct senses of "liberty" ', the fundamental moral sense and the socio–political sense.

[10] See 'Two Concepts of Liberty' in *FE*, 124–6 for some examples.

[11] See ibid. 118–21, 124–8; and his 'Introduction' to *FE*, pp. xlviii–lxiii.

'liberty' as a concept is not easy. Berlin states that the concept is 'protean' and 'porous'. He claims that two hundred or more senses of the word can be identified in the history of ideas. Yet what concerns him are two major uses in the history of political thought. Either use, he says, has its own pedigree; but one is older than the other: the positive liberty of democratic self-governance stretches back to the ancient city-states; while freedom from interference is a modern conception of liberty. These two senses of liberty compete as solutions to the problem of political obligation. They also refer to two different models of human nature and society which, in their extreme formulations, are incompatible.[12]

Berlin begins the analysis by categorizing liberty according to two related, yet distinct, sets of questions. The first set includes questions such as 'Who is master?' and 'By whom am I governed?'[13] or, 'Who governs me?' and 'Who is to say what I am, and what I am not, to be or do?'[14] or more generally, 'What, or who, is the source of control or interference that can determine someone to do, or be, this rather than that?'[15] The answers point to the notion of self-mastery and 'the positive liberty of self-realization'.[16] Berlin includes here all doctrines of self-direction and self-realization, from plain self-mastery, to the personal doctrines of salvation propounded by the Stoics, as well as the collectivist doctrines of self-realization found in Rousseau and Marx.

Apart from plain self-mastery,[17] what is common to all these doctrines is that liberty is linked to an over-arching goal, a teleological enterprise. This end may be the *ataxia* of the stoic, the rational harmony and self-perfection of Plato's *Republic*, Aristotelian entelechies, the duty prescribed by God and the Church, the social justice and class harmony of Marxian communism, the realization of one's rational and proper self, as with Spinoza, Rousseau, Kant, Fichte, Hegel, and T. H. Green, or the self-realization of the person as a member of a democratic polity, a group, a tribe, a class, a

[12] The All Souls and Athenaeum interviews. See 'Two Concepts of Liberty' in *FE*, 121–2, 129, 134, 166; and 'Introduction' to *FE*, pp. xl–xlii, xlviii–lxiii.

[13] 'Introduction' to *FE*, p. xliii.

[14] 'Two Concepts of Liberty' in *FE*, 130.

[15] Ibid. 122.

[16] 'Introduction' to *FE*, p. lvi.

[17] As when I say that I am following my own will, my own lights, but without any particular overall goal, save to be free.

nation.[18] In such positive doctrines, liberty is a part of a hierarch of goods or moral ends. This hierarchy is constructed according to a fixed understanding of human nature and its potentials; or theory of our eternal place in and potential harmony with nature society, the cosmos. Political life is said to be objectively and correctly founded when it conforms to an eternal plan for human nature in society. From this perspective, liberty is a means to achieve this order: it is true to its purpose when it helps one arrive at the eternal order of things.[19]

Berlin's conceptual net is cast very wide. But these doctrines are held together by their particular claims that freedom must be *for* something, to achieve some greater goal. On the positive view freedom of movement is often a necessary but never a sufficient condition of real freedom. Freedom is authentic only when someone is in full charge of himself and acts nobly or well or justly or in any manner deemed praiseworthy and correct according to his intrinsic nature, or to the eternal dictates of reason, or those of one's religion or tribe or nation or class.[20] Positive liberty is the freedom lauded by Leo Strauss, to take one contemporary exponent, when he says that 'liberty consists in doing in the right manner the good only'.[21] For Berlin 'positive' liberty is self-determination and the freedom *to* do something.[22] What concerns Berlin is that teleological conceptions of liberty may subsume civil liberty. To avoid what he regards as an all too common pitfall, Berlin points to a non-teleological or open-ended concept of liberty. This concept of liberty is negative and figures centrally in the classical liberal conception of liberty.

This second conception of liberty is identified by questions which ask, 'Over what area am I master?' and 'How much am I governed?', or 'How wide is the area over which I am, or should be, master?'[23] or 'How far does government interfere with me?' and 'What am I free to do or be?'[24] or more generally 'What is the

---

[18] Berlin bunches all these moral and political theorists together (see his 'Two Concepts of Liberty' in *FE*, 135–62).

[19] Ibid. 145–54.   [20] Ibid. 131–41

[21] Leo Strauss, 'What is Political Philosophy?' in *What is Political Philosophy? and Other Studies* (Chicago, 1959), 51. Berlin has little sympathy for Strauss's essentialism (correspondence, 27 Sept. 1989). See the Jahanbegloo interview (31–3 109), where Berlin equates Strauss's method with that of a magician or shaman.

[22] 'Two Concepts of Liberty' in *FE*, 131.

[23] 'Introduction' to *FE*, pp. xliii–xliv.

[24] 'Two Concepts of Liberty' in *FE*, 130.

area within which the subject—a person or group of persons—is or should be left to do or be what he is able to do or be, without interference by other persons?'[25] The answers to these questions point to the 'negative liberty of non-interference'.[26] By contrast with those of 'positive' liberty, these questions are concerned with the limits of power, and not with the source of power. What is at issue are spheres of non-interference and not principles of democratic participation. Nor is 'negative' liberty concerned with the reasons and goals of action. What is important is freedom of action, and less *who* does what, and *what* one does with one's liberty.[27]

Undeniably, Berlin's definition of negative liberty is based on a physicalist model of human agency. His concept refers to civil freedom, to movement of persons in civil society.[28] Its roots are Hobbesian: negative liberty is what both Thomas Hobbes and Benjamin Constant designated as the liberty of modern, civil men.[29] That Berlin follows this tradition is most evident in the following quotation:

The fundamental sense of freedom is freedom from chains, from imprisonment, from enslavement by others. The rest is extension of this sense, or else metaphor. To strive to be free is to seek to remove obstacles; to struggle for personal freedom is to seek to curb interference, exploitation, enslavement by men whose ends are theirs, not one's own. Freedom, at least in its political sense, is co-terminous with the absence of bullying or domination.[30]

Negative liberty therefore is concerned with the opportunities for action. One is free in the negative sense when one is not obstructed. Negative freedom is freedom *from* obstacles.[31] The negative

---

[25] Ibid. 121–2. [26] 'Introduction' to FE, p. lvi.

[27] 'Two Concepts of Liberty' in *FE*, 129–31, 166.

[28] See 'Introduction' to *FE*, pp. xxxvii–xxxviii.

[29] See Thomas Hobbes, 'Of the Liberty of Subjects' in C. B. Macpherson (ed.), *Leviathan* (London, 1968), ch. 21 esp. at 261–2, 266; and Benjamin Constant, 'De la liberté des anciens comparée à celle des modernes' [1819], in M. Edouard Laboulaye (ed.), *Cours de politique constitutionnelle*, vol. ii (Paris, 1872), 539–60 at 541. The latter is now translated into English as 'The Liberty of the Ancients Compared with that of the Moderns' in Biancamaria Fontana (ed. and trans.), *Constant: Political Writings* (Cambridge, 1988), 309–28. For a discussion of these views, see Miller, 'Introduction' to *Liberty*, 7–8, 15.

[30] 'Introduction' to *FE*, p. lvi.

[31] See 'Two Concepts of Liberty' in *FE*, 131. In 'From Hope and Fear Set Free' (in *CC*, 190) he writes: 'freedom is to do with the absence of obstacles to action'.

concept of liberty is, to quote Charles Taylor, an 'opportunity concept'.[32]

As is apparent in the quotation above and the one below, negative liberty denotes freedom of movement. It is unconnected with the ends of liberty, such as moral and spiritual self-perfection.[33] Berlin disconnects negative liberty from such ends in order to underline the importance of outward obstacles as impediments to action, especially in civil society. In fact, Berlin's 'negative liberty' stands for what we ordinarily call civil or political liberty, of which he writes that,

The sense of freedom, in which I use the term, entails not simply the absence of frustration (which may be obtained by killing desires), but the absence of obstacles to possible choices and activities—absence of obstructions on roads along which a man can decide to walk. Such freedom ultimately depends not on whether I wish to walk at all, or how far, but on how many doors are open, how open they are, upon their relative importance in my life, even though it may be impossible literally to measure this in any quantitative fashion. The extent of my social and political freedom consists in the absence of obstacles not merely to my actual, but to my potential choices—to my acting in this or that way if I choose to do so. Similarly absence of such freedom is due to the closing of such doors or failure to open them, as a result, intended or unintended, of alterable human practices, of the operation of human agencies; although only if such acts are deliberately intended (or, perhaps, are accompanied by awareness that they may block paths) will they be liable to be called oppression.[34]

In short, negative liberty varies according to the numbers of doors through which one may pass. The concept does not cover, let alone evaluate, the moral chambers into which the doors open; only whether or not they are open.

Negative liberty is presupposed by any positive doctrine of liberation. Regardless of the fact that one often wishes to be free *to do something*, such a freedom cannot exist if one faces barriers to action. In a conceptual sense, negative liberty is basic to positive

[32] Charles Taylor, 'What's Wrong with Negative Liberty' in Alan Ryan (ed.), *The Idea of Freedom* (Oxford, 1979), 175–93 at 177.

[33] Berlin emphasizes this point in an unpublished letter to Beata Polanowska-Sygulska (24 Feb. 1986, 3–5). See also his 'Introduction' to *FE*, p. xxxix.

[34] 'Introduction' to *FE*, pp. xxxix–xl. On measuring freedom see ibid., p. xlviii; and 'Two Concepts of Liberty' in *FE*, 130.

liberty. But the converse is not true. Not all demands for freedom from obstacles need be demands of freedom to do something in particular. One can want to be free of chains only, and not for any particular or fixed set of ends.[35] This formulation of freedom has come under attack from various quarters. The most famous criticism is that of Gerald C. MacCallum, who argues that when we speak of freedom we always refer to a triadic relationship, and not to a dyadic one, as Berlin's treatment indicates. When we say someone is free, we say that X is free from A to do or be Z. For MacCallum it is best to drop the physicalist and liberal formulation and recognize the underlying logic of statements about freedom. For him, a triadic relationship is common to all conceptions of liberty.[36] Berlin has responded by arguing that one can desire freedom in itself. We understand this best when we consider persons and nations struggling against fetters, or oppressors. People who struggle against chains want freedom, plain and simple.[37] It is immaterial what they wish their freedom for.[38] Thus MacCallum's formulation hides an important aspect of civil liberties; namely, their open-endedness.[39] And it is this aspect which Berlin considers essential to any definition of freedom, and centrally the concern of liberals.

Puccini gives us a good representation of this problem. In Act III of his opera *Tosca* (1900), the protagonists, Cavaradossi and Tosca, are trapped in the Castel Sant'Angelo. Cavaradossi, Tosca's lover, has been sentenced to death by the police chief of Rome, Scarpia. Cavaradossi has had no trial; Scarpia sentenced him in order to have Tosca for himself. While visting her lover in the Castel, Tosca tells Cavaradossi of her plan to release him. Soon, she says, they will both be free. They sing of their eternal love and exclaim together: '*Liberi. Via pel mar!*' (Freedom. Away by Sea!) The tragic end results from their betrayal by Scarpia. Yet this betrayal is due to political conditions (no less than covetousness and jealousy), due in part to the lack of civil liberties in Rome, in particular the freedom

[35] All Souls interview.
[36] See Gerald C. MacCallum, jun., 'Negative and Positive Liberty' in Peter Laslett, W. G. Runciman, and Quentin Skinner (eds.), *Philosophy, Politics and Society*, 4th series (Oxford, 1972), 174–93.
[37] All Souls interview.
[38] See 'Introduction' to *FE*, p. xliii n. 1.
[39] See Kocis, 'Reason, Development, and the Conflicts of Human Ends: Sir Isaiah Berlin's Vision of Politics', 42–4.

from arbitrary arrest. Amongst other things, the opera is about the unfree state of Italian institutions in the early nineteenth century.

Now, we would not approach this situation by asking the protagonists *why and for what* they wish to be free. We do not question Tosca's on her motives. We do not point out that she is proud and jealous. We do not say that her jealousy will probably doom her union with Cavaradossi. We do not judge her virtue. Likewise, we do not question Cavaradossi's social role. We do not say that, as an artist and bohemian, his love for Tosca may not last. It burns brightly but may burn out quickly. Neither partner may be suited for conjugal relations. We do not reflect upon the immoderate aspects of their love when speaking of the justice in their demand for liberty. Instead, we reflect on the fact that in this situation there are no fundamental liberties, such as freedom from arbitrary arrest and due process under the law. Their fate hangs on the whim of prefects and informers. Yet the freedom that is lacking is not the freedom from prefects and informers *in order to love*. Rather, it is freedom *from* the arbitrary acts of prefects and informers. What the lovers need are spheres of non-interference, or areas of independence. They need to come and go as they please; do what they desire. What they demand is an open-ended freedom, a freedom *from* prefects, *from* arbitrary measures of all kinds, and *from* political oppressors of all types.

There is no need for a triadic formulation here; a dyadic one will do. When speaking of political liberty, we do not have to ask how one will live apart *from* political oppressors, or for what one wishes *to* live when free; only that to be politically free one ought at least be free *from* compulsion and chains.[40] This is the conception of liberty found in classical liberal thought. It is what is sought in all doctrines of rights to resistance and rights against oppressors.[41] It is what Berlin considers to be the core of 'negative' conceptions of liberty.[42] For example, removing obstacles is clearly what is meant by giving people fundamental freedoms of association and expression. Such liberties are open-ended. We do not grant such rights with stipulations that people must enter associations, or enter

---

[40] For a supporting argument, see Gray, 'On Negative and Positive Liberty', 49–50.
[41] See 'Introduction' to *FE*, p. lxii and 'Two Concepts of Liberty', 122–31. See also John Plamenatz, 'Introduction' to his selection of *Readings from Liberal Writers: English and French* (New York, 1965), 11–18.
[42] All Souls interview.

particular associations. Nor do we say that they must express certain things in particular media. Rather, constitutional principles of rights to association and expression are rules of non–interference. They allow people to act without restriction. They give them opportunities to act. What people in fact do is, at the level of rules, unprescribed. But are all obstacles juridical ones? Are limits to freedom always kinds of coercion, force, or threats of violence? Obviously, this is not the case.

In his essay 'From Hope and Fear Set Free' Berlin states that impediments may be of many kinds. He points to political, social, economic, even psychological, barriers to action. Thus one may be said to be unfree if and when one lacks 'rational self-control', when one is burdened by neuroses. If psychoanalysis is to be credited with any discoveries, one is surely that our psychological state, our past experience and memories, curtail our field of action.[43] From the psychological point of view, to be free is to make use of certain capacities for action; action guided by one's reason, for example. One is free when one is master of one's emotional problems. Or free when one is self-directed. It is not absurd to point to internal obstacles.[44]

However, in the 'Two Concepts' essay, Berlin relegates 'self-mastery' to a version of the positive concept of liberty.[45] Moreover, he considers a lack of will, neuroses, and lack of economic powers to be the absence of conditions of liberty, and not the absence of liberty itself.[46] Is Berlin being too restrictive, as some believe?[47] Is there something wrong with the concept of negative liberty because of this, as Charles Taylor, for one, maintains?[48] I think not. Taylor argues that a concept of liberty must include pointers about intellectual capacities, such as rational self-control and rational self-mastery. Only in this way can we imagine people judging between ends, considering some more significant than others.[49] This is what is meant by autonomy, to say that one

---

[43] 'From Hope and Fear Set Free' in *CC*, 190–1.

[44] See Peter Gay, 'Freud and Freedom: On a Fox in Hedgehog's Clothing' in Alan Ryan (ed.), *The Idea of Freedom*, 41–59.

[45] 'Two Concepts of Liberty' in *FE*, 131–4.

[46] See ibid. 122 ff; and 'Introduction' to *FE*, pp. xlv–xlvii, lix–lxii.

[47] See e.g. C. B. Macpherson, 'Berlin's Division of Liberty' in *Democratic Theory: Essays in Retrieval* (Oxford, 1973), 95–119 at 101–3.

[48] See Taylor, 'What's Wrong with Negative Liberty', 175–93.

[49] Ibid. 179.

follows one's own law and purposes, and not those of others. To be autonomous, however, we need to be knowledgeable about our ends and how best to achieve them. We may need to demonstrate moderation and show proper judgement. In addition, other people, say, our friends, can help us in this regard. A friend may be uniquely positioned to know what impedes my aims and projects, since we are both on intimate terms. A friend may help me shake my irrational sentiments, such as resentment or spite, and help me attain greater freedom to pursue my most significant and prized goals.[50]

Because we may speak of freeing a person in the above sense, Taylor concludes that the physicalist conception of liberty is limited; indeed inadequate given that it misses a whole range of behaviour linked to the exercise of freedom. Given that we must speak of capacities for action, Taylor concludes that a concept of liberty must be properly an 'exercise-concept' and not solely an 'opportunity-concept'. We must be able to speak of internal as well as external obstacles to action; psychic and character-based ones as well as those linked to coercion. What is wrong with negative liberty, therefore, is that the concept includes only talk of external obstacles. It relies exclusively on a physicalist model of human agency. Such a model does not allow us to think about discriminating judgement between motivations; to think about the way in which persons determine which motivations, which plans, are or are not crucial to their 'long-lasting needs'.[51]

Yet none of these points weakens Berlin's position. He does not claim that negative liberty is the only concept of liberty; nor that it captures every sense of liberty. He admits that negative and positive liberty start 'at no great logical distance from each other'.[52] Second, he does not reject the positive liberty of self-direction and self-mastery.[53] We rightly speak of persons as autonomous agents, in full possession of their powers and particularly adept in finding what they consider to be their true path in life. And Berlin concedes that internal obstacles can exist to autonomy. It is not absurd to say that a man is constrained by his passions and that these psychological obstacles impede him from being a good husband, bank

[50] Taylor, 'What's Wrong with Negative Liberty', 184–91.
[51] Ibid. 177, 179, 186, 188, 192–3.   [52] 'Two Concepts of Liberty', 131.
[53] All Souls and Athenaeum interviews. See also 'Introduction' to *FE*, p. xliii; and 'Two Concepts of Liberty', 131, 135–9.

manager, or whatever. However, none of these issues concern civil liberties. The lack of rational self-control, due to a lack of knowledge and discriminating judgement, or due to a poor character and feeble will, do not impinge upon one's civil liberties. What they do affect are the conditions of one's enjoying civil liberties. A constitutional liberty of self-expression is obviously without value for the person who cannot speak in public or write a coherent sentence because he suffers from a neurotic condition. Yet it remains true that a polity is significantly free when its laws and institutions assure the liberty of self-expression; and unfree when the polity does not. Neurotics can be educated and helped with therapy; once cured they will come to enjoy, if they choose, the liberty of self-expression that all can equally enjoy by law. But they will remain unfree in a significant sense if they are restricted by the authorities from expressing themselves in public, in print or on the airwaves. Sanity and good character are distinct conditions from these barriers to liberty.

There is a misunderstanding on Taylor's part in that his criticisms do not focus on this issue of civil liberties which is Berlin's target. In his article he gives no examples of problems relevant to public authority; his examples of persons being liberated from 'motivational fetters'[54] all refer to face-to-face relations, such as those concerning relations between a husband and wife and friendly debates about the most rational way to satisfy one's preferred lifestyle. None of these examples deal with the relationship between citizens and government; rather, the focus is on autonomy instead of civil liberty.

In all his writings Berlin never discounts the importance of personal relationships, or the utility of friendly advice. Nor does he disparage the notion of self-mastery and self-determination. What his analysis principally covers are problems of public authority, and not personal psychology. Moreover, Berlin could accept all that Taylor says and still maintain that in modern polities it is imperative to have negative liberties. The latter are often a condition for autonomy. It is the protection of spheres of non-interference that assures people the freedom to debate and discuss amongst themselves about what may or may not be the best course in life. Indeed, without such spheres of non-interference, fewer

[54] Taylor, 'What's Wrong with Negative Liberty', 193.

options are likely to come to the fore and less debate will occur over the ends of life.[55] For this reason, there is nothing wrong with negative liberty as a concept of civil liberties. Berlin is not being inconsistent in speaking of inner freedom as a condition for autonomous acts, and yet distinguishing this positive liberty from civil liberties. Nor is he being too restrictive. The two different conceptions of liberty exist; yet they pull in opposite directions. The first concerns autonomy and self-perfection; the latter denotes spheres of non-interference in which to realize one's autonomy, to perfect or not perfect oneself. And it is useful to distinguish these two senses. For to equate both senses is to confuse matters. It is quite appropriate to speak of the importance of negative freedom in political society. However, it is inappropriate to include the goal of rational self-direction when formulating constitutional rules to determine the relationship between subjects and their sovereign. We do not speak of a constitutional liberty from neuroses. Nor do we speak of rights to reason or of rights to psychic health. This is because both rational autonomy and self-realization are different from being left alone by the state, or not being coerced by thugs. The former may or may not issue from the presence of civil liberty. The relationship between autonomy and civil liberty is complex; conditional on the education, character, and the culture of subjects. Clearly, to grant persons civil liberties does not necessarily give them autonomy.[56]

Even if we speak of rights to education, which are related to the cultivation of autonomy, these rights are entitlements. These entitlements may ensure the cultivation of reasonable subjects, however defined. But they refer to positive state action to procure certain goods. They do not refer to the limits on state action, as rights to liberty do. Such public goods are part of the conditions for the enjoyment of civil liberties. And while it is true that educating everyone to read and write gives equal worth to the liberty of self-expression, this egalitarian end is distinct from ensuring a sphere of non-interference.[57] The same holds for all other entitlements, such

[55] See Sidney Morgenbesser and Jonathan Lieberson, 'Isaiah Berlin', 22–3.

[56] This is the main criticism that Berlin has of J. S. Mill. The latter presumed that civil liberties were both a necessary and sufficient condition for the pursuit of autonomy, of truth, and creativity. Yet the latter are contingent goods and distinct from civil liberty (see 'Two Concepts of Liberty', 128–30).

[57] For this argument about the equal worth of liberties, see John Rawls, *A Theory of Justice*, 204–11.

as economic rights to welfare. These are not civil liberties, but conditions for the equal enjoyment of civil liberties.[58] In this case, Berlin argues that an assimilation of negative liberty with economic conditions depends on one's preferred theory of social and economic development.[59] The question is not just conceptual, but empirical as well; indeed, often speculative, because it refers to how a different order of property distribution would affect the sum total of liberties available in a society.[60] In any case, there are widely differing arguments about which economic system best ensures individual autonomy, or equalizes power and capacities for action. Some have argued that socialism would increase aggregate liberties in society, and not just the equal distribution of existing liberties. C. B. Macpherson, in particular, has criticized Berlin for missing this important aspect of social liberty.[61] But it is uncertain—at least not as certain as Macpherson asserts[62]—that socialist systems can equalize conditions for civil liberties, as well as increase the aggregate sum of liberties. It could just as well be argued (and with much empirical evidence) that collective ownership of property actually reduces autonomy as well as the sum of liberties. Historically, collective ownership has meant a great restraint on civil liberty.[63]

Berlin wishes to keep the distinction between liberty *and* the conditions for its use. He considers their conflation fatal to a liberal order. In his review of C. B. Macpherson's book, *The Political Theory of Possessive Individualism*,[64] Berlin criticized Macpherson for reducing all liberties to their conditions and understanding rights solely as the political expression of a bourgeois order.[65] Berlin asserts that natural rights to liberty are analytically distinct from

[58] See 'Introduction' to *FE*, pp. xlv–xlviii, xlix, liii–lv; and 'Two Concepts of Liberty', 123–6.

[59] See 'Two Concepts of Liberty', 123; and Gray, 'On Negative and Positive Liberty', 61–2.

[60] For this argument, see G. A. Cohen, 'Capitalism, Freedom and the Proletariat' in Alan Ryan (ed.), *The Idea of Freedom*, 9–25 at 15–16.

[61] See C. B. Macpherson, 'Berlin's Division of Liberty', 95–119.

[62] See C. B. Macpherson, 'Problems of a Non-Market Theory of Democracy' in *Democratic Theory: Essays in Retrieval* (Oxford, 1973), 39–76.

[63] For a survey of these arguments and for his own argument that private property, and not common property, best assures personal autonomy, see Gray, *Liberalism*, 62–72.   [64] Oxford, 1962.

[65] Macpherson continued to do this throughout his writings, see e.g. 'Natural Rights in Hobbes and Locke' in *Democratic Theory*, 224–37 at 236–7.

supporting arguments for any particular economic arrangement in
political society. Rights of resistance and rights to non-interference
are irreducible to economic arrangements, socialist or capitalist:
either kind of economic society can violate them.[66]

It is clear that Berlin holds to the distinction between liberty and
its conditions for historical reasons. There is much evidence that a
zealous pursuit of equality of conditions in fact reduces civil
liberties. Attempts to administer civil society for equality invariably lead to the development of large bureaucratic and police
organizations which attempt to control all aspects of civil life. To
equate liberty with its conditions, as Macpherson does, is to make
all controls over civil action acts of liberation.[67] That this is patently
not the case is evident from the experience of all existing socialist
regimes.[68]

If the negative concept of liberty is interpreted as the concept of
liberty found in classical liberal conceptions of political order, then
what is it that has been so contentious about the distinction
between positive and negative liberty, or between liberty and its
conditions? Some of these debates, as I have said, are the result of
misunderstanding. This is especially the case with negative liberty.
Other criticisms have been correct, particularly with respect to
Berlin's treatment of positive liberty.[69] C. B. Macpherson has
noted three different kinds of positive liberty discussed by Berlin.
The first kind is the liberty of self-direction or self-mastery (PL1).
The second is the idealist and rationalist versions of self-realization
(PL2). The third is a collective form of self-realization, such as the
status one enjoys as a democratic agent, as a participant in
sovereign decision-making (PL3).[70]

An example of PL1 is Stoicism. In Stoical thought liberty is
equated with self-abnegation. For a liberal, the problem with this
formulation is that spiritual freedom can become consistent with
political despotism. If one is free by eliminating psychological

---

[66] See I. Berlin, 'Hobbes, Locke and Professor Macpherson' in *Political Quarterly*,
35 (1964), 444–68; and the veiled criticism of Macpherson's book by Plamenatz,
'Introduction' to *Readings from Liberal Writers*, 12–13.
[67] See C. B. Macpherson, 'Problems of a Non-market Theory of Democracy',
70–6 and 'Berlin's Division of Liberty', 112–19.
[68] See 'Introduction' to *FE*, pp. l–lv; and Gray, *Liberalism*, 37–42, 84–9.
[69] See the conclusion to this chapter, below.
[70] C. B. Macpherson, 'Berlin's Division of Liberty', 108–9.

obstacles, then the fewer desires and passions one has, the freer one will be. Thus the Stoic can claim that even though he is in prison, or is a slave, he is freer than his gaolers and masters. Nothing in the external world impinges upon him. If one achieves the ideal of *ataxia*, of spiritual autarky, then one is said to be fully human and truly free regardless of one's social and legal status.[71] Clearly, the Stoical ideal has nothing to do with civil or political liberties. Indeed, once freedom is equated with controlling one's desires, a significant sense of the term is lost into the bargain. Once the equation is made, then all one has to do to be free is to extinguish one's desires. Moreover, if a despot, tyrant, or religious leader is successful in convincing people that their desires for civil liberties are false desires, then, on this psychological formulation of freedom, citizens are rendered free once they extinguish their so-called false desires. This formulation forces us to concede, absurdly, that one can be free while being socially and politically enslaved and ordered about by the authorities.[72]

To avoid this absurdity, Berlin seeks to distance his formulation of liberty from psychological theories of freedom. He claims that freedom is best understood as a function of the lack of 'possible' and 'potential' human and institutional obstacles to choice. The 'absence of frustration', therefore, will not do as a coherent formulation of liberty.[73] Liberty, he says, must be computed by measuring the 'range of objectively open possibilities, whether these are desired or not'. Otherwise, without objective measures, liberty can be perverted into its opposite.[74]

What is at issue here are descriptions of free societies, and not just conceptual formulations of liberty. Something more than a subject-specific measure of liberty is needed if we want to avoid the pitfalls of Stoical thought. This is because desires for whole classes of freedom can be extinguished. Soviet or other totalitarian systems of government have shown how this is possible. Propaganda can condition people to consider themselves free regardless of the lack

---

[71] Epictetus' *Manual* is the most systematic expression of Stoicism we possess. See Nicholas P. White (ed. and trans.), *The Handbook of Epictetus* (Indianapolis, 1983).

[72] See 'Introduction' to *FE*, pp. xxxviii–xxxix; and 'From Hope and Fear Set Free', 193.

[73] 'Introduction' to *FE*, pp. xxxix–xl.

[74] 'From Hope and Fear Set Free', 193.

of civil liberties in their society. In such societies, most people do consider themselves free.[75] How can we say that they are unfree? Or, specifically, in what *sense* are they unfree? To show how, Berlin has to rely on an objective measure of liberties; he cannot rely on subjective appraisals. The best measure is institutional.[76] In an institution-specific formulation, we can easily point to the existence or absence of freedoms. We can determine whether or not a polity has civil liberties. We need only count those institutions that assure civil liberties. These may be constitutional rules, courts, legislative acts, the behaviour of executive bodies and the police, of the press, and so on. On such grounds we may say that consent to a totalitarian order is voluntary, but that it amounts to a loss of civil and political liberties. Or, to take a hackneyed case: someone may freely sell himself into slavery, but he will no longer enjoy the legal status of a free man.

My point is that we do not need to appeal to what a rational subject can or must do in such circumstances. What rational agents, however understood, must do is beside the point. When the free institutions are lacking, or they exist in name only, a polity cannot be said to be free in the civil sense of the term. In fact, in such societies, there are clear barriers to freedom, in the form of prohibitions against unauthorized publications and debate, or the reproduction of foreign books.

In this sense, Berlin's concept of negative liberty denotes the core constituents of a specific kind of free society: namely, a liberal and democratic society ordered under the rule of law. No matter how abstract, the concept can be read as an abridgement of the workings of actual liberal-democratic institutions.

This focus on negative liberty is important because it places Berlin within a specific tradition of liberal thought, the classical one of Locke, Voltaire, and Benjamin Constant. As John Plamenatz reminds us, the classical liberal is concerned firstly with institutions which secure individual liberty and secondly with the self-cultivation of subjects. This is not because the classical liberal is

[75] Berlin argues that the 'psychological machinery' presupposed by Soviet propaganda is the same as that of Stoical thought; one that relies on self-conditioning, on internalizing outward commands or making them one's own (see 'Introduction' to *FE*, p. xxxix n. 1). For a description of conditioning based on the Soviet model, see Václav Havel, *Living in Truth* (London, 1989), 36–122.

[76] See 'Two Concepts of Liberty' in *FE*, 162–6; and Kocis, 'Reason, Development, and the Conflicts of Human Ends', 49.

unmindful of self-improvement. It is only that he thinks that little self-improvement is possible in a polity that cannot assure the security of the person and other basic civil liberties.[77] Both his strong attachment to negative liberty, and his willingness to defend it against any distortion, put Berlin amongst those in the classical camp. The classic nature of his liberalism makes him wary of concepts of liberty which speak, on the one hand, of freedom as rational self-improvement and freedom as rational self-control, and on the other, of freedom as collective self-assertion and freedom as collective self-determination. These concepts differ from what is meant by civil liberties, even though they are found in the work of some liberal thinkers.[78]

Berlin does not dispute the worth of self-realization (PL2) or that of participation in collective decision-making (PL3). He is no supporter of irrationalism, nor is he specifically undemocratic. He objects, however, to political theories which assert that there is one and only one true path to moral and political life. This assertion he encounters in most advocates of PL2, be they within or outside the liberal tradition. Because advocates of PL2 usually assert one fixed and true end for people, these theories are easily transformed into justifications of authority.[79] The cause of these distortions has been the belief in monism. According to Berlin, PL2 theories often split the self into two: with the higher level being equated with the rational side of the psyche, while the lower level is equated with the desirous and empirical parts. Thinkers as disparate as Plato, Epictetus, Rousseau, Kant, Spinoza, Fichte, and Hegel have all split human nature in this way. They have all claimed that following one's desires is to be in a condition of heteronomy; while in contrast, autonomy and true freedom amount to following one's reason, one's highest faculties.[80] As a philosophy of life this may well be unproblematic. It is good to govern onself, to follow one's

[77] See Plamenatz, 'Introduction' to *Readings from Liberal Writers*, 14–18.
[78] See 'Introduction' to *FE*, pp. lvi–lix. Plamenatz (see n. 77) divides liberals into 'ordinary' and 'high-minded' liberals on this very idea of autonomy and self-cultivation. John Gray follows him and claims that 'revisionary liberals', such as T. H. Green and L. T. Hobhouse, differ from 'classical' liberals, such as David Hume, John Locke, and Benjamin Constant, in that the former camp is more interested in the capacities and powers of citizens than in the limits of sovereign authority over their lives. J. S. Mill is a pivotal representative of both camps (see *Liberalism*, 7–36).
[79] See 'Two Concepts of Liberty' in *FE*, 145–6, 167–72.
[80] See 'Introduction' to *FE*, p. xliv; and 'Two Concepts of Liberty', 131–54.

own laws; it is wise to follow one's reason. But it is the political
implications of such philosophies that concern Berlin. For, if and
when the ends of rational persons are said to converge in all
instances, then disagreements about good ends are taken to be
species of irrationalism. On such grounds, coercing recalcitrants
amounts to putting them on the rational, true, and right path.
Indeed, the use of force amounts to liberating them from their
errors. The political implications is that coercion becomes the
handmaiden of liberty.[81]

Berlin identifies such paternalistic and authoritarian tendencies
throughout the Western, but especially the rationalist, tradition,
from Plato[82] to Leo Strauss.[83] He finds these tendencies in such
illiberal thinkers as Marx and Lenin,[84] as well as liberal thinkers,
such as Montesquieu, Kant, Burke, T. H. Green, even Locke.[85] He
writes that,

> The common assumption of these thinkers . . . is that the rational ends of
> our 'true' natures must coincide, or be made to coincide, however
> violently our poor, ignorant, desire-ridden, passionate, empirical selves
> may cry out against this process. Freedom is not freedom to do what is
> irrational, or stupid, or wrong. To force empirical selves into the right
> pattern is no tyranny, but liberation . . . In the ideal case, liberty coincides
> with law: autonomy with authority.[86]

In contrast to these thinkers, Berlin holds strongly to the view that
all infringements of liberty are limits on liberty. He will have no
truck with arguments which make prohibitions into extensions of
liberty. While it is true that rules and laws often increase aggregate
liberty, it does not follow that a law is anything but a limit on some
specific liberty or set of liberties. He holds with Bentham on this
score: 'Every law is an infraction of liberty'. To say otherwise is to
turn the concept of liberty into something else.[87]

The same problem of distortion can be detected with PL3 (i.e.
participation in sovereign decision-making). Briefly, the problem

---

[81] 'Two Concepts of Liberty', in *FE*, 145–54.   [82] Ibid. 151–4.
[83] All Souls interview; and the Jahanbegloo interview, 51–4.
[84] See 'Political Ideas in the Twentieth Century' in *FE*, 15–28.
[85] 'Two Concepts of Liberty' in *FE* 133 n. 1; and 'Introduction' to *FE*, p. xlix n. 1,
and p. lxi.
[86] 'Two Concepts of Liberty' in *FE*, 148–9.
[87] Ibid.; and the All Souls and Athenaeum interviews.

revolves around identifying oneself with a collective entity, such as a master race, or the democratic assembly, or the nation in arms.[88] Berlin argues that if and when liberty is taken to have a fixed end and to be realizable only within a specific group, then once again, coercion may be justified on the grounds that it is really not coercion, but liberation. Hence the patriot says that one is truly free only when subject to the dictates of the nation. Or the democrat tells us that we are truly free only in following the dictates of the assembly. If you disagree, you go against your true self. One could go even as far as Rousseau and claim that it is right and proper for you to be forced to be free; such coercion is for your own good, and once you become reasonable, you will come to recognize it as such. Here freedom becomes synonymous with authority.[89]

These are the doctrines that Berlin considers fatal to liberal institutions and contrary to liberal conceptions of freedom. None of the formulations of positive liberty are concerned with spheres of non-interference. The concern is with who is acting, with right and good deeds, and with capacities and agent-relative ends. The focus is on one, or several, of the following: self-mastery, the will, power, goals, self-development, self-improvement, self-perfection, and goals other than individual liberty, such as doing one's democratic or religious duty. All of these are at odds with the negative libertarian conception of freedom. Here the focus is on barriers to the use of power, limits on authority. The liberal may be concerned with autonomy and self-improvement, with democratic and religious duty, or with doing what is reasonable and rational; but she will come close to justifying authority, possibly unlimited authority, if she speaks of these things and forgets to speak of limits on power as well.

Conclusion

In this chapter I have argued that Isaiah Berlin's concept of negative liberty is best understood as a conceptual tag for civil liberties. This does not imply that liberty can only be understood negatively; but that civil liberty is negative liberty as Berlin defines it. Nor does

---

[88] I deal in detail with Berlin's critique of democratic theories in Chs. 6 and 7.

Berlin consider positive liberty and social egalitarianism as unworthy ends; only that these ends, if zealously pursued, can subvert liberal institutions. When these points are understood, Berlin's distinctions between negative liberty and positive liberty are easy to grasp. Negative liberty deals with spheres of non-interference, such as freedom from arbitrary arrest; positive liberty deals with self-mastery and what one does, what one achieves, with liberty. Furthermore, negative and civil liberties are different from the conditions of their enjoyment. The point is not to take equality to be liberty, or consider good and rational behaviour to be freedom.

There are advantages to Berlin's distinction, especially with regard to his use of negative liberty as a tag for civil liberties. Formal-legal or juridical liberties are good empirical markers of freedom in modern polities. This distinction allows him to determine the nature of a political society, whether it is authoritarian or despotic, liberal or free; and to what degree it may be free or less so.[90] In fact, the freedom of a polity can be verified by using the marker of negative liberty. We can point to the protection of negative freedom in civil and constitutional law, in the workings of courts and the decrees of executive bodies, or in the effective limits on the power of sovereigns and legislatures—in short, in the actual workings of constitutional regimes. Thus Berlin can easily claim (as we all can) that a modern polity is significantly free if and only if there are institutional protections against arbitrary force, where the rule of law exists, and where the constitution is ordered to protect the lives and views of minorities and individuals.

Yet for all this, Berlin's understanding of liberty does not exclude autonomist versions of liberty such as those concerning individual self-mastery or the self-determination of a nation.[91] This point has unfortunately been concealed by Berlin's own rhetoric; by the way he lumps the principles of self-determination and self-realization with monism; by the way he links, rather unfairly, such disparate thinkers as Kant and Locke with Marx and Lenin. But none of this is needed, nor follows from the concept of negative liberty and the critique of positive liberty. As John Gray argues, Berlin failed in his famous essay to discriminate between kinds of positive liberty, and hence made all kinds a species of monistic thought. Gray adds that

[90] The Jahanbegloo interview, 40–2.
[91] Correspondence (18 Mar. 1991).

it is possible to subscribe to a conception of autonomy 'which does not have the feature of requiring access to a single body of objective moral truths, but instead demands simply the free exercise of the human intelligence'. In fact, such a conception is invoked in dealing with the specific 'modern threats to freedom—propaganda, media manipulation, and the tyranny of fashion'. In addition, such 'an open conception of autonomy . . . avoids the rationalist metaphysic of the self of the sort criticized by Berlin'. To be autonomous is to live according to one's reason, to use one's critical powers of analysis, and to live according to one's guiding light.[92]

None of this is foreign to Berlin, as I showed in Chapters 2 and 3; but it is not the focus of the 'Two Concepts' essay. In fact, his other works show that he is a proponent of enlightenment and critical reason. So long as we add the rider that autonomous beings are unlikely to converge on one pattern of life, then Berlin has no qualms with principles of self-determination and self-realization.[93] Nevertheless, autonomy, self-determination, and self-improvement are different from civil liberties. To be self-directed, rational, and a good person is different from living in a free society.[94] People can be free in the negative, civil sense and be unfree in the positive sense. Berlin's point is that autonomy and self-improvement are poor markers for civil and political liberty. They refer to what one may do with civil liberty, and not to whether civil liberties exist in a polity. At best, the latter are institutional conditions for autonomy and self-realization.[95]

In sum, Berlin considers the concept of negative liberty to be 'basic' to all kinds of liberties, to all free acts, even those seeking 'self-realization', whether individual or collective. Negative liberty is a necessary condition of positive freedom. Hence a polity without negative or civil liberties is unfree in a basic and fundamental sense. This is true even if the polity exhibits a great deal of social justice, or democratic solidarity, or religious sentiment, or its subjects are disposed to correct behaviour. However, it is one thing to say what liberal freedom is, or how it allows people to develop, and quite another to assert that negative freedom is what we need. In the next two chapters I will analyse Berlin's historical,

---

[92] Gray, *Liberalism*, 59–60.
[93] Correspondence (5 Jan. 1991).
[94] All Souls and Athenaeum interviews.
[95] See also Gray, *Liberalism*, 60–1.

sociological, and political defences of classical liberalism and negative libertarianism. My claim is that his conception of freedom is adequate for what we know about human needs, about our historical development in Western culture, and the nature of modern politics.

5

PLURALISM AND THE
LIBERAL POLITICAL ORDER

[C]ollisions of values are of the essence of what they are and what we are. If we are told that these contradictions will be solved in some perfect world in which all good things can be harmonized in principle, then we must answer, to those who say this, that the meanings they attach to the names which for us denote the conflicting values are not ours. We must say that the world in which what we see as incompatible values are not in conflict is a world altogether beyond our ken; that principles which are harmonized in this other world are not the principles with which, in our daily lives, we are acquainted; if they are transformed, it is into conceptions not known to us on earth. But it is on earth that we live, and it is here that we must believe and act.

(Isaiah Berlin, 'The Pursuit of the Ideal')

Pluralism, with the measure of 'negative' liberty that it entails, seems to me a truer and more humane ideal than the goals of those who seek in the great, disciplined, authoritarian structures the ideal of 'positive' self-mastery by classes, or peoples, or the whole of mankind. It is truer, because it does, at least, recognize the fact that human goals are many, not all of them commensurable, and in perpetual rivalry with one another. To assume that all values can be graded on one scale, so that it is a mere matter of inspection to determine the highest, seems to me to falsify our knowledge that men are free agents, to represent moral decision as an operation which a slide-rule could, in principle, perform. To say that in some ultimate, all-reconciling, yet realizable synthesis, duty *is* interest, or individual freedom *is* pure democracy or an authoritarian state, is to throw a metaphysical blanket over either self-deceit or deliberate hypocrisy. It is more humane because it does not (as the system builders do) deprive men, in the name of some remote, or incoherent, ideal, of much that

they have found to be indispensable to their life as unpredict-
ably self-transforming human beings.

(Isaiah Berlin, 'Two Concepts of Liberty')

At this point, my presentation leaves conceptual distinctions aside,
and looks at the empirical and practical aspects of Berlin's defence
of political liberalism. As I have stated, the debate sparked by the
essay 'Two Concepts of Liberty' has been too concerned with the
cogency of Berlin's analysis of the concepts of liberty, to the point
that his other arguments have received scant attention, if not been
overlooked entirely. It is my contention that moral but also
historical and practical arguments, no less than conceptual ones,
form parts of Berlin's defence of liberalism. Some of these moral
and empirical arguments can be found in 'Two Concepts of
Liberty'; others elsewhere. In this chapter I discuss the political
implications of Berlin's theory of moral pluralism, as well as his
ethical naturalism. In Chapter 6 I discuss Berlin's understanding of
the difference between ancient and modern liberty, and then turn to
his interpretation of the problem of political power in modernity,
with particular reference to popular sovereignty, Bonapartism, and
totalitarianism. In Chapter 7 I discuss his views on the founding of
a new nation, Israel. While Berlin does not discuss Israel in the
'Two Concepts' essay, his Zionist writings offer an interesting
application of the pluralist and liberal principles expressed in this
famous essay.

'The One and the Many'

Berlin ends his 'Two Concepts' essay with a section entitled 'The
One and the Many'. In it he links value pluralism to the importance
of negative liberty and to a decent, free society. This is not
surprising; as I argued in Chapter 3, value pluralism is a central idea
in his thought. That is, Berlin argues that our moral universe is
made up of a plurality of goods, not all of which are compatible, or
can be combined without loss. There are many ways to live a good
life, no one standard can appraise all goods, and no society can
unite all good ways of life. If this model is true—and Berlin believes
that there is sufficient empirical cause to accept it, rather than all its
Ionian-inspired opposites—then it offers strong support for an
open political order; in fact, support for a liberal polity.

As with most of his arguments, this one begins with a critique of the position of opponents. As discussed in Chapter 3, Berlin argues that monism is incoherent in theory. Yet this has not stopped the practice of monistic politics. By focusing on practice, Berlin shifts ground to the historical and empirical realm of political studies. Monism is prevalent in the history of political movements, having inspired much ancient thought and politics, most religious movements, and in modern times, utilitarians, socialists, communists, and religious fundamentalists. Berlin even considers dogmatic libertarians to be monistic, for they wish to sacrifice all values to liberty. Monism has also underpinned social Darwinism, much nationalist thought, most revolutionaries and authoritarian populists, and certainly all Fascists.[1] What predominantly concerns Berlin, and motivates his critique of monism, are the political implications of such ideologies. He does not spare the rod (nor the polemics) in denouncing their effects. In 'Two Concepts of Liberty' he states bluntly that,

One belief, more than any other, is responsible for the slaughter of individuals on the altars of the great historical ideals—justice or progress or happiness of future generations, or the sacred mission or emancipation of a nation or race or class, or even liberty itself, which demands the sacrifice of individuals for the freedom of society. This is the belief that somewhere, in the past or in the future, in divine revelation or in the mind of an individual thinker, in the pronouncements of history or science, or in the simple heart of an uncorrupted good man, there is a final solution.[2]

The last two words amplify Berlin's belief that monistic thought has led, from its first conception amongst Ionian philosophers, to the worst of all crimes against humanity, the 'final solution' of the Nazis. Indeed, it is as if what Berlin calls this 'ancient faith' in monism[3] had revealed all its faults in the twentieth century, aided by the development of weapons and organizations of mass

---

[1] See 'Political Ideas in the Twentieth Century' and 'Two Concepts of Liberty', both in *FE*, 1–40 and 145–72, respectively. See also 'Herzen and Bakunin on Individual Liberty' in *RT*, 82–113; 'The Pursuit of the Ideal' in *CTH*, 1 and *passim*; and 'Joseph de Maistre and the Origins of Fascism' in *CTH*, 91–174. For discussions of the rise and spread of fundamentalism in the Jewish, Catholic, and Islamic worlds, see Albert Memmi, 'Intégrisme et laïcité' in *Le Monde Diplomatique* (Mar. 1989), 3; and Didier Foucault, 'Jusqu'où faut-il respecter l'autre?' in *Le Monde Diplomatique* (Apr. 1989), 16–17.

[2] 'Two Concepts of Liberty' in *FE*, 167.   [3] Ibid.

destruction. It is for this reason that its logic must be exposed, undermined, falsified.

Berlin argues that, regardless of its comfort to the mind and soul,[4] monism is a 'metaphysical chimera' which runs contrary to ordinary experience. Common sense correctly judges human affairs as having few, if any, ultimate solutions to moral problems. Instead, 'ordinary experience is one in which we are faced with choices between ends equally ultimate, and claims equally absolute, the realization of some of which must inevitably involve the sacrifice of others'. Not only is it contrary to ordinary experience to think otherwise, but it is imprudent, and often frightfully barbaric, to act on such principles and ideologies. For if one 'final state' can be achieved, one in which all values, or all putatively true and correct values, are realized, then the sacrifice of some values, liberties, even persons today will no doubt be worth it tomorrow.[5]

It is this kind of justification for sacrifice which Berlin seeks to end; first by showing the falsehood of the belief in an ideal state, and second by pointing to the inhuman consequences of acting on such beliefs. Without a priori guarantees of the existence of a perfect state, crusading for it becomes unjustifiable. What one is left with are 'the ordinary resources of empirical observation and ordinary human knowledge', both of which paint a complex, finite, pluralistic, and untidy moral universe rather than a complete, or near complete, monistic and harmonious one.[6] On this point, Berlin is adamant. He drops scholarly distance and states candidly that,

[I]t seems to me that the belief that some single formula can in principle be found whereby all the diverse ends of men can be harmoniously realized is demonstrably false. If, as I believe, the ends of men are many, and not all of them are in principle compatible with each other, then the possibility of conflict—and of tragedy—can never wholly be eliminated from human life, either personal or social. The necessity of choosing between absolute claims is then an inescapable characteristic of the human condition. This gives its value to freedom as Acton had conceived of it—as an end in itself, and not as a temporary need, arising out of our confused notions and irrational and disordered lives, a predicament which a panacea could one day but right.[7]

[4] 'Two Concepts of Liberty' 170, 172.   [5] Ibid. 168.
[6] Ibid.   [7] Ibid. 169.

Pluralism is a fact of our moral condition. As such, it implies a fundamental place for liberty in moral life. For without liberty, one cannot choose between goods. In this sense, freedom from interference, room to choose, is prior to other goods.[8] It is for this reason that Berlin considers negative liberty to be basic to moral life. It is also the reason why he criticizes positive libertarian doctrines. Because many such doctrines presuppose an ideal order, or prescribe a *good* way to act in order to *truly* be free, they can validate the suppression of a great many liberties. Indeed, choice is superfluous once a conception of life which takes all ends to be harmoniously set, either above or behind ordinary experience, is accepted. The same is true of doctrines which hold that history is unfolding toward a complete realization of human ends. Choice is error, grave error indeed, and must be suppressed in order to live in *truth*, if and when the course of society is set on the road to a perfect state. Under such schemes, the suppression of liberty is not injustice, but rather a means towards the full realization of all values, including liberty, or at least its *proper* form. This point can be taken further still: once the utopia is achieved, liberty need no longer exist. This is because when all goods are harmoniously realized, the necessity of choice 'withers away'.[9]

Once we deny the truth of the ideal, the means to achieve it are suspect. And suspicion mounts as we tally the inhuman results of holding to monism. But Berlin's aim is not just to denounce barbaric acts committed in the name of lofty principles, more is sought. The aim is to point out how freedom from interference, negative liberty, respects a fundamental characteristic of the human condition, which is the pluralism of moral values. For if people are given sufficient liberties, then space is granted for persons to identify themselves with various goods present in life. In fact, Berlin argues for negative liberty because he believes that pluralism is true, and not because he has a dogmatic adherence to personal liberty. He thinks that a political order which grants individual liberties, in sufficient number, best fits the pluralistic reality of our moral condition. This is so because a liberal order is tolerant of

---

[8] See John Gray, 'On Negative and Positive Liberty' in Gray, *Liberalisms*, 64–6.
[9] See 'Introduction' to *FE*, pp. l–lii. The reference to Engels is obvious, and implies that moral life and personhood would be altered beyond recognition in a communist society.

differences.[10] To reiterate, Berlin holds that monism is incoheren[
at the conceptual level, as well as untrue to ordinary experience. I[
contrast, moral pluralism is conceptually valid, and also a fact o[
the human condition—in his own words, 'an inescapable charac[
teristic of human nature'.[11] One only need add the claim tha[
freedom of the will is presupposed by our moral talk, to come clos[
to Berlin's defence of political liberalism. Freedom is part of huma[
nature, and pluralism typifies our moral universe. Moreover, it i[
the plurality of goods that shows the importance of liberty t[
human existence. A polity which is true, formally and empirically
to human nature, will go some way toward recognizing an[
respecting both pluralism and liberty. Inasmuch as liberal politie[
recognize and respect these aspects of human nature, they are true[
to our natures than other polities based on principles which den[
the centrality of either pluralism or liberty. And to make his poin[
resonate in practice, Berlin completes his defence with a critique o[
monistic politics. His argument has ostensive import: it points t[
practice, is political, and relies on history. This will be furthe[
explored in the following two chapters. As the second quotation a[
the beginning of this chapter shows, Berlin holds the view tha[
once history and political events are taken into account, one realize[
that a good amount of negative liberty renders a polity humane, o[
at least more so than others which fail to recognize and respect bot[
pluralism and individual liberty. A polity which allows for negativ[
liberties, for choices free from interference, respects two aspects o[
our nature: our freedom as moral beings and the plurality of mora[
goods, bundles which form our identities as unique cultural being[
and individuals.

'A Common Public World of Values'[12]

In the liberal tradition, talk of what persons need *qua* human being[
has usually been based on conceptions of natural right and natura[
law. For instance, rights to life and liberty are considered to b[
basic claims that citizens make on their governments, not becaus[
they are citizens, but in light of their humanity or their nature a[

[10] Correspondence (15 Apr. 1991). See the Jahanbegloo interview, 43–4.
[11] 'Two Concepts of Liberty' in *FE*, 169.
[12] See 'Introduction' to *FE*, p. xxxi.

moral beings. Such a defence of the right to liberty is long standing, part of the social contract tradition which stretches from Hobbes and Locke, in the 16th and 17th centuries, to H. L. A. Hart and John Rawls in the 20th.[13] It is present in all contemporary defences and declarations of human rights.

Berlin's historicism, his sympathy for Vico and Romanticism, and his belief in pluralism, would seem to suggest that he could not believe in natural laws, in moral claims based on universal values.[14] If true, this would surely damage his defence of liberalism, because the values of liberty and variety would be contingent, without foundation beyond our modern social formation.[15] In other words, if there are no eternal axioms of morality, or overarching standards of morality, then how can one defend the correctness of liberal institutions, their fit with human interests? If values like liberty are historical and culturally specific, what is valid in liberalism?

Of course, Berlin the historicist may be at odds with Berlin the proponent and philosopher of liberalism. But while there is a tension here, there is no incoherence. As I said in the conclusion to Chapter 3, Berlin's moral and political theory is best understood as working on two levels. The first deals with universal statements about human nature, human interests, and the foundations of morality; the second deals with histories, conventions, practices, and mores. While analytically distinct, these two levels are intertwined in his moral and political thought.[16] It is important to separate them, especially to show the limits of Berlin's pluralism, where he draws the line between his moral theory and relativism or nihilism.[17] In fact, Berlin believes in the moral unity of the human

[13] H. L. A. Hart, 'Are There Any Natural Rights?' in Antony Quinton (ed.), *Political Philosophy* (Oxford, 1967), 53–66; and John Rawls, *A Theory of Justice*. See also the introduction to Ch. 6.

[14] See e.g. Berlin's discussion of Vico's critique of natural law in *VH*, 86–7; and the interchange between Ronald McKinney and Berlin, *Journal of Value Inquiry*, 26 (1992), 395–407, 557–60.

[15] Berlin poses this problem at the end of 'Two Concepts of Liberty' but offers no solution (see *FE*, 172).

[16] Berlin makes a distinction between a universal 'common public world of values', the 'foundations of human morality' as opposed to 'notions of custom, or tradition, or law, or manners, or fashion, or etiquette . . .' The former offer us a minimum core of common values, while the latter are mutable, ever changing (see 'Introduction' to *FE*, pp. xxxi–xxxii).

[17] Due to his pluralism, some critics label him a relativist. See Michael Sandel, 'Introduction' to *Liberalism and its Critics* (New York, 1984), 7–8; and Leo Strauss, 'Relativism' in *The Rebirth of Classical Political Rationalism* (Chicago, 1989), 13–19.

species. He has a theory of human nature which includes the capacity to make moral decisions and the common (or virtually universal[18]) acceptance of a set of core values. These include, for example, justice, compassion, mercy, strength, liberty, equality, and the like. There are certain basic human needs as well, many of which are easily translated into basic moral claims, such as the need for shelter, food, security, possibly belonging 'to a group of one's own' if we accept Herder's views; and if we accept the claim of classical liberalism, a minimum of liberty to act and express oneself, to create, to love, and to worship.[19] The fact that some of these, such as valuing diversity, arise in history and were not held by the ancients, is no argument against the common worth of the value. There is a difference between questions of fact and questions of validity; and Berlin believes that the modern genesis of the acceptance of pluralism affects neither the truth pluralism expresses about our moral condition, nor the validity and worth of judgements based on pluralism, such as the respect of diversity.[20]

Thus common values arise not only out of a theory of human needs; they can arise in history. Moreover, their fundamental nature is often revealed to us in extreme situations. Berlin relates that the importance of universal moral claims is most evident in the face of ethical catastrophes, such as wars, pogroms, and holocausts. If the Nazis and Soviets proved anything, Berlin tells us, it is that there are absolute limits to political action. To transgress these limits is to fall into barbarism and inhumanity. If Stalinism offers us any lessons, surely one of them must be that the ruthless and total management of human beings falls outside any justifiable moral behaviour. When moral limits are transgressed, the moral unity of the species is violated, and we properly recoil in horror. For Berlin,

For a full discussion of these critiques, see my unpublished Ph.D. dissertation, 'Isaiah Berlin's Liberalism: An Exposition and Defense' (University of Toronto, 1990), 259–75.

[18] Correspondence (16 May and 15 Apr. 1991). Berlin qualifies this assertion with an empirical rider. We hold such values to be correct, but know that experience could falsify our certainty in their universality. In the meantime, we are confident about their widespread acceptance across time and cultures. See 'Introduction' to *FE*, pp. xxxi–xxxii and liii.

[19] Unpublished letter to Beata Polanowska-Sygulska (24 Feb. 1986), 2–3. See 'Introduction' to *FE*, p. liii; and 'European Unity and Its Vicissitudes' in *CTH*, 205–6.

[20] Correspondence (17 Nov. 1988), 2. See 'Two Concepts of Liberty' in *FE*, 172; and the Jahanbegloo interview, 43.

he experience of moral horror exposes the truth of natural law.
'hock at such horrors would be impossible without intimations of
uch laws. Without natural law we could not make ultimate moral
laims against governments, nor understand the horror and pain
elt by the victims of inhuman acts.[21]

This is different from a theory which derives universal values, a
•riori, from a fixed image of human nature, revealed to reason, or
•y revelation. Such theories usually miss the complexities of
ultural life, and tend to be anachronistic; thinkers such as Vico
vere correct in criticizing their limitations.[22] Rather, the theory
•ropounded by Berlin is thoroughly empirical, related to the
indings of 'moral psychology and historical and social anthropo-
ɔgy'.[23] These empirical disciplines do uncover universal charac-
eristics to human life, as well as falsify previous assumptions
•r claims about such universality. This is how these sciences
rogress, and correct our knowledge of human nature. None
he less, there remains some things which are fundamental to
uman existence, and we know this to be fact (at least, until our
xperience proves otherwise). In this sense his historicism comple-
nents, rather than conflicts with, his ethical naturalism.[24]

[21] See 'European Unity and its Vicissitudes' in *CTH*, 202–6; O. Utis [Berlin's
ɔm de guerre], 'Generalissimo Stalin and the Art of Government' in *Foreign Affairs*,
ɔ (1952), 197–214. See also his 'Does Political Theory Still Exist?' in *CC*, 166; and
ħationality in Value Judgements' in Carl J. Friedrich (ed.), *Nomos 7, Rational
'ecision*, 221–3. Of course some will point out that this commits the naturalistic
llacy because it derives normative claims from empirical ones, 'ought' from 'is'.
ɔr a defence of ethical naturalism, see Stuart Hampshire, *Morality and Conflict*, 6–8,
ʒ–100, 168–9.
[22] See *VH*, 87–9.
[23] 'Introduction' to *FE*, p. xxxii.
[24] See 'Introduction' to *FE*, pp. lii–liii. In an unpublished letter to Beata
ɔlanowska-Sygulska (24 Feb. 1986, 2), Berlin admits that: 'I do not believe that all
ten are in the relevant respects the same "beneath the skin", i.e., I believe that
ɪriety is part of human existence and in fact—though this is quite irrelevant—that
ɪis is a valuable attribute, though that is a very late idea, probably not to be met
ιuch before the eighteenth century.' Yet he also asserts that: 'I think that common
round between human beings must exist if there is to be any meaning in the
ɔncept of human being at all.' And while the category of human being presumes
nity, and for this reason we can discern some uniformity in characteristics amongst
ιman beings, the really interesting parts of human nature are cultural and thus
ιutable. Hence Berlin continues (p. 3) by stating that: 'I believe in the permanent
ɔssibility of change, modification, variety, without being able to state that there is
ɔme central kernel which is what is being modified or changed—but there must be
ιough in common between all the various individuals and groups who are going
ιrough various modifications for communication to be possible; and this can be

While the history of events and ages plays a role in this theory, by adding flesh to the basic moral skeleton, history also confirms the existence of the moral skeleton. For example, the carnage of this century and the totalitarianism of some regimes have made plain that we should operate 'as if' natural law were true. Our censure of Nazism is intelligible on this basis, because it is framed by universal moral language. We need to abide by these laws, if we wish to avoid immeasurable human suffering—this is what Berlin takes to be the needed translation of natural-law doctrines from their old theological foundations into *empirical* as opposed to a priori claims about our fundamental needs as moral beings.[25] In this respect, Berlin subscribes to a minimum content theory of natural law. He often writes of 'the common public world of values', or 'the central values . . . common to human beings as such, that is, for practical purposes, to the great majority of men in most places and times'.[26] He believes that there exist basic moral rules, the lack of which makes civil life intolerable *and* impossible.[27] But such requirements are minimal indeed.

Herein lies a problem with all natural-law doctrines: they *underdetermine* actual moral and political life. Their field of concern is the foundations of morality as such, and the basic requirement for civilization. Yet there exists a significant variety of moral sanctions and prescriptions apart from the basic conditions needed for moral and civilized life.[28] We know these are the conventions

expressed by listing, almost mechanically, various needs—"basic" for that reason—the various forms and varieties of which belong to different persons, cultures, societies, etc. The need for food is universal, but the way I satisfy it, the particular foods I crave, the steps I take to obtain it, will vary: so with all the other basic needs—my mythology, metaphysics, religion, language, gestures, will widely vary, but not the fact that these are attempted ways of trying to explain to myself, to find myself at home in, a puzzling and possibly unfriendly environment, or indeed world.'

[25] Athenaeum interview; correspondence (17 Nov. 1988 and 16 May 1991); 'Reply to Ronald H. McKinney', 557–8. See the Jahanbegloo interview, 37–40, 108–14; and 'European Unity and its Vicissitudes' in *CTH*, 204.

[26] 'Introduction' to *FE*, pp. xxxi–xxxii; see also p. liii.

[27] All Souls interview; correspondence (17 Nov. 1988 and 16 May 1991). See 'Introduction' to *FE*, pp. xxxi–xxxii; and the Jahanbegloo interview, 141–2. On minimal content theories of natural law see Gray, *Liberalism*, 50; and Hart, 'Are There Any Natural Rights?', 55–66.

[28] See the Jahanbegloo interview, 61. For a discussion of other problems—e.g. how many exist, whether they are natural or social, what to do when they conflict—see Gray, *Liberalism*, 46–8.

customs, practices, and institutional rules of actual societies and polities.[29] While natural-law doctrines are crucial in contesting the claims of moral relativists, and denouncing certain inhuman practices and evil regimes, natural-law doctrines provide 'no direct route from a theory of human nature to the superiority of a liberal society'.[30]

Berlin acknowledges this problem. He believes in the truth of some claims for human rights, but he does not know how many such rights exist.[31] He knows that there are some basic human needs and basic moral conditions necessary to make society workable, decent, tolerable; but such conditions do not necessarily prescribe liberalism.[32] For example, basic moral claims do not say how much *liberty* we need, let alone entail the large amount offered by contemporary liberal–democratic governments. Something more is needed. With Berlin, these additions amount to a fully developed moral theory which captures all aspects of persons, in particular their histories, and their lives within cultures, and actual political societies. With respect to liberty, it points to the development of persons in Western societies, typified by social complexity, with attachments to individuality, and respect for cultural and religious variety. As Berlin says, the right measure of liberty can be assessed only after one grasps the 'total patterns of life' within a culture or society.[33]

Hence persons are defined not only universally, as human beings, but also according to their differences, based on cultural affiliation. This is the essence of his theory of cultural pluralism, and follows from his interest in the history of ideas, in the development of human cultures. We are cultural animals who live and develop in historically formed and unique societies. Customs, practices, and institutions form part of our identities and moral make-up. In fact, most moral rules and practices, such as tolerance, can only be understood fully in the context of institutional development, of moral progress in resolving major ethical conflicts. Hence it is not incorrect, but fitting, to appeal to such historical

[29] See Hampshire, *Morality and Conflict*, 117, 126–39.
[30] Gray, *Liberalism*, 50.
[31] Unpublished letter to Beata Polanowska-Sygulska (24 Feb. 1986), 5; the Jahanbegloo interview, 142.
[32] All Souls interview.
[33] 'Two Concepts of Liberty' in *FE*, 140 n. 1.

118 *Pluralism and the Liberal Political Order*

examples when justifying various practices. In some cases, these
may be the fullest appeals we have.[34]

Different from basic claims about natural justice or utility, it is
this second realm of practical activity and codes of institutional
behaviour that justifies most of what occurs in actual political
societies.[35] With Berlin, it is what justifies much of liberal-
democratic practice, including the respect and preservation of
moral pluralism and a large amount of personal liberty.

Conclusion

Given Berlin's criticisms of the natural-law tradition, of monism,
and his acceptance of moral pluralism, one could conclude that his
defence of liberalism lacks firm moral foundations. This is not so.
While Berlin denies that a fixed set of moral laws exists to cover all
civilized behaviour, he does not deny the existence of a core set of
moral values, 'a public world of common values'. The question is
one of range and scope. According to the old objectivist theories of
ethics, such as the natural-law tradition, all moral phenomena
could be resolved into a set of natural laws good for all times.
Berlin considers this too strong a theory, for it hides the
incompatibility of values, the pluralism of moral life. Hence Berlin
sees limits to reason, to theory, to revelation, in ethical reflection.
Yet it does not follow from this that no universal moral claims can
be made with respect to some actions, and according to some
values.[36]

One can hold to a theory of the limits of reason (or revelation or
intuition) in moral life, and still maintain that a core set of values

[34] As John Plamenatz reminds us, the liberal principle of tolerance arose out of the
religious wars of the 16th and 17th centuries, after which most reasonable men
realized the frightful consequence of acting on ultimate principles derived from
revelation. Tolerance was first a prudential principle, only to be defined as a
fundamental right much later by liberal theorists. The principle makes better sense
once the history of its genesis is known. See Plamenatz, 'Liberalism' in Philip P.
Wiener (editor in chief), *Dictionary of the History of Ideas* iii, 41–3; and ch. 2, 'Liberty
of Conscience' in Plamenatz's *Man and Society* (New York, 1963), 45–88. For a
summary of the historical development of the liberal principles of religious
tolerance, liberty of conscience, and limited government, see D. J. Manning,
Liberalism (London, 1976), 31–80.
[35] See Hampshire, *Morality and Conflict*, 4–9, 101–25, 148–69.
[36] 'Reply to Ronald H. McKinney', 557–60.

typifies human nature and the human condition. There is nothing inconsistent in this. One can deny the applicability of one theory of morality to all civilized and praiseworthy behaviour, and still hold that there are universal moral claims on some aspects of human activity. This is what Berlin does when he speaks of liberty as a fundamental characteristic of human nature, a thing which human beings, based on our knowledge of them, have valued for millennia. In this sense, Berlin is an ethical naturalist: he holds to a minimum content theory of natural law, one that includes liberty as a fundamental value. With this core theory, Berlin judges some regimes to be inhuman because they go beyond the limits of justifiable authority. He takes some acts to be barbaric, beyond the scope of what is recognizably human and decent. The pogroms and the holocausts of the 20th century are examples of such inhuman acts. Moreover, our shock at the excesses of Nazism are for him a sign of moral progress, the virtually universal recognition that there are limits to political action, beyond which persons are debased and violated *qua* human beings.[37]

While Berlin knows that some of these core values are Western, he none the less finds it hard to imagine others not holding to them.[38] It is difficult to think of persons who would prefer for themselves despotism over liberty, torture over due process, the killing of their children instead of long life for them, instability over stability, evil over good, and so on. It is not to deny the existence of such persons; many such have been powerful agents of history. Rather such persons for Berlin lack moral discrimination, operate outside rules necessary for civilized life; and for that, can easily be judged insane, or barbaric, and justifiably in need of being locked up.[39]

These appeals to fundamental values and a theory of human nature cover only the basic operating rules and principles of civilized life. They do not distinguish morally between, say, a feudal and a liberal order.[40] They may distinguish between

---

[37] 'European Unity and its Vicissitudes' in *CTH*, 202–6.

[38] Correspondence (17 Nov. 1988 and 16 May 1991).

[39] Correspondence (15 Apr. 1991 and 16 May 1991); 'Reply to Ronald H. McKinney', 557–60. See also 'Introduction' to *FE*, p. xxxi.

[40] A feudal order, run by an 'easy-going or inefficient despot' may allow for a great deal of liberty, as Berlin states himself (see 'Introduction' to *FE*, pp. lvii–lviii). Some feudal cities were quite safe and enjoyable. Yet on other scores, such as respect for the equality of persons, feudalism fares much worse, and liberal-democracies

communist or fascist regimes and liberal ones, because the former
overly repress freedom and pervert their citizens. To go beyond
this, and in particular, to defend a liberal order, Berlin must use
other arguments and appeal to a wider range of facts. This he does
when he says that liberal regimes are truer to our condition than
theocratic regimes, because the former respects value pluralism
while the latter denies it on principle. A liberal order allows for
pluralism, allows people enough freedom from interference to
choose the way of life which is good for them.[41] However, if
pluralism is valid and true to experience, then liberty is a prior
value in some measure among other values. Berlin is quick to point
this out: he is no dogmatic, immoderate, uncom-promising
negative libertarian. He recognizes the importance of other values
such as equality and social justice, and argues for them, especially
to make a society decent, just, and tolerable for all. It is only that a
balance, a working compromise, must be struck between these
values.[42]

But what of the balance between negative and positive liberty?
Here the issue is complex, and not determined by hard-and-fast
rules.[43] Rather, history and practical judgement about political
history must come into play. So must the trial-and-error application of solutions to moral conflicts. As the above discussion of
monistic politics shows, Berlin is concerned about the authoritarian
tendencies in positive libertarian doctrines. This is not a formal,
conceptual argument, but one related to a historical and practical
point: namely, that positive libertarian doctrines have too often
justified the concentration and unlimited use of political power.[44]
The next two chapters deal with these empirical points in Berlin's
work.

better. This, I take it, is what Berlin means by comparing 'total patterns of life', and
not just discrete values or scales based on one value, such as liberty or security.

[41] See Bernard Williams, 'Introduction' to *CC*, p. xviii. For a full exposition of
the links between pluralism and a liberal political order see Joseph Raz, *The Morality
of Freedom* (Oxford, 1986), Pt. V.

[42] 'Two Concepts of Liberty' in *FE*, 170; and 'Introduction' to *FE*, pp. xlv–xlvii,
liii–lvii, lx–lxiii.

[43] See 'Introduction' to *FE*, pp. xlviii–l.

[44] Ibid., pp. xliv–xlviii, lxi–lxii.

6

BERLIN AND FRENCH LIBERALISM

The desire not to be impinged upon, to be left to oneself, has been a mark of high civilization both on the part of individuals and communities. The sense of privacy itself, of the area of personal relationships as something sacred in its own right, derives from a conception of freedom which, for all its religious roots, is scarcely older, in its developed state, than the Renaissance or the Reformation. Yet its decline would mark the death of a civilization, or an entire moral outlook.

(Isaiah Berlin 'Two Concepts of Liberty')

When you establish that the sovereignty of the people is unlimited, you create and toss at random into human society a degree of power which is too large in itself, and which is bound to constitute an evil, in whatever hands it is placed. Entrust it to one man, to several, to all, you will still find that it is equally an evil. You will think that it is the fault of the holders of such power and, according to the circumstances, you will accuse in turn, monarchy, aristocracy, democracy, mixed governments or the representative system. You will be wrong: it is in fact the degree of force, not its holders, which must be denounced. It is against the weapon, not against the arm holding it, that it is necessary to strike ruthlessly. There are weights too heavy for the hand of man.

(Benjamin Constant, *Principles of Politics Applicable to all Representative Governments* (1815))

Larry Siedentop, a former student of Berlin's, has identified two dominant traditions in liberal thought.[1] The first is the British tradition which is typified by a priori forms of argument, such as those of natural law. Berlin draws from this tradition, as I showed

[1] Larry Siedentop, 'Two Liberal Traditions', in Alan Ryan (ed.), *The Idea of Freedom* (Oxford, 1979), 153–74.

in the previous chapter. But he also borrows from a second principally French tradition.[2] In reaction to the French Revolution and capitalist modernization, French liberals developed a new defence for limited government. In the early 19th century, writers and politicians such as Mme de Staël, Benjamin Constant, François Guizot, Alexis de Tocqueville, and a group named the *Doctrinaires*, debated the view that liberal forms of government could be defended successfully with sociological, cultural, and economic arguments. Unlike writers in the English tradition, these thinkers used dynamic models of human nature and society, centring on social, economic, and cultural considerations. They claimed that modern conditions were specific, unique, and thus in need of a kind of government adapted to the times. Their opponents fell into two camps, the Jacobins on the left and the Royalists on the right. The liberals argued that while the Royalists reminisced about a feudal order and the Jacobins yearned for republican politics based on ancient norms, both were misdirected because they did not adequately understand the changed conditions of French society.[3]

According to the French liberals, neither aristocratic nor ancient republican forms of government were political orders fitting to the new distribution of property, the egalitarian sentiments amongst the middle classes, and the concentrated nature of power in the modern state. Instead, these thinkers argued that limited government under the rule of law, or a liberal order, was best suited to modern times. Only this kind of political order responded to the growth of commercial activity in civil society, the differentiation of social roles, and the development of individualism. Only limited government under the rule of law could fit with a free civil society.[4]

This defence has significant advantages over natural-law doctrines, though it need not supplant them. English liberalism has often been criticized for being individualistic, a priori, abstract, unhistorical, and insensitive to social reality. French liberalism, on the other hand, overcomes these deficiencies by grounding political

[2] This is not to say that British liberalism is lacking in empirical method. One need only point to Locke, Hume, and J. S. Mill as examples. But Berlin does not rely explicitly on their work, not even on that of Mill. Rather, a close reading of 'Two Concepts of Liberty' shows an extensive use of 19th-century French liberal thought.

[3] Siedentop, 'Two Liberal Traditions', 157–62, 169–70.   [4] Ibid. 154–71.

prescriptions in theories of social change. The theories are partly empirical because they appeal to social facts. Social and cultural context becomes as important, if not more so, as normative arguments. Indeed, these thinkers assert that the normative arguments found in the natural-law tradition fail to represent the nature of political choice and action within contemporary society: they lack grounding in social and political facts.[5]

A developed historical and sociological sense overcomes the deficiencies of abstract political theory by showing what can and cannot be achieved given a particular social condition, or the material conditions, of a nation. At the time, French liberals tried to suppress the grand and hubristic politics of the Jacobins, which had been guided by abstract doctrines of natural law as well as ideal views of human beings as republican citizens. They also sought to undermine the prescriptions of the Royalists in the post-revolutionary period, who claimed that France ought to return to the feudal order of the *ancien régime*. Neither option seemed sociologically sound and thus these liberals asserted that neither option should be given serious political attention. The material and cultural conditions of the times would not allow for political orders devised according to archaic understandings of society.[6]

Berlin's debt to this tradition is evident in the 'Two Concepts' essay: in the section entitled 'Liberty and Sovereignty' he draws from Benjamin Constant's work.[7] Yet no critic has discussed or developed this aspect of Berlin's thought, possibly because of the over-emphasis amongst critics on the conceptual aspects of the essay. Whatever the cause, it should be no surprise that, as a historian of ideas, Berlin looked to the French liberal tradition for supportive arguments in addition to ones derived from natural law. Given his desire to avoid anachronistic readings of cultures, both past and present, there is a clear affinity between Berlin's historical orientation and that of French liberalism.[8]

Below I discuss the historical, sociological and political aspects of Berlin's defence of political liberalism. This will show that the 'Two Concepts' essay is not restricted to an analysis of the meaning and use of words, but contains a defence of substantive views.

[5] Ibid. 153–6, 162, 172–4.   [6] Ibid. 156–62, 169–72.
[7] 'Two Concepts of Liberty' in *FE*, 162–6.
[8] He has pointed this out to me in the All Souls and Athenaeum interviews, and to Jahanbegloo, 40–3, 142–4.

The Historical Nature of Liberty

Valuing individual freedom is fundamental to any liberal philosophy, and is modern in genesis.[9] The ancients, for example,
placed no premium on individual independence; indeed, they could
not. The ancient Greeks knew only the positive liberty of
democratic self-governance. Their term for freedom does not refer
to the liberty of personal independence. They understood freedom
to mean freedom from slavery and the legal status to participate in
public decision-making.[10] If Aristotle is accurate about the spirit of
the times, the ancients considered participation in collective
decision-making as the satisfaction of man's highest capacities.[11]
Women and slaves lacked the capacities for deliberation and
reasoned discourse; hence they were of no use to public debate and
could be legitimately excluded from public affairs. By Aristotle's
ranking, women and slaves were inferior, somehow not fully
human because they could not operate in the public realm.[12] Thus
Berlin relates why the Greek word *idiotes* is pejorative: it points to
the half-wit who cannot or does not want to participate in the
affairs of the *polis*. At least until the Stoics, liberty was valued solely
in the positive, republican sense.[13]

Berlin places the birth of the notion of personal independence
with the Stoics, but the great value placed on it in social and
political thought does not pre-date the Renaissance.[14] The claim
that the modern experience of liberty and democracy differs from
that of the ancients was first popularized by Enlightenment
thinkers, in particular the Scottish political economists. In addition,
this historiographical point became a touchstone of many defences
of liberal institutions.[15] But it was Benjamin Constant who most

[9] See 'Introduction' to FE, pp. xxxxviii–xli; 'Two Concepts of Liberty', 129; and
the Jahanbegloo interview, 42.

[10] For an etymological study of the word 'free' see C. S. Lewis, *Studies in Words*
(Cambridge, 1960), 111–32.

[11] Aristotle, *The Politics of Aristotle*, trans. Ernest Barker (Oxford, 1948), 1252a1–
1253a16. See also on this point, Jean-Pierre Vernant, *Les origines de la pensée grecque*
(Paris, 1975), 131–3.   [12] Aristotle, *Politics*, 1260a1–1260b16.

[13] All Souls interview. See also the Jahanbegloo interview, 56.

[14] See 'Two Concepts of Liberty' in FE, 129.

[15] See Biancamaria Fontana, 'The Shaping of Modern Liberty: Commerce and
Civilisation in the Writings of Benjamin Constant' in *Annales Benjamin Constant* V

succinctly stated the difference and made the argument clearest.[16] In his famous speech and essay of 1819, 'De la liberté des anciens comparée à celle des modernes', Constant distinguishes between ancient and modern liberty, and then argues that many of the excesses of the French Revolution were due to the fact that the revolutionaries were unaware that ancient republican forms of liberty ill fitted modern social conditions.[17] The ancients, Constant states, could easily participate to the fullest extent in collective affairs because their city-states were small and cohesive. Slavery enabled a class of citizens sufficient leisure time to dedicate to public affairs. Moreover, the ancient city-states were perennially at war with one another. Debating in common was a matter of collective survival, and not just a common preference for public life.[18]

None of these conditions are present in modern times, Constant tells us. The modern nation-state is vast and diversified; it is not made up of extended families living within the confines of a small city. Most nation-states are made up of a large citizenry, making face-to-face politics impossible. Politics becomes an abstraction, a matter of reflection rather than of widespread practice; only a few professionals are charged with political roles. Moreover, the modern individual has little of the influence of ancient citizens: 'his personal influence is an imperceptible part of the social will which impresses on the government its direction.'[19]

The Judaeo-Christian tradition, commerce, and 'the moral and intellectual progress of the human race' have eradicated slavery, at least in the European nations. Commerce and industry have

(1985), 3–15. See also 'Two Concepts of Liberty' (in *FE*, 129), where Berlin cites his debt to this tradition.

[16] At least according to Berlin (All Souls interview). See also the Jahanbegloo interview, 42.

[17] Benjamin Constant, 'De la liberté des anciens comparée à celle des modernes' in E. M. Laboulaye (ed.), *Cours de politique constitutionnelle* ii (Paris, 1872), 539–60. See also Fontana, 'The Shaping of Modern Liberty', 4–8. For the English translation of Constant's speech, see *Constant: Political Writings*, trans. and ed. B. Fontana (Cambridge, 1988), 309–28. Throughout the following discussion, I will refer, whenever possible, to Fontana's translations of Constant's works.

[18] Constant, 'The Liberty of the Ancients Compared with that of the Moderns', 312–13 (Fontana trans.). Jean-Pierre Vernant (in *Les origines de la pensée grecque*, 33–64), situates the development of Greek democratic practice and political ideals in the context of an aristocratic and warrior culture.

[19] Constant, 'The Liberty of the Ancients Compared with that of the Moderns', 314.

liberated the masses, giving them 'a vivid love of individual independence' and now occupy most of their time. Indeed, commerce has started to displace war. The tendency of modern states is toward increasing trade, and extending peaceful competition rather than fostering bellicose relations and perpetual warfare. For moderns, profit and luxury are more important than glory on the battlefield, or virtuous conduct and honour in the *agora*.[20] In modern times private life, life in civil society, has expanded and grown in prestige and worth. Correspondingly, public life has lost much of its former glory, lustre, and appeal. The modern citizen is more bourgeois-minded than civic-minded. For this reason, he is less willing to trade his private affairs for public honour. He is more willing to sacrifice a direct influence on politics for an indirect one. Thus representative democracy and laws protecting individual liberties have replaced the ancient forms of direct participation in politics. The political interference by all into the private affairs of each other is frowned upon, and moreover, strongly resisted. Censorship, ostracism, and the public control of wealth and trade are anathema to modern sentiments, not to mention extremely difficult to enforce.[21]

According to Constant, modern liberty is about 'the peaceful enjoyment of one's private independence'.[22] Correspondingly, modern politics is focused on securing personal freedom and eliminating unjustifiable interferences in the private realm of life. In essence, Constant's modern liberty is what Berlin calls 'negative liberty'. Ancient liberty is a kind of 'positive liberty', for it is composed of 'an active and constant participation in collective power' (PL3 to use Macpherson's classification[23]). In the ancient *polis* each was beholden to all; the discretionary powers of the collectivity were vast and uncontested. Politics was about the collective determination of all acts, both private and public. No one was free from interference.[24]

---

[20] Constant, 'The Liberty of the Ancients Compared with that of the Moderns', 314–15. Of course, with respect to the decline in warfare, Constant proved to be overly optimistic.   [21] Ibid. 314–20.

[22] This is my translation of 'la jouissance paisible de l'indépendance privée' (Constant, 'De la liberté des anciens comparée à celle des modernes' in the Laboulaye edn., 547).

[23] Constant, 'The Liberty of the Ancients Compared with that of the Moderns', 316. For a discussion of Macpherson's classification, see Ch. 4.

[24] Constant, 'The Liberty of the Ancients Compared with that of the Moderns', 310–11, 316.

Constant asserts that the ancient and modern forms of liberty and democracy are different in that they aim at different ends, support different needs. Different sacrifices therefore are demanded on the part of the citizen. The ancient citizen sacrificed all his private life for a rich political one. This was a small sacrifice since civil life was undeveloped. Thus 'the ancients when they sacrificed [private] independence to their political rights, sacrificed less to obtain more'.[25] The modern citizen has a different relationship to his civil existence. He enjoys a rich and varied private life. He values his independence because it is rich and varied. Hence he would give up more than the ancients could have if he were to trade his private enjoyments for a public life.[26] With this kind of argument Constant hoped to undermine the political prescriptions of civic humanists. On his reading of modern conditions, it is untrue that little would be lost, and everything gained, should modern men reinstate ancient republican forms of government. Lost would be a rich private life. Hence if we were to exchange our private life for a public one, 'we would give more to obtain less'[27] and the exchange would be quickly discredited.

Yet such sacrifices were asked for by the French revolutionaries. Constant blames both Rousseau and the Abbé de Mably for propagating the myth that ancient forms of government were the only adequate ones for man. He blames the revolutionaries for confusing the battle against the *ancien régime* with the attempts to morally regenerate men and re-order modern politics according to ancient models. Constant concludes that the Terror was the result of this cult of antiquity. Because of this case in particular, he concluded generally that what is adequate for one age may not be so for another.[28]

The experience of statecraft bear this out. Modern developments, such as a strong central state born of royal absolutism, have left us with enormous concentrations of political power. Borrowing from the ancient republics is no answer to the problems raised by such concentrations of power. Indeed, an appeal to republican or civic values only justifies concentrations of power. In modern

[25] Ibid. 317.
[26] Ibid. 310–18 and *passim*.   [27] Ibid. 317.
[28] Ibid. 318–28. On the presence of classical models of politics during the French Revolution, see Lynn Hunt, *Politics, Culture, and Class in the French Revolution* (London, 1986), 20, 28–9, 33, 51, 60–1.

times, if it is held that the collectivity is supreme, unlimited numbers of individuals can be ordered about, even sacrificed for the greater glory of the nation. Experience shows, argues Constant, that order and stability, let alone a cohesive *ethos*, do not result from politics based on civic virtue. Social discord, arbitrary force, fanatical squabbles, factional strife, and above all, terror are the more likely result. In fact, ancient liberty in modern conditions is more arbitrary and unjust than the rule of monarchs. This is because it extends over all individuals without discrimination, without intermediary institutions to resist the popular will or its putative representatives. Once modern citizens pretend that they are ancient republicans, they willingly sacrifice their security and individual liberty; political participation becomes perverted into the promotion of collective despotism.[29] After his historical analysis, Constant exhorted his audience:

Let us mistrust, Gentlemen, this admiration for certain ancient memories. Since we live in modern times, I want a liberty suited to modern times; and since we live under monarchies, I humbly beg these monarchies not to borrow from the ancient republics the means to oppress us.

Individual liberty, I repeat, is the true modern liberty. Political liberty is its guarantee, consequently political liberty is indispensable. But to ask the peoples of our day to sacrifice, like those of the past, the whole of their individual liberty to political liberty, is the surest means of detaching them from the former and, once this result has been achieved, it would be only too easy to deprive them of the latter.[30]

Berlin accepts the arguments presented in Constant's famous essay.[31] The negative liberty of non–interference includes all the individual liberties upheld by Constant. And the ancient liberty of direct and full participation in public affairs is identical with Berlin's positive liberty of democratic self-governance.[32] Like

---

[29] Constant, 'The Liberty of the Ancients Compared with that of the Moderns', 317–23.   [30] Ibid. 323.

[31] All Souls and Athenaeum interviews. See the Jahanbegloo interview, 40–3.

[32] These similarities and agreements are true with respect to political and civil liberties, but not with regard to economic freedoms. Unlike Constant, Berlin does not stress the development of commerce·and industry. Nor does he speak of the importance of property rights in the development of a free society. In the list of fundamental rights mentioned in his 'Two Concepts' essay, he does not include the right to property (see 'Two Concepts of Liberty' in *FE*, 165–6). This list covers

Constant, Berlin states that the ancient Greeks could not hold individual liberty as a central value in their civilization.[33] This is because individual liberty and the importance of free will are 'by-products' of a particular 'stage of social development', of the Judaeo-Christian civilization. Free will and autonomy have become crucial things in light of the experience of cultural heterogeneity in modern times, the sophistication of tastes and mores.[34] As Western civilization has developed, cultural norms, including those related to liberty, have altered. Berlin relates that, '[t]he sense of privacy itself, of the area of personal relationships as something sacred in its own right, derives from a conception of freedom which, for all its religious roots, is scarcely older, in its developed state, than the Renaissance or the Reformation'.[35] This does not mean that the ancients experienced little or no personal freedom; only that the high value placed on individual liberty is modern. The point is that the ancients valued negative liberty differently from the way we moderns do. They placed positive liberty higher on their list of virtues than we do. Indeed, if we are to look at ancient Greek sources, negative liberty figures very little in their outlook on freedom.[36]

Berlin's historicism is crucial to the argument, since it allows him to contest the ancient ranking. He accepts that human needs develop in history and follow different courses. For this reason, some political values will retreat in importance, while others will become primary. This seems to be the case with negative and positive liberty. However, this is not just a question of valuation; it

solely what are known today as civil rights, or 'human rights' (the All Souls interview). The word 'property' only appears once in his essay, in reference to Constant (p. 126). In fact, 'property' does not appear in the index of *Four Essays on Liberty*. Nor does it figure prominently anywhere in Berlin's writings. In the All Souls interview Berlin explains that: 'I don't agree that we have a right to property, or that we have a natural right [to it].' Whether or not he supports a capitalist polity depends on the circumstances, but in general he says that: 'I'm not pro-capitalist.'

[33] See 'Introduction' to *FE*, pp. xl–xli. In 'Two Concepts of Liberty' (in *FE*, 129), Berlin writes that 'There seems to be scarcely any discussion of individual liberty as a conscious political ideal (as opposed to its actual existence) in the ancient world. Condorcet had already remarked that the notion of individual rights was absent from the legal conceptions of the Romans and Greeks; this seems to hold equally of the Jewish, Chinese, and all other ancient civilizations that have since come to light.'

[34] 'Introduction' to *FE*, pp. xli–xlii.

[35] 'Two Concepts of Liberty' in *FE*, 129.

[36] See 'Introduction' to *FE*, pp. xl–xli.

concerns the context of social development, of what fits when. Along with other historicists, such as Herder and Hegel, Berlin suggests that modern attempts to reinstate ancient forms of self-government are impracticable because they do not fit contemporary social conditions. Like Constant, Berlin denies the claim that the ancient experiences of liberty and democracy are suited to modern conditions. This is because cultural, sociological, and political conditions have changed. What was good and fitting for one age is out of place in another. Political theory should be aware of such limits. As Berlin puts it, in political and moral affairs, 'choices are limited by the circumstances of men and their environment'. Specifically,

[T]he attempt to turn to some classical ideal is impractical, indeed, absurd, for reasons excellently stated by Herder—we are what we are, and although we change and develop, mankind is not infinitely malleable: to return to the past is impossible, an ideal both utopian and false.[37]

One must assume a great deal of human malleability if one wishes to prescribe ancient forms of self-government for modern societies. Berlin judges such prescriptions wrong and imprudent. Stronger still, he judges as 'immoral' those who attempt to make modern persons live by such ideals.[38] Trying to turn modern individuals into *citoyens* on the ancient model treats individuals as means to a collective project, as minors who must be forced to practise a republican life for their own and, perhaps, society's good.[39] This violates what we now hold dear, our freedom to choose the best life for ourselves. On both historical and moral grounds, Berlin objects to projects which would jettison this modern, Kantian value of autonomy.[40] Furthermore, those who advocate such projects commit the Ionian fallacy. Berlin argues that civic humanists wrongly hold that the *best* life is the political life. As a pluralist, he does not believe that only one form of life need be lived. In response to Machiavelli's faith in *civisme*, for example, Berlin praises Christian thinkers and modern liberals for comprehending the worth of a private existence, apart from the public sphere.[41] On

---

[37] 'Reply to Kocis', 391.
[38] Ibid. 391–2.   [39] Ibid. 387–93.
[40] See 'Two Concepts of Liberty', 170–1. This is an example where he accepts positive liberty, but of an open-ended kind.
[41] 'The Originality of Machiavelli' in *AC*, 60–1.

this question, natures and 'temperaments differ'.[42] A public life and a private life are often incompatible so one must choose a path: some will prefer privacy to a public life. Yet each path is equally good and ennobling; neither is absolutely better than the other.

Here, as we know, lies the value of individual liberties, and their protection. Personal liberties enable each person to make his choices, to form his own accommodations in a moral world of plural ends. It is for this reason that we demand individual liberties, guarantees of spheres of non-interference.[43] Here also lies the utility of representative institutions. In a representative democracy, one can choose proxies for one's political opinions, attendants and promoters for one's interests as well as the general interest. Not everyone need be directly and constantly involved in the affairs of state. In a liberal-democratic polity, one can choose to be either a private or a public person.

Of course there is some loss in this new order. What a liberal polity excludes is republican forms of self-discipline and corporate unity. As Hegel describes it, the ancient city-state was characterized by an immediate or unreflective unity between citizens and the corporate spirit of their city. Such solidarity could not outlive the demise of city-states and is impossible in modern culture. Modern self-consciousness is typified by its alienation from collectivist and civic virtues, from those direct forms of participatory politics which are both cause and effect of the corporate unity of a small state. In modernity, any and all attachments to these things and practices are reflective, never immediate, always potentially freely chosen.[44] In other words, modern civil society is greatly differentiated along occupational, status, and class lines. There is a high degree of individualism and social mobility, as well as ethnic and religious diversity. The art of modern government is very much based on brokering without eliminating such social, economic, and

---

[42] 'Introduction' to *FE*, pp. lvii–lviii.

[43] See 'The Originality of Machiavelli' in *AC*, 66–7, 78–9.

[44] For this story, see Hegel's *Phenomenology of Spirit*, A. V. Miller (trans). (Oxford, 1977), paras. 446–86. In the *Philosophy of Right*, Hegel writes that ancient philosophy lacked 'the principle of subjective freedom', or in Berlin's terms, negative liberty (see *Philosophy of Right*, trans. T. M. Knox (Oxford, 1942), para. 185, commentary). For more on this phenomenological story, see Jean Hyppolite, *Genèse et structure de la Phénoménologie de l'esprit de Hegel* (Paris, 1946), 232–412; and Hyppolite's *Introduction à la philosophie de l'histoire de Hegel* (Paris, 1983).

cultural cleavages. It is not based on uniting everyone into a collective democratic project, assembling all into a forum to debate the affairs of state.

Berlin prizes what is now part of Western culture: individualism, the desire for personal freedom and the toleration of religious and ethnic minorities. And to preserve these principles and freedoms, Berlin argues that it is important to be concerned with the limits of governance, and not just with its source or its ends. This is why he makes the distinction between negative and positive liberty, and why he argues that an uncritical attachment to the positive liberty of self-governance can justify democratic tyranny. All attempts at regenerating people through politics have failed miserably. Jacobin, fascist and communist movements only succeed in contorting their subjects, in creating terror, holocausts, and gulags.[45]

Berlin does not imply that political participation and the virtues attendant on such practices cannot be present in liberal-democratic polities.[46] Rather, Berlin says that the positive liberty of self-governance is a good thing and that it is often instrumental in preserving freedom, both civil and political. In fact, liberal polities do not exclude democratic forms of activity. Positive and negative liberty are not mutually exclusive in all situations; they may overlap and they may be combined. What is important is a proper balance between them.[47]

In sum, it is less a question of whether solidarity and civic virtues are superior to individualism and liberalism, but of what is *possible* and *desirable* under modern conditions.[48] The question is not about what is fitting and desirable in the abstract, or what armchair republicans can tell us we must have in order to be fully human, but about *what fits when and what fits where*, and *what works* to avoid the evils of authoritarian or totalitarian rule. Berlin is not against

[45] See 'Two Concepts of Liberty' in *FE*, 129, 148, 165–6; and 'Political Ideas in the Twentieth Century' in *FE*, 39–40.

[46] This is the view that Quentin Skinner attributes, falsely, to him. See Skinner, 'The Idea of Negative Liberty: Philosophical and Historical Perspectives' in Richard Rorty, J. B. Schneewind, and Quentin Skinner (eds.), *Philosophy in History* (Cambridge, 1984), 193–8, 208, 217–19.

[47] 'Two Concepts of Liberty', 130, 156–7, 165. See John Gray, 'Negative and Positive Liberty, 48–51.

[48] From a normative perspective, the question is whether a republican life or some other life, say that of a monk, is superior. For a pluralist like Berlin, both are part of the set of valuable lives.

positive liberty and democratic participation. Rather, he is against theories which equate liberty with democratic participation. This is not only false in theory; in practice it amounts to sacrificing civil liberties for only one type of freedom.

Democracy and Unlimited Sovereignty

In 'Two Concepts of Liberty', Berlin focuses on the problems of positive libertarian doctrines for historical and polemical reasons. He holds that, on balance, negative liberty has shown itself to be less pervertible than positive liberty, less likely to justify intolerable levels of interference in the lives of individuals and minorities.[49] While each concept may 'seem liable to perversion into the vice which it was created to resist', negative liberty has shown itself more resistant. This is because the major focus of negative liberty is the expansion of opportunities for action, and the erection of barriers against interference by social and political agents.[50] The negative concept of liberty affords one the ability to speak about 'a wall against oppressors'.[51] Conversely, the positive notion of liberty gives no consideration to limitations on social and political power. For this reason the concept of positive liberty can turn into the opposite of liberty, into the 'apotheosis of authority'. Indeed, Berlin writes that such a perversion of the meaning of freedom has for 'a long while been one of the most familiar and depressing phenomena of our time'.[52]

He goes on to state that the rise and fall of the two concepts of liberty are historically sensitive. Which concept is emphasized over the other depends on the nature of the enemy that is being fought.[53] At the time he wrote his 'Two Concepts' essay, the 'oppressors' were obvious to him. The essay arose from talks and lectures he gave throughout the 1950s and he willingly admits that his emphasis on negative liberty was due to his fear of recent and contemporary dictatorships, in Nazi Germany, in the Soviet Union, in parts of

---

[49] See 'Introduction' to *FE*, p. xlvii; see also the Jahanbegloo interview, 40–3. In the All Souls interview, he explains that his aim was to make a historical point, and not to dismiss positive liberty. He says that both senses 'are perfectly valid uses of liberty'.

[50] See 'Introduction' to *FE*, pp. xlvi–xlvii.   [51] Ibid. p. xlv.

[52] Ibid. p. xlvii.   [53] Ibid. pp. xlvi–xlvii.

Africa, and in Latin America. As late as 1988 he still considered himself proudly to be a Cold-War warrior.[54]

Yet this position is more than just a phlegmatic reaction to contemporary events. Thinking as a historian of ideas, Berlin has tried to uncover the roots of contemporary forms of authoritarian politics. He has found them in 18th-century political thought, in the debates between the right and left. With respect to the left,[55] Berlin concerns himself with the new themes of 'popular sovereignty' that arose in the 18th century, best expressed in Jean-Jacques Rousseau's *Du contrat social* (1762). In criticizing Rousseau, Berlin stands alongside other liberals who worry about the possible excesses of democratic politics. This line begins with liberal critics of Rousseau and the French Revolution, such as Benjamin Constant, and runs throughout the 19th century.[56] Amongst 19th-century liberals, Berlin gladly claims to follow the writings of the Third Republic scholar Henry Michel.[57] Michel reiterated

[54] Anthony Arblaster seeks to give a pejorative sense to Cold War liberalism. He denounces Berlin, along with other ostensible fellow-travellers, such as Raymond Aron, Albert Camus, Karl Popper, Daniel Bell, and Seymour Martin Lipset for being anti-left and anti-communist liberals (see Anthony Arblaster, *The Rise & Decline of Western Liberalism* (Oxford, 1984), 308–32). In response, Berlin accepts that he has been a 'Cold-War Liberal'; indeed, he is rather proud of having been one (All Souls and the Athenaeum interviews). Berlin has not hidden his politics. In 1949 he argued that the United States was the main guarantor of civil liberties in the Western world. It was the major power resisting the communist threat from Russia and Eastern Europe. For this reason, he argued that Britain should accept the new worldhistorical position and pre-eminent role of the United States (see 'The Anglo-American Predicament' in the *Listener* 42 (29 Sept. 1949), 518–19, 538, and his letters, 20 Oct. 1949, 681, and 10 Nov. 1949, 813–14). Berlin's anti-communism was strongly expressed at the outset of the Cold War (see 'Attitude on Marxism Stated: Dr Berlin Amplifies His Remarks Made at Mount Holyoke', letter to the *New York Times*, 8 July 1949, 18). His views remained strong throughout the Cold War: he was reluctant to denounce (though he did not praise) the American war effort in Vietnam (see Cecil Woolf and John Bagguley (eds.), *Authors Take Sides on Vietnam* (New York, 1967), 60–2). Only after the 'Velvet Revolution' in late 1989 did he soften his stand, and permit himself some hope for the future of Eastern Europe and Russia (see Berlin's contribution to 'The State of Europe: Christmas Eve 1989' in *Granta 30* (Winter, 1990), (*New Europe!*), 148–50). Unfortunately, the problem of communism has been displaced by that of nationalism, giving different reasons for despair (correspondence, 8 July 1992).

[55] With respect to the right, see 'Joseph de Maistre and the Origins of Fascism' in *CTH*, 91–174.

[56] Correspondence (17 Nov. 1988).

[57] See Henry Michel, *'L'Idée de l'état: essai critique sur l'histoire des théories sociales et politiques en France depuis la révolution* (Paris, 1896), 37–45 and *passim*. In addition, Michel surveys and critically evaluates the thinking of liberals, democrats, and socialists in England and the Continent, from Hume and Voltaire onwards. In the

Constant's criticisms of Rousseau, and Berlin continues the line into the 20th century along with critics of totalitarian democracy such as Sir Karl Popper, F. A. von Hayek, and Jacob Talmon, whom Berlin often praises. What for Berlin is crucial in these fellow-travellers is their emphasis on the 'greater importance of civil liberties than of the authority of majorities'.[58] None of them believes that democratic self-governance automatically guarantees the enjoyment of civil liberties for all citizens. Each is worried about the excesses of democratic government. Each points to the experience of the French Revolution, to Jacobinism and the Terror, as archetypical instances of the tendency of modern democratic movements to become authoritarian, if not totalitarian. And each understands the Rousseauian theory of democracy to be 'proto-totalitarian'.[59]

This is not to say that Berlin is against universal suffrage; far from it.[60] It does mean that he is concerned particularly with the justifiable limits on all kinds of sovereignty, including popular sovereignty. He knows, as did Constant, that it matters little to those being oppressed whether the authorities are monarchs or parliaments.[61] None the less, Berlin is not against democratic participation in political affairs. He knows that 'participation in decision making is some guarantee against oppression or loss of

All Souls and Athenaeum interviews, Berlin recommended Michel's large work in the history of ideas. His praise for it is evident in a letter to me (dated 19 Sept. 1988), where he writes that 'I admired [Michel] because he was one of the most temperate and coherent and convincing critics of Rousseau, in moderate language, that I came across'.

[58] Correspondence (17 Nov. 1988).

[59] Correspondence (19 Sept. 1988). Berlin often points to Jacobinism and Bonapartism as the first examples of totalitarianism in modern times (see his 'Herzen and Bakunin on Individual Liberty' in *RT*, 101–2; 'Generalissimo Stalin and the Art of Government' in *Foreign Affairs*, 30 (1952), 202–4; and 'Political Ideas in the Twentieth Century' in *FE*, 1–40, *passim*). In the Athenaeum interview, Berlin admits to being influenced by K. Popper's two-volume study, *The Open Society and Its Enemies* (London, 1945). He states that the study 'gave me a fillip'. He also mentions that he is sympathetic to F. A. von Hayek's similar work, *The Road to Serfdom* (Chicago, 1944), but does not accept the latter's economic liberalism. He also admires J. L. Talmon's work on the origins of totalitarianism (see *The Origins of Totalitarian Democracy* (New York, 1970); and Berlin's eulogy to Talmon, 'A Tribute to my Friend', *Forum*, 38 (1980), 1–4). See D. J. Manning, *Liberalism* (London, 1976), 81–118, for a short summary of the liberal polemics against popular sovereignty and totalitarianism from Constant to Hayek and Popper.

[60] Correspondence (19 Nov. 1988).

[61] See 'Two Concepts of Liberty' in *FE*, 163–4.

individual liberty'.[62] Political participation is often instrumental in and critical to the protection and promotion of civil liberties. Like Constant, he is aware of the interrelations of negative and positive liberty.[63] Yet he does not want us to forget the converse: civil liberties (such as liberty of speech, of the press, of association) are needed in order to influence political authorities democratically. Hence Berlin states that 'unless you have a certain amount of negative liberty, you cannot take part in self-government'.[64] Negative liberty is basic to democratic government. In short, positive and negative liberty 'play at both ends' of a continuum. For this reason Berlin is adamant in his claim that 'it is . . . wrong to accuse me of being *against* positive liberty'.[65] If well represented and properly balanced, positive and negative liberty support each other.

There are cases when positive liberty oversteps proper bounds, and harms negative liberty. An example is when a democratic assembly abrogates civil liberties, or when it legislates the policy preferences of a national majority against an ethnic minority. In fact, a democratic polity can just as easily abrogate civil liberties as can an oligarchy or a monarchy. Berlin's point is that without strong guarantees of civil liberties, any regime can be repressive. We speak of despotism with regard to oligarchies; tyrannies with respect to monarchies; but we can equally speak of the tyranny of the majority in democracies.[66] In general, democracies have a tendency to act in a tyrannical fashion if their sovereignty over individuals and minorities is not tempered by laws, conventions, political forces, institutions, and a political culture, all of which act in concert to protect civil liberties. As Berlin writes, individual liberty

has little to hope for from the rule of majorities; democracy as such is logically uncommitted to it, and historically has at times failed to protect it, while remaining faithful to its own principles. Few governments, it has

[62] Correspondence (19 Nov. 1988).

[63] Athenaeum interview; Constant, 'The Liberty of the Ancients Compared with that of the Moderns', 326–7.   [64] Athenaeum interview.

[65] Ibid. See also 'Introduction' to *FE*, p. xlvii; and 'Two Concepts of Liberty' in *FE*, 165.

[66] Berlin believes that 'on the whole democracies do tend to value personal liberty more than authoritarian regimes, but, of course, they have trampled on them historically—but less than monarchies or oligarchies' (correspondence, 17 Nov. 1988).

been observed [by Constant], have found much difficulty in causing their subjects to generate any will that the government wanted. 'The triumph of despotism is to force the slaves to declare themselves free.' It may need no force; the slaves may proclaim their freedom quite sincerely: but they are none the less slaves. Perhaps the chief value for liberals of political— 'positive'—rights, of participating in the government, is as a means for protecting what they hold to be an ultimate value, namely individual— 'negative'—liberty.[67]

Once again Berlin's argument is informed by politics and history. In his view, one's participation in sovereign decision-making (either directly or through representatives) is an insufficient guarantee of individual liberty.[68] This is especially the case when it is argued that all manner of interference with individuals is justified on democratic grounds. According to thinkers such as Constant, Henry Michel, and Berlin, it is dangerous to argue that political power should be 'unlimited' because sovereignty emanates from the people. It helps little, and adds insult to injury, to argue as Rousseau did, that if everyone gives up their natural liberty, each is protected from everyone else.[69]

Constant, for one, denounced Rousseau's political doctrine for this metaphysical sleight-of-hand. He argues that Rousseau's social-contract doctrine hides the institutional fact that concentrations of power further the cause of tyranny and not that of liberty. Rousseau's doctrine is concerned only with the consensual bases of sovereignty and not its limitation. To claim, as Rousseau did, that the general will can do no wrong to any particular member conflates liberty with authority. Such a view of sovereignty is concerned exclusively with democratic consent to authority. But once there is a 'practical organization of authority', the problem of its limitation arises. According to Constant, a modern political theory must be concerned with limitations on democratic authority; otherwise, a doctrine of the democratic will becomes a justification for unlimited rule, for a species of tyranny.[70]

[67] 'Two Concepts of Liberty' in *FE*, 165.
[68] See 'Introduction' to *FE*, pp. lvii–lviii; and 'Two Concepts of Liberty' in *FE*, 129–30.
[69] See 'Two Concepts of Liberty' in *FE*, 164. See also Jean-Jacques Rousseau, *Du contrat social* (Paris, 1966), book i, chs. 5–7; and Benjamin Constant, 'Principes de politique' (1815), in Laboulaye (ed.), *Cours de politique constitutionnelle*, i, 10–12 (pp. 177–8 in the Fontana trans.); and Henry Michel, *L'Idée de l'état*, 37–45.
[70] Benjamin Constant, 'Principes de politique', 7–17 (pp. 175–83 in the Fontana trans.). With regard to Rousseau's arguments in book i, chs. 6–7 of *Du contrat social*,

Like most liberal critics, Constant is unimpressed by Rousseau's assurance that the people cannot harm themselves. The theory of democratic consent or the formal basis of democratic political obligation amounts to one thing. The actual practice of democratic politics, or that of the delegates of the people, is a different thing entirely. Democratic theory takes the arrogation of political power by a monarch, or a retinue of oligarchs, to be illegitimate and unjust. This is a positive advance over the doctrine of the divine right of kings. Yet the democratic theory of political obligation says nothing of the limits of popular authority over individuals. Of course, democratic theory speaks about guarantees of popular sovereignty, but these are formal guarantees. Democratic rule is a principle of legitimacy concerning the bases of legitimate rule. Political power ought, of course, to originate from the people. The people must formally rule. This is done by democratic election, where political authority is vested in the people, and not a king or a priest, and delegated (on trust) to representatives. But this is not a principle of individual liberty: it does not speak of limits to public authority, only of who legitimately can use political authority.[71]

In practice, democratic rule is unlimited, and therefore it is as dangerous as the rule of princes.[72] In effect, Rousseau's doctrine of popular sovereignty merely substitutes the myth of benevolent popular rule for the myth of the divine right of kings.[73] From the vantage point of the individual and his liberty, unlimited democratic

---

Constant states the following: 'The people, Rousseau says, are sovereign in one respect and subject in another. But in practice, these two relations are always confused. It is easy for the authority to oppress the people as subject, in order to force it to express, as sovereign, the will which the authority prescribes for it.

No political organization can escape from this danger' (pp. 179–80 of the Fontana trans.). For Berlin's similar point about the conflation of liberty with authority in Rousseau's work, see 'Two Concepts of Liberty' in *FE*, 148.

[71] See Constant, 'Principes de politique', 7–17 (pp. 175–83 in the Fontana trans.) and 275–87. In his additions to his 'Principes de politique', Constant (275–6, n. 2) elaborates that *'Les droits individuels, c'est la liberté: les droits sociaux, c'est la garantie. L'axiome de la souveraineté du peuple a été considéré comme un principe de liberté: c'est un principe de garantie. Il est destiné à empêcher un individu de s'emparer de l'autorité qui n'appartient qu'à l'association entière; mais il ne décide rien sur la nature et les limites de cette autorité'*.

[72] Speech by Constant (10 Mar. 1820), cited by Laboulaye in his edition of 'Principes de politique', 10 n. 1.

[73] Constant, 'Principes de politique', 9–13 (pp. 177–80 in the Fontana trans.). See also, Henry Michel, *L'Idée de l'état*, 44, 300.

political power is no different from the power of absolute monarchs. As Constant puts it: 'Popular government is simply a violent tyranny, monarchical government only a more concentrated despotism'.[74] The importance of Constant and other French Liberals, is to have pointed out this fact to their compatriots, and to have deflated the claim of democratic consent as a guarantee of individual freedom, security, or political stability.

In 'Two Concepts of Liberty', Berlin certainly agrees with Constant on this score and follows him very closely, often paraphrasing his work or citing translated phrases. Like Constant, he points to similar dangers in the theory of popular sovereignty. Hence Berlin writes of probable authoritarian consequences if and when positive liberty is said to circumscribe all kinds or senses of liberty. Inasmuch as we are concerned with individual liberty, Berlin exhorts us to resist the view that democratic liberty is the only sense of liberty. For to identify oneself fully with a democratic body can result in a great loss of personal freedom. All the more so if limitations are taken on voluntarily.[75]

As I pointed out in Chapter 4, Berlin is especially suspicious of the view of liberty that equates freedom with 'self-mastery'. Such a view demands that one fully identify oneself with a sovereign principle and its embodiment. Yet this can only occur, or so Rousseau had to argue, in an unsophisticated and simple society. It is only in such societies that desires, wants, and needs are relatively undifferentiated, more immediately related to the survival of everyone as part of a corporate body. Because this was not the case in the France of his day, Rousseau demanded that his contemporaries discipline themselves and forget many of their civilized desires. His aesthetic and moral senses were somewhat Spartan, and contrary to the sophistication of his times. According to him, one's true self lies in simpler times, within a small community of equals. Thus only by returning to a simpler collective existence can we become part of a noble enterprise that seeks to realize the coherent sovereign principle of public virtue. In a simple and homogeneous community, one will be likely to act in concert with others. Rousseau considered such a return to simpler times to be a great liberation,

---

[74] Constant, 'Principes de politique', 282 (trans. Fontana, p. 178). In 'Two Concepts of Liberty' (in *FE*, 164), Berlin cites his own translation of this sentence.
[75] See 'Two Concepts of Liberty' in *FE*, 162–6.

for it amounts to following one's better and truer self, a self uncorrupted by civilized tastes and mores.[76]

Berlin has no sympathy for this ideal, since it equates liberty with self-discipline and self-abnegation.[77] He also echoes Voltaire's original criticism of Rousseau's *Du contrat social*. Voltaire had argued that Rousseau's ideal society could only be tribal, a step back in time.[78] Rousseau did presuppose this: in *Du contrat social*, he states that his ideal of democratic politics presupposes 'much simplicity of mores'.[79] But for a pluralist, this goal is incoherent in principle: there is no fundamental unity of interests and goods, and politics cannot create it, except by eliminating the desire for a great many goods. Self-identification with a sovereign principle does not necessarily lead to liberation. It is more likely to entail self-immolation in the name of abstract principles, such as those discovered by one's putatively rational and 'true' self, or one's leader, or those exhibited by one's country, or polity, or religion, or race.[80]

Because he is aware of the dangers of civic republicanism, Berlin approvingly points to Mill's argument that, in practice, 'democratic self-government is not the government "of each by himself" but, at best, of "each by the rest" '.[81] It is because of such realistic appraisals of politics that liberals are suspicious of democratic theory and support democratic practice only conditionally. Berlin correctly observes that for liberals (such as Constant and Mill),

[76] See Rousseau, *Du contrat social*, book i, chs. 7, 9; book ii, chs. 8–9; and book iii, ch. 4.

[77] In correspondence (17 Nov. 1988), Berlin has elaborated his views on Rousseau in the context of his thinking about positive liberty. He writes: 'Rousseau: I think that his is a kind of attempt to dissolve self in Self. The tribal voice which talks through me, and I who talk through the tribal voice, is an attempt to remove conflict between individuals, or individuals and institutions, by melting the whole thing into one homogeneous source of everything. I expect this could be called an unjust attribution of primitivism to Rousseau. Yet I suspect that that is a genuine, indeed a dominant, element in the "removal of obstacles". '

[78] For perhaps the earliest criticism of Rousseau as an archaic thinker, see Voltaire's letter (dated 30 Aug. 1754) to Rousseau upon the former's reading of the *Discours sur l'origine et les fondements de l'inégalité parmi les hommes* (1754). This letter is reprinted in *Discours sur les sciences et les arts/Discours sur l'origine de l'inégalité* (Paris, 1971), 237–40.

[79] Rousseau, *Du contrat social*, book iii, ch. 4 (my trans. of 'une grande simplicité des moeurs').

[80] See 'Two Concepts of Liberty' in *FE*, 145–54, 165–6.

[81] Ibid. 163. See J. S. Mill, *Utilitarianism, Liberty and Representative Government*, A. D. Lindsay (ed.) (London, 1964), 67–8.

personal fulfilment in democratic politics does not necessarily mean that one is freer because of it.[82] It may be that one has chosen to be a slave to the polity and has gladly accepted such a status; or even exclaimed it as the apotheosis of freedom. But we should not call this a complete realization of freedom, since it is compatible with a great deal of authority and restrictions on individual liberty. Following in line, Berlin argues that Rousseau's version of the social contract is monistic and highly repressive. It is unlikely that a uniform moral subject of collective proportions can be created by a political act. This is not because we are essentially immoderate and avaricious beings, Hobbesian in nature. It is due to the nature of moral life itself. There are too many possible divergencies in moral and civil life which politics cannot overcome. The moral universe is not harmonious and politics will not make it so it can only purchase unity by means of repression.

Citizens or their representatives may forge compromises and agreements in politics, and limit the range of goods, or opportunities available to individuals. But one does not liberate a political actor by forcing him or her to follow the dictates of a democratic assembly. Force is force, and coercion is not liberty. In this way, Berlin's critique of monism carries over into a critique of extreme democratic theories, such as those of Rousseau and his followers.[83] The result is support for limited government and for modern forms of pluralist politics. The tendency is away from attempts to find moral salvation in civic republican forms of government, and towards constitutional regimes based on liberal–democratic principles.[84]

---

[82] All Souls and the Athenaeum interview. See 'Two Concepts of Liberty' in *FE*, 162–6.

[83] For a contemporary follower, see Benjamin R. Barber, *Strong Democracy: Participatory Politics for a New Age* (Berkeley, Calif., 1984). I discuss this work in Ch. 8.

[84] See 'Introduction' to *FE*, pp. x, l–lxiii; 'Political Ideas in the Twentieth-Century' in *FE*, 1–40; and 'Two Concepts of Liberty' in *FE*, 141–54 and 167–72. For Henry Michel's criticisms of Rousseau, see *L'Idée de l'état*, 37–45. Constant also finds that Rousseau's doctrine of popular sovereignty rests on a false metaphysic, and an overly optimistic view of human infallibility in politics. He responds with an institutional and realistic view of politics which supports pluralist and liberal forms of social and political organization. His 'Principes de politique' is concerned with articulating the constitutional arrangements necessary for a liberal–democratic and bourgeois polity.

Robespierre, Bonaparte, and Totalitarianism

The above argument concerns the positive liberty of democratic self-government. Berlin's critique states that if one accepts the doctrine of the social contract, and acts on it, one risks losing the very liberties sought in the first place by demanding participation in political decision-making.[85] But this is not the only problem with doctrines of 'popular sovereignty'. Berlin is also on guard against political leaders who wish to sanctify their power by claiming that it emanates from the People, the Nation, or the Race. Once again he draws resources from French liberal thinkers.

Benjamin Constant, François Guizot, Alexis de Tocqueville, and Mme de Staël were acutely concerned with finding ways to avoid a repeat of the Terror and the age of Napoleon. They tried to understand the power of a Robespierre or a Napoleon, over the French people. They argued that such leaders were a new kind of despot; one that claims to act for 'the people' and subsequently demands, and receives, unlimited power in the name of 'the people'. This legitimation of power is not the same as monarchical claims to sovereignty, which are founded on divine right. The situation is different when a prince states that his power is supreme and unlimited *because* the people consent to it being so. Here sovereignty is no longer divinely sanctioned. It is limited neither by natural law nor by the authority of other institutions like the Church and the aristocracy. Sovereignty is now taken to be secular and limited only by what one says is the people's will. According to the liberals of the period, such a form of sovereignty becomes virtually limitless because the people's will can be interpreted to justify any action. All one needs is to be accepted by a majority of the people in order to act extensively in their name.

For Constant, for other liberals of his generation, and, later, for Henry Michel, this new form of sovereignty is most insidious because it seeks to make people consent to a despotic government.[86] Berlin updates this position by pointing to modern forms

---

[85] See 'Introduction' to *FE*, p. lxii; and 'Two Concepts of Liberty', 160–2.

[86] See Constant, 'Principes de politique', 13 and n. 1; and Michel, *L'Idée de l'état*, 39–40, 300–3. For a discussion of the views of other French liberals, see Manning, *Liberalism*, 89–92.

of Bonapartism such as Leninism, Stalinism, and Peronism. Beginning with his 1939 book on Karl Marx, but especially after the Second World War, Berlin has been concerned with the transformation of revolutionary thought into totalitarianism.[87] In his 1949 article for *Foreign Affairs*, 'Political Ideas in the Twentieth Century', he discusses the common traits of modern revolutionaries: namely, their fanaticism, appeals to national sentiment, intolerance of social diversity, and desire completely to transform human nature along some predetermined plan.[88] In another article for *Foreign Affairs*, 'The Silence in Russian Culture' (1957), he argues that the Russian penchant for grand moral theories is a breeding ground for the perfectibilian and totalitarian tendencies in socialist, and in particular Marxist, thought.[89] In a 1952 article, 'Generalissimo Stalin and the Art of Government', also written for *Foreign Affairs*, he identifies similarities between Jacobin and Bonapartist tactics and those of Bolshevik leaders and, later, Stalin. The political aims of these ideologues is to control all facets of social life in the name of an ideal claimed to be held by the people themselves.[90] The dangers to individual liberty are evident. For such great, perfect, glorious, and massive political projects, any and all means need to be used including revolutionary violence, terror, propaganda, and the constant call of the nation to arms. If individual liberties are an impediment, they should be dispensed with; in fact, this is no great loss because greater freedom will result once the classless society, or national purity, is established. With the perfectibility of persons and society in sight, no sacrifice is too great, and certainly not that of individual liberty.[91] The logic of

[87] See Berlin's *Karl Marx: His Life and Environment* (Oxford, 1939). This book is now in its 4th edn. (1978). For a critical review, see G. A. Cohen, 'Isaiah's Marx, and Mine', in Edna and Avishai Margalit (eds.), *Isaiah Berlin: A Celebration*, 110–26.
[88] Repr. in *FE*, 1–40.
[89] Berlin, 'The Silence in Russian Culture', *Foreign Affairs*, 36 (Oct. 1957), 1–11. In 'The Road to Catastrophe' in the *Times Literary Supplement* (30 Mar. 1962), 216, Berlin writes of 'the fanatical faith in absolute moral intellectual truths, by which Russia is to this day sustained'. This experience of Soviet and Stalinist politics is a decisive biographical fact. It gave direction to Berlin's scholarly career (see 'The Three Strands of My Life', 5–6, and 'The Pursuit of the Ideal' in *CTH*, 1–19).
[90] O. Utis (Berlin's *nom de guerre*), 'Generalissimo Stalin and the Art of Government', *Foreign Affairs*, 30 (1952), 197–214. At that time, Berlin wrote about Soviet affairs under the cover of anonymity to protect his relatives residing in the Soviet Union.
[91] See 'Political Ideas in the Twentieth Century' in *FE*, 15–21; and 'The Silence in Russian Culture', 1–11.

such beliefs is insidiously compelling as well as dangerous. Berlin imaginatively reconstructs the logic thus:

[T]o make mankind just and happy and creative and harmonious for ever—what could be too high a price to pay for that? To make such an omelette, there is surely no limit to the number of eggs that should be broken—that was the faith of Lenin, of Trotsky, of Mao, for all I know of Pol Pot. Since I know the only true path to the ultimate solution of the problems of society, I know which way to drive the human caravan; and since you are ignorant of what I know, you cannot be allowed to have liberty of choice even within the narrowest limits, if the goal is to be reached. You declare that a given policy will make you happier, or freer, or give you room to breathe; but I know that you are mistaken, I know what you need, what all men need; and if there is resistance based on ignorance or malevolence, then it must be broken and hundreds of thousands may have to perish to make millions happy for all time. What choice have we, who have the knowledge, but to be willing to sacrifice them all?[92]

Berlin believes that modern forms of perfectibilian politics result from the simplistic models of human nature and society common in social thought since the 18th century. Most of this simplicity is due to borrowings from scientific methods, both empirical and formal. Berlin argues that these models ill fit our ordinary understanding of the lives of individuals and the workings of societies,[93] and thus distort ordinary experience. Likewise, state-craft cannot be scientific; it is more akin to an art. One must know the limits of one's material and come to understand which actions are needed under which circumstances. This knowledge is born of practical experience, not scientific experiments or abstract reflection. For this reason, Berlin states that the 'gift' of the politician is 'wholly incompatible with faith in the supremacy of some idealized model, which, in the case of fanatical ideologies, takes the place of genuine capacity for responding to impressions'.[94]

Berlin admonishes radical politicians, such as Robespierre and Lenin, for misunderstanding the limits of the human material they wished to alter. He considers the moral rectitude of Joseph II of Austria equally simplistic, though benign. He points to Bismarck, Lloyd George, and Roosevelt as moderate and realistic politicians.

---

[92] 'The Pursuit of the Ideal' in *CTH*, 15.
[93] Berlin, 'Realism in Politics' in *Spectator* (17 Dec. 1954), 774–6 at 775.
[94] Ibid. 776.

Because they knew the limits of human malleability, their politics were more successful and less bloody. They did not lack doctrines, purposes, and aims, but their sense of what could and could not be done was correct. They practised a politics of the possible and succeeded where others, no less well-intentioned, failed. Perfectibilist schemes and the revolutionaries who follow them lack a realistic appraisal of individuals, society, and politics. As a consequence, most revolutionaries since the 18th century have achieved very little of lasting value.[95]

The experience of modern political movements demonstrates to Berlin that one must pay attention to the protection of individual liberties. One has to think about how much political power can be wielded against individuals. An exclusive focus on who has political power, and for what ends, ignores the question of how much political power is being accumulated by individuals and groups. Like Constant, Berlin is watchful of the unlimited 'acquisition' of political power, either by mobs, elected majorities, authoritarian populists, communists, or fascists.[96] Although the tyrants and the forms of repression may change, the problem of unlimited authority remains the same. Hence Berlin adheres to his liberal yardstick and distinguishes negative liberty from positive liberty, and pushes for the protection of the former kind of freedom.

He identifies himself with negative libertarians and their concern to limit sovereignty for two reasons: first, to preserve a balanced appraisal of the needs of persons in society, and second, to protect the 'inner life of man' as much as liberty of movement for individuals. Modern politics lead him to criticize those political doctrines founded on an unqualified adherence to positive liberty. Times may change but for now he is more concerned with preserving and promoting the worth of negative liberty though, as he admits on numerous occasions, this does not mean that negative liberty is the one thing he values to the exclusion of all other values.[97] Negative liberty is rather a concept of liberty that he

---

[95] Athenaeum interview. See 'Realism in Politics', 774–6; and 'Political Ideas in the Twentieth Century' in *FE*, 37–40.

[96] Correspondence (17 Nov. 1988).

[97] All Souls and the Athenaeum interview. See also 'Introduction' to *FE*, pp. lxi–lxiii.

believes must be represented in any contemporary society, if that society is to be called free and decent.[98] Paris and the Vendée under the Terror, and Germany under Nazi rule do not pass this test; nor did the former Soviet Union and the now defunct Eastern Bloc; nor does much of Africa, Latin America, and the Far East today.

Accumulation of too much political power is clearly the main threat perceived by Berlin in the modern age. His response is that of a classical liberal, prescribing effective limits on government action, and the rule of law—in short, prescribing negative liberties. As such, Berlin situates himself in a long line of liberal political philosophers who have been sceptical and wary of authority in the modern age, and all political philosophies that promote its concentration. Berlin is less concerned with *who* holds sovereign power, than with its limitation. What matters is *how much* power is concentrated in government. Too much power in any hands is too much power; the glory of the ends will not alter this problem.[99]

Conclusion

The question of power is in fact the 'cardinal issue' that separates negative from positive liberty.[100] As should be evident from the analysis in this chapter, the reasons behind the analytical distinctions discussed in Chapter 4 are partly historical and practical, not exclusively conceptual. Indeed, much in Berlin's argument has been missed by critics because their focus has principally been on the coherence of his conceptual distinctions. The full purpose of the distinction between negative and positive liberty is apparent only once it is related to Berlin's reading of political history and his sense of our fundamental interests as individuals living in modern societies.

With this said, now we can deal with the problem raised in Chapter 5. There I pointed out how natural-law doctrines underdetermine the argument for political liberalism. Berlin understands this problem, and it is for this reason that he uses empirical

---

[98] Correspondence (17 Nov. 1988).
[99] See 'Introduction' to FE, pp. lxi–lxii; and 'Two Concepts of Liberty' in FE, 164–5.   [100] 'Two Concepts of Liberty' in FE, 166; see also 129–31.

rguments to support his case. By analysing the history of the idea
f liberty and pointing to its uses in political history, he strengthens
he case against the positive conception of liberty. It is not that he
onsiders the conception wrong as such, only that it must be
omplemented with protection of civil liberties. And once he
oints to the cultural conditions of modern societies, the case is
urther strengthened with respect to negative liberties. Liberal
egimes are most suited to social and cultural conditions found in
modern civil societies. Hence not only do 'facts' about our moral
ife such as liberty and pluralism entail some negative liberties; the
istory of civilizations such as the Western one point to the need for
 great deal of civil liberty.[101]

There is no doubt that Berlin's aim in the 'Two Concepts' article
vas to clarify the use of the concept of 'liberty'; but, at the same
ime, he also sought to defend liberal-democratic governments
rom attack by left-wing and communist writers who argued that
true liberty' *is* the participation in politics, or identification with a
reat collective cause such as the class war, or identification with a
ational leader such as Lenin, Stalin, or Peron.

Berlin concluded from history that the concept of negative
iberty has been historically less perverted than the concept of
ositive liberty. This is because negative liberty refers to limits on
uthority, or what we now call civil rights; while positive liberty
loes not have the same focus, and deals principally with capacities
nd good ends. Inasmuch as we are concerned with preserving
iberty, we should be at least promoting civil liberties. This appeal
o history follows the methods of 19th-century French liberals,
uch as Benjamin Constant, but it also updates the case by looking
t 20th-century examples. Moreover, Berlin did not forget that
oth-century civilization could be socially progressive by promoting
quality and social justice. In this sense, he distinguishes himself
rom classical liberals, and approaches the position of welfare

[101] In answering a query about how much negative liberty is needed in society,
erlin (correspondence, 17 Nov. 1988) responds in this fashion: 'How does one
llow for these [negative] rights and liberties? The best I can do is to say that they are
quired for a minimal "decent society". Of course what the minimum is is difficult
 determine, but it must be directly related to the actual inescapable wants and
spirations of the human beings in given times and places; and we are then required
 explain the empirical errors, or departures from psychological normality, which
n account for the lack of such recognition in other societies and cultures.'

liberalism. His main thrust, however, is to defend substantive views, in particular the principles of limited government under the rule of law against those who argue that true liberty could be found under communist rule, or that of churches, classes, or nations. On this score, history continues to prove Berlin right.

7

A NEED TO BELONG

When men complain of loneliness, what they mean is that nobody understands what they are saying: to be understood is to share a common past, common feelings and language, common assumptions, possibility of intimate communication—in short, to share common forms of life. This is an essential human need: to deny it is a dangerous fallacy. To be cut off from one's familiar environment is to be condemned to wither.

(Isaiah Berlin, 'The Three Strands in My Life')

So far, I have discussed three aspects of Berlin's political thought and theory of human nature: liberty, pluralism, and history. To this list must be added his belief that belonging is a human need, no less important than liberty. This is another respect in which he distinguishes himself from much of the liberal tradition, in particular contemporary Anglo-American liberal thought.

Many liberals are, or have been understood to be, proponents of individualism and thus on guard against any collective values such as the importance of belonging to a people or nation. There now exists a substantial body of literature critical of this tendency in liberal thought. The major conclusion of this 'communitarian' literature is that liberals are committed to social atomism and have little understanding and even less regard for the moral demands of communal life. Liberalism, in this critical reading, is devoid of historical sense, unsophisticated about society, and promotes an empty cosmopolitanism.[1] Berlin is no such liberal. His work has

---

[1] Most of this literature has focused on the left-of-centre liberalism of John Rawls and the libertarian views of Robert Nozick. For summaries of these debates, see Amy Gutmann, 'Communitarian Critics of Liberalism' in *Philosophy & Public Affairs*, 14 (1985), 308–22; Chantal Mouffe, 'Le libéralisme américain et ses critiques' in *Esprit* (Mar. 1987), 100–14; and John R. Wallach, 'Liberals, Communitarians, and the Tasks of Political Theory' in *Political Theory*, 15 (1987), 581–611. However, liberals have begun to respond by reconstructing their tradition to better reflect

communitarian and collectivist facets which few have recognized.[2] This is understandable given his attachment to civil liberties.[3] However, on methodological and substantive issues, Berlin's thought has no trace of atomistic individualism. As a historian of ideas, he argues that to understand much of human behaviour we must reconstruct in our imagination the mentalities of the people under study. Only when we have entered into the spirit of a people and the spirit of an age, can we understand and explain past and contemporary events. It is not by adding up the behaviour patterns of individuals that we understand action and events; but rather by coming to know the whole range of attitudes, norms, and motivations held by a group, including its leaders. Therefore, on this methodological front, Berlin can be considered a methodological holist, whereas most other contemporary liberals cannot.

Substantively, he considers belonging to a place and a people to be a fundamental human characteristic, in fact, a human need. From this follows his acceptance of the moral value of political liberty for a people. Berlin is a liberal who knows that freedom usually is *for* something; often, in particular, for the expression of values and virtues that are intimately tied to unique cultures.[4] Even though he claims that negative liberty is crucial for modern polities,

its communitarian aspects (see Will Kymlicka, *Liberalism, Community, and Culture* (Oxford, 1989)).

[2] In his criticisms of Berlin's liberalism, Charles Taylor (in 'What's Wrong with Negative Liberty') misses these facets altogether. So does C. B. Macpherson, who claims that Berlin's distinction between negative and positive liberty is based on 'the postulate of an atomized market society' (see 'Berlin's Division of Liberty', *Democratic Theory*, 104; for the same charge repeated, see Macpherson's 'Pluralism, Individualism, and Participation' in *The Rise and Fall of Economic Justice* (Oxford, 1985), 92–100 at 94–5). Stuart Hampshire, for one, correctly sees the collectivist side of Berlin (see 'Nationalism' in Edna and Avishai Margalit (eds.), *Isaiah Berlin: A Celebration*, 127–34).

[3] Another explanation for this is that the vehicles he chose for the most collectivist of his writings, those that deal with Zionism, are relatively obscure journals with low circulation.

[4] He has gone so far as to claim that belonging is a basic need, one that ennobles and enlightens free persons. When exhorting his fellow Jews to travel to Israel, he writes that, 'The first thing that a man must know, if he is to function freely, and not under the influence of delusions or ignorance—if he is to know what he is and what is his place, in his time and social environment (particularly if he wants to change this)—is to know where he comes from, the history of the group to which he belongs, how he and his family and community and people have come to feel and to think and to act as they do' ('Go There to Find Your Identity', in *Jewish Chronicle*, supplement (16 Apr. 1974), p. i).

he does not consider individual liberty to be the sole end of good government. He is concerned that other admirable ends be met and satisfied, especially a sense of belonging to a culture, speaking a particular language, being tied to a people by common bonds of history and locality. It is in common institutions, including political ones, that such a sense of belonging is expressed. This is one reason why he takes positive liberty to be an important value.[5]

Like contemporary communitarians, Berlin is critical of much liberal thought because it discounts the importance of collective sentiments.[6] He sympathizes with principles of 'cultural self-determination', and with nationalist movements animated by such principles.[7] But he travels only so far with these movements. He parts company with aggressive forms of nationalist and religious politics, the most extreme being Nazism, Italian fascism, and theocratic governments such as that of Khomeini in Iran. He argues that while modern polities can make room for national self-expression, some guarantees of individual liberty must exist. 'Non-aggressive nationalism', such as that promoted by Herder, Mazzini, Verdi, Clemenceau, Cavour, Roosevelt, and Weizmann is humane, tolerant, and thus acceptable. It is ultra-nationalist, totalitarian, and theocratic politics that are his main foes. These positive libertarian movements err in subscribing to an overarching principle or purpose, and then seeking to impose it on everyone within their control. It is these extremes from which we need protection, not ethnic and cultural self-affirmation. And to avoid these extremes of nationalist aggression and religious intolerance, cultural aspirations must be tempered by a constitutional order that preserves liberties for individuals and minorities.[8] In short, Berlin's political thought responds to the human need to belong but also guards against extremes of aggressive nationalist and theocratic politics. In this way, he avoids any charge of insensitivity to the social or cultural

[5] See 'Two Concepts of Nationalism: An Interview with Isaiah Berlin' in *New York Review of Books* (21 Nov. 1991), 19–23 (and Berlin's letter listing corrections to this interview, printed in *New York Review of Books* (5 Dec. 1991), 58); and 'The Cost of Curing an Oyster' in *Jerusalem Post* (10 Feb. 1986), 8.
[6] See 'The Three Strands in My Life' in *Jewish Quarterly*, 27 (London, 1979), 5–7.
[7] See the interview, 'Two Concepts of Nationalism'.
[8] Correspondence (5 Jan. and 15 Apr. 1991). See the interview, 'Two Concepts of Nationalism'; and 'The Bent Twig: On the Rise of Nationalism' in *CTH*, 238–61; 'Nationalism: Past Neglect and Present Power' in *AC*, 333–55; and 'Two Concepts of Liberty' in *FE*, 155–62. See also Stuart Hampshire, 'Nationalism', 132–4.

aspects of life; yet does not err in claiming that they are primary and exclusive considerations for the legitimacy of authority.

Berlin is therefore both communitarian and liberal, advocating a mixture of negative and positive liberty, individualism and communal affiliation, individual liberty and collective self-determination. His liberalism is focused principally on avoiding excesses of authority and concentrations of power; it is antithetical to publicly organized religion, unlimited democracy, and of course, totalitarian government. Conversely, it is open to cultural needs, the variety of customs, the claims of locality, and the exigencies of language.

Zionism and Liberalism

The communitarian aspects of Berlin's political thought are most prominent in his Zionist writings. These works deal with the origins of Zionist thought, its prominent advocates, the birth of the state of Israel, that country's leaders, and his own activities in support of the Zionist cause.[9] They also reflect a tension in his

[9] On this topic, Berlin's writings fall into four categories: (a) studies on Jewish and Zionist thinkers; (b) the history of the founding of Israel; (c) the leaders of modern Zionism: and (d) his own reflections on the fate of Jews in history. Regarding (a) see 'The Life and Opinions of Moses Hess' and 'Benjamin Disraeli, Karl Marx and the Search for Identity' in AC, 213–51 and 252–95, respectively. Regarding (b) see 'The Origins of Israel' in Walter Z. Laqueur (ed.), The Middle East in Transition (London, 1958), 204–21; 'Zionist Politics in Wartime Washington: A Fragment of Personal Reminiscence',. the Yaacov Herzog Memorial Lecture (Jerusalem, 1972); 'A Nation Among Nations' Jewish Chronicle, colour magazine (4 May 1973), 28–34. Regarding (c) see 'Dr Chaim Weizmann' (supplementary obituary), The Times (17 Nov. 1952), 8; 'Men Who Lead' in Jerusalem Post (2 Nov. 1954), 5–6; (with Miriam Rothschild) 'Mr James de Rothschild' (supplementary obituary), The Times (13 May 1957), 15; 'Chaim Weizmann' [1958], repr. in PI, 32–62; 'L. B. Namier' [1966] repr. in PI, 63–82; 'A Generous Imaginative Idealist' in Edward Victor (ed.), Meyer Weisgal at Seventy (London, 1966), 89; 'The Biographical Facts' in Meyer W. Weisgal and Joel Carmichael (eds.), Chaim Weizmann (London, 1962), 17–56; 'Felix Frankfurter at Oxford' [1964] repr. in PI, 83–90; 'Portrait of Ben-Gurion', Jewish Chronicle (25 Dec. 1964), 7, 22; 'Weizmann as Exilarch' in Chaim Weizmann as Leader (Jerusalem, 1970), 13–21; 'Dr Jacob Herzog' in Jewish Chronicle (14 Apr. 1972), 28, 43 (repr. under the same cover with 'Zionist Politics in Wartime Washington . . .', 3–6); 'Einstein and Israel' [1979] repr. in PI, 144–55; and For Teddy Kollek (Jerusalem, 1981). Regarding (d) and in addition to all the preceding, see 'Jewish Slavery and Emancipation' in Norman Bentwich (ed.), Hebrew University Garland (London, 1952), 18–42; 'Go There to Find Your Identity' in Jewish Chronicle, supplement (16 Apr. 1974) p. i; 'The Three Strands in My Life'

thought between negative and positive liberty. This results from advocating both civil liberty and collective self-determination, two fundamentally divergent moral principles. Such conflict is not surprising, for only simplistic and doctrinaire political thought avoids altogether intricacy and entanglements. And given Berlin's advocacy of moral and cultural pluralism, one would expect to find in his political thought and affiliations a complex set of principles and moral sentiments.

In one of the few autobiographical pieces extant, Berlin tells us that his 'sympathies had been pro-Zionist since my schooldays'.[10] Maurice Bowra confirms this when he says of his friend that although 'he would never himself have migrated to Palestine, he felt its struggles as his own and knew that it was his own kin who were suffering from the indecision and vagaries of British policy' in the inter-war years.[11] In another autobiographical reflection, Berlin includes Judaism as a crucial 'strand' of his own identity, along with the British and Russian ones.[12]

It is not surprising, therefore, to discover that he has interested himself in Jewish studies as a lecturer and essayist. Some of his reflections are intimate because they deal with the actions of Zionist leaders whom Berlin knew personally, such as Dr Chaim Weizmann, David Ben-Gurion, and the American Supreme Court Justice, Felix Frankfurter. His 1972 lecture, 'Zionist Politics in Wartime Washington: A Fragment of Personal Reminiscence', is remarkable for its grasp of the personal qualities of Zionist leaders and their opponents. It is a fascinating example of personal history interwoven with reports of confidential diplomatic affairs. In the lecture Berlin recounts some of his work as a British information officer posted to New York and Washington during the Second World War. In addition to his description of the Byzantine intrigue of wartime American and American-Jewish politics, Berlin discusses his own political views.[13] He says that he was, and

---

in *The Jewish Quarterly* (London, 1979), 5–7; 'Greetings' to the editorial board of *Secular Humanistic Judaism* (Jerusalem, 1986), 2; and 'The Cost of Curing an Oyster' in *Jerusalem Post* (10 Feb. 1986), 8.

[10] 'Zionist Politics in Wartime Washington', 15.

[11] Maurice Bowra, *Memories: 1898–1939* (London, 1966), 184.

[12] 'The Three Strands in My Life'.

[13] For more on wartime Washington, see the collection of Berlin's despatches, in H. G. Nicholas, *Washington Despatches 1941–1945: Weekly Reports from the British Embassy* (London, 1981).

remains, a committed Weizmannite. Weizmann 'gave shape to my views', he says. It was Weizmann who expressed best for him pragmatic solutions to the abandoned fate of the Jewish people.[14] Weizmann practised moderate and non-violent politics, and travelled a patient diplomatic course in both Britain and America. Berlin clearly preferred this option, especially as a substitute for any armed activity by Jews in Palestine.[15] Thus he says of Weizmann:

His realism, his moderation and his political genius lifted him above any other statesman I ever knew well. I remained devoted to him to the end of his days, and adhere to his principles and outlook to this day. In Washington, he and his immediate followers seemed to me to be at once the most farsighted and the most effective. The extremists, both of the Right and the Left, who, out of bitterness or for temperamental reasons, advocated ruthless policies, I never found congenial; they seemed to put the satisfaction of their own emotional needs above the attainable goals of the cause which they supported. The extremists regarded the moderates as craven, the moderates repaid them by regarding them as lunatics. This is perhaps the situation in every movement to promote radical change against great odds. I knew where I stood. The politics of the extremists seemed to me the politics of despair at a time when sanity could still prevail; their goals seemed to me utterly utopian, their methods horrifying, and likely to lead to results which only fanatics could desire. I was, and remain, an incurably sceptical liberal, a convinced gradualist. The attractiveness to me, therefore, of Dr. Weizmann's outlook was obvious.[16]

Later in the same lecture, Berlin tells us that in the 1930s and 1940s he was, like Weizmann, 'a convinced believer in the Anglo-Zionist connection'.[17] This implied that Jews should support the British war effort. Hitler was the common enemy of mankind, and after the war, with Churchill's help, one could expect the British to act correctly. No matter the slowness of British response, regardless of

[14] 'Zionist Politics in Wartime Washington', 6.
[15] Such as the need for an army of stateless and Palestinian Jews, proposed by the Bergson group in the USA during the early 1940s. Berlin and other moderate Zionists effectively resisted this proposal advocated by the followers of Ze'ev Jabotinsky. For the story, see Louis Rapaport, 'The Hoskins Affair' in *Jerusalem Post* (23 Nov. 1984), unpag.
[16] 'Zionist Politics in Wartime Washington', 16–17. For more on Berlin's assessment and praise of Weizmann's gradualism, political realism, courage, freedom from chauvinism and cant, and strong sense of civilized ideals and humanism, see Berlin's 'Weizmann as Exilarch' and 'Men Who Lead'.
[17] 'Zionist Politics in Wartime Washington', 55.

he setbacks with the Foreign and Colonial Offices, it was the British and no other nation that would grant the Jews a homeland in Palestine.[18] Events did not unfold in this way, and it was America, not Britain, that eventually came to the rescue of Jewish interests. None the less, the Weizmannite goal has remained dear to Berlin, even if at the crucial historical moments the chosen diplomatic tactics failed.[19]

In the 'Zionist Politics' lecture, in the biographical sketches of his political hero and in his other Zionist writings, Berlin often refers to Weizmann's political goals. Briefly, they centre around the principal goal of all Zionists, from Moses Hess and Theodor Herzl onwards: the creation of a nation state, of a political homeland, for the Jewish people. This need was obvious: Weizmann saw that the liberties granted to Jews in host nations were precarious; he could not accept the solution of assimilation.[20] Nor could Hess, since Jewish characteristics would always be noticed by members of host nations.[21] As Berlin was to argue elsewhere, Jews could not expect to count on being welcomed anywhere but in their own homeland: host nations would always treat them to some degree as strangers.[22] The problem was always one of being singled out, no matter the attempts to assimilate. For Berlin, the Holocaust proved this once and for all.[23] Thus to avoid situations in which the Jews were left to the good grace of hosts, or worst of all, at their mercy, Weizmann concluded that the Jewish people needed a homeland (the same solution reached by Hess and Herzl), or, as Berlin puts it: 'a free, self-governing Jewish commonwealth, preferably under British auspices, in Palestine.'[24] Weizmann embodied this ideal and struggled to achieve it. He sought a state on the British model, with liberties to preserve modern achievements, in particular in science and the arts. It was to this design that Weizmann dedicated his life.[25]

---

[18] Ibid. 16–38.
[19] Ibid. 57–67; and 'Men Who Lead', 6. For another detailed discussion of the diplomacy behind the founding of Israel, see Berlin's biographical essay on Weizmann, 'The Biographical Facts'.
[20] 'Weizmann as Exilarch'.
[21] 'The Life and Opinions of Moses Hess' in *AC*, 213–51.
[22] 'Jewish Slavery and Emancipation', 31–3.
[23] Jahanbegloo interview, 19–22.
[24] 'The Biographical Facts', 13.
[25] See 'Weizmann as Exilarch' and 'The Biographical Facts'.

In the 1930s and 1940s Berlin embraced these views. He still does. In the All Souls interview (1988), he states that 'my Zionism—which is quite strong—is ultimately an English conception of why people need a country'. This is another reason why Berlin is not against positive liberty; he wholeheartedly believes in Herder's claim that belonging is a human need, for some, the greatest of human needs.[26] And it is only within a territory under collective set of institutions that a people can be self-governing, positively free, or can determine its own destiny.[27] Again like Herder, Berlin holds that it is within states, and not as individuals scattered around the world, that ethnic groups can find a home.[2] Ethnicity and culture are thus fundamental to him. Political orders are meant to preserve and express these collective values of individuals. As he puts it in the All Souls interview, individuals 'are born into' and shaped by their culture; one's culture is the condition for self-identity, the basis upon which one flourishes. In reality 'you can't totally emerge from the stream in which you were born'.[29] It is only within nation states that ethnic groups acquire *secure* existence; only within states can nationalities be protected.[3] Not only cultures, but individuals as well, are granted a secure existence in nation states.[31]

The source of this communitarianism is Berlin's own experience of Judaism. He credits his 'Jewish roots' for protecting him from what he considers to be the main deficiency of the liberalism of Enlightenment thinkers like Immanual Kant and Voltaire: their

[26] All Souls interview. For Berlin's treatment of Herder's notion of belonging and concept of 'populism', see *VH*, 153, 156–64, 180–94; and for how he related Herder's notions to Zionism, see 'Benjamin Disraeli, Karl Marx and the Search for Identity' in *AC*, 252–60, esp. 257–8.
[27] See 'The Cost of Curing an Oyster'. In 'Weizmann as Exilarch' (p. 17), Berlin accepts Herzl's political vision and praises the latter because it was he 'who arrived a a clear vision of who his brethren were and what they lacked most, namely, political autonomy, without which, in our day, a free cultural life cannot be lived'. Berlin adds that: 'If Herzl had not insisted so strongly on the primacy of the political factor it is very doubtful whether the secular framework for the maintenance of Jewish education, culture and tradition, both religious and secular, could have survived.'
[28] See 'Two Concepts of Nationalism: An Interview with Isaiah Berlin'.
[29] All Souls interview.
[30] 'The Three Strands in My Life', 7.
[31] See 'Benjamin Disraeli, Karl Marx and the Search for Identity' in *AC*, 252–60; 'Jewish Slavery and Emancipation', 18–42; 'A Nation Amongst Nations', 217–21; 'The Cost of Curing an Oyster'; and 'Two Concepts of Nationalism: An Interview with Isaiah Berlin'.

bstract and atomistic individualism, their cosmopolitanism.[32]
3ecause of his Jewish roots he tells us that:

have never been tempted, despite my long defence of individual liberty
. . to march with those who, in the name of such liberty, reject adherence
ɔ a particular nation, community, culture, tradition, language, the
nyriad impalpable strands', subtle but real, that bind men into identifiable
roups. This rejection of natural ties seems to me noble but misguided.
When men complain of loneliness, what they mean is that nobody
nderstands what they are saying: to be understood is to share a common
ast, common feelings and language. Common assumptions, possibility of
itimate communication—in short, to share common forms of life. This is
n essential human need: to deny it is a dangerous fallacy. To be cut off
rom one's familiar environment is to be condemned to wither. Two
iousand years of Jewish history have been nothing but a single longing to
elong, to cease being strangers everywhere; morning and evening, the
xiles have prayed for a renewal of the days of old—to be one people again,
ving normal lives on their own soil—the only condition in which
idividuals can live unbowed and realise their potential fully; no men can
ɔ that if they are a permanent minority—worse still, a minority
verywhere, without national base. The proofs of the crippling effect of
iis predicament, denied though it sometimes is by its very victims, can be
:en everywhere in the world.

I grew up in the clear realisation of this fact; it was awareness of this that
iade it easier for me to understand similar deprivation in the case of other
eoples and other minorities and individuals. Such criticisms as I have
iade of the doctrines of the French Enlightenment and of its lack of
ympathy for emotional bonds between members of races and cultures,
nd its idealistic but hollow doctrinaire internationalism, spring, in my
ase, from this almost instinctive sense of one's own roots—Jewish roots,
i my case—of the brotherhood of a common predicament—utterly
ifferent from a quest for national glory—from a sense of fraternity—
erhaps most real among the masses of the poor and socially depressed,
specially my ancestors, the poor but literate and socially cohesive Jews of
astern Europe—something that has grown thin and abstract in the West
where I lived my life.[33]

---

[32] To quote a recent interview ('Two Concepts of Nationalism', 22): 'Like
lerder, I regard cosmopolitanism as empty. People can't develop unless they
elong to a culture. Even if they rebel against it and transform it entirely, they still
elong to a stream of tradition. . . . But if the streams are dried up, as, for instance,
vhere men and women are not products of a culture, where they don't have kith and
in and feel closer to some people than to others, where there is no native
anguage—that would lead to a tremendous desiccation of everything that is
uman.'   [33] 'The Three Strands in My Life', 7.

In short, Berlin is no proponent of abstract individualism. Unlik
some liberals, he does not grasp for all the liberty he can get
especially if this means suffering from anomy or the creation of a
empty culture. In fact, the melancholic tone at the end of th
passage above discloses this sympathy and preference for a ric
cultural life; something that is losing ground in the mechanical an
electronic age.[34]

This communitarian streak has led him not only to criticize th
abstract tenor of Enlightenment thinkers and the homogenizin
tendencies of contemporary societies, but also to justify the natio
state on cultural and psychological grounds. Berlin argues that th
Diaspora status of Jews led to common pathologies. Without
collective home, Jews had to attempt to assimilate into foreig
cultures; or seek to express their uniqueness, at times rathe
aggressively. Since assimilation was rarely accepted by hosts, Jew
had always been overly self-conscious, abnormally so, according t
Berlin. While cultural estrangement did allow for great achieve
ments, often born of suffering or a will to succeed, the Jew
remained a distorted people. To quote him:

the works of talent or genius were often disturbed, tormented in a peculia
fashion. They were voices of exiles, those who look in from the outside
and sometimes have a clearer view of the life of the majority, a view o
which their own security relies, than the majority has of itself. A deepe
insight on the part of gifted individuals, purchased by untold suffering c
entire communities, surely could not be accepted as natural or unavoid
able.[35]

What the Jews lacked was a polity in which they would not stan
out; a polity in which they could be recognized as ordinary huma

---

[34] Berlin is hardly anti-modern, but he is sensitive to the decay of culture in ou
age of quantitative methods, mechanical models, and bureaucratic administratior
He notes gloomily that the 'Bazarovs have won' the day. Turgenev's portrait o
these scientific philistines and nihilists (in *Fathers and Sons*) is no longer novel, but th
norm (see 'Fathers and Children' in *RT*, 261–305 at 300). And in the 'Two Concept
of Nationalism' interview, he makes a point of arguing, in line with his pluralism
that a universal world culture is a vacuous ideal. To the claim that world trad
patterns, international popular music, and modernization are eliminating minorit
cultures and languages, he responds (p. 23) with sad irony: 'If you think that all thi
[i.e. cultural and linguistic variety] will one day give way to one universa
language—not just for learned purposes or politics or business, but to conve
emotional nuances, to express inner lives—then I suppose that this would not be on
universal culture, but the death of culture. I am glad to be as old as I am.'
[35] 'The Cost of Curing an Oyster'.

eings, with shared virtues and foibles, and not be expected either
ɔ disappear or seek approval by excelling at all manner of arts and
ɔience. This was achieved with the founding of Israel: the 'Zionist
ure' for collective entrapment in a minority status, as perennial
utsiders the world over.[36] With the founding of Israel, the Jews
ɔund their home and were liberated from 'social uneasiness', free
ı a society of cultural equals and no longer in need of extra-
rdinary recognition or forced to put on the airs of a foreign culture
ı order to blend into the society of their hosts. In this sense, they
ʌere no longer 'slaves' to foreign societies and cultures.[37]

In effect, the creation of Israel was a 'self-liberation' for Jews.[38] In
ɨrael Jews around the world can find a spiritual and ethnic home,
ıat is, if they so desire to emigrate. There they can practise their
ɛligion and speak their language. Berlin makes much of the fact
ɪat Weizmann's ideal of cultural unity for the Jews is now assured
y public policies which encourage the use of Hebrew in all facets
f public life.[39] The solidarity of the Jews, which was born of the
xperience of persecution and hardship, is now based on positive
xperiences: the building of a national culture in a politically
ɛfined territory.[40]

None the less, Berlin remains wedded to liberal principles. The
ɛed for belonging never derogates in his thought from the need
ɔr basic individual liberties. He faces the fact that liberal and
ɔmmunal values can conflict, but he sides with liberalism when
xtreme cases arise. In matters of life and death, law and order,
asic liberty and fundamental justice, he stands as an ethical
ɪdividualist and proponent of limited government. His nationalism
ıus is tempered by a liberal sense of the just limits of authority.
ıasmuch as he is a communitarian, he is so only up to the point
ıat communal sentiments begin to justify the repression of
ɪdividuals, minorities, or worse, pogroms and holocausts.[41]

[36] Ibid., Berlin writes that: 'The Zionist cure for this was the possibility, whether
ken advantage of or not, of leading the life of a free people in its own land. Hegel's
ɪmous definition of freedom—"to be at home"—would alone heal the wounds
hich this abnormal condition inevitably caused'.
[37] Ibid.; and 'Jewish Slavery and Emancipation', 39, 42.
[38] 'Weizmann as Exilarch', 13.
[39] 'The Biographical Facts', 21–6, 30; and 'A Nation Among Nations', 33–4.
[40] 'Jewish Slavery and Emancipation', 34–42.
[41] Berlin calls himself a 'moderate populist', by which he means a supporter of
ɔme preservation of communal traditions', but not to the point of sanctioning
pressive regimes (correspondence, 15 Apr. and 16 May 1991).

Fortunately, so Berlin tells us, the founding members of Israe
were steeped in the liberal and socialist traditions of the West. H
underlines the fact that a significant number of the Russian an
Polish Jews who emigrated to Palestine were liberal humanists an
left-of-centre intellectuals. As he puts it: 'their vision was humane
individual liberty, social justice and self-government were th
values inherent in all they said and thought.'[42] Along with French
American, and British Jews, this group of founders initiall
determined Israeli political culture. Their principles ordered th
Israeli constitution, made it secular, democratic, liberal, an
socially progressive. In the early 1950s Berlin concluded that Israe
was 'a kind of welfare state—the kind of state which, by the end o
the war, many people wished to see—a country which is neithe
communist, nor moving in a communist direction—nor yet one i
which rampant individualism breeds a great deal of violent socia
injustice'.[43] Between the extremes of capitalism and communism
between sterile individualism and enforced collectivism, Israe
stood for Berlin as the last shining example of the 'Italia
Risorgimento: on the whole, left of centre, of a kind rightl
admired by English liberals and radicals in the nineteenth century'.[44]

Still, the founding of the nation might never have occurred. I
his various studies on the history of the Zionist movement, Berli
stresses the leadership of great men, such as Weizmann and Ben
Gurion.[45] He points to the contingency of events, to how the tid
of events could have gone against the Zionists. Yet the founding o
Israel is, for Berlin, a test case in the triumph of ideals. Withou
Herzl and his followers, without the ideals of Zionism whicl
animated leaders and all immigrants alike, without internationa
support for the idea of a nation state, Israel would never have bee
founded. In fact, Israel is testimony to, and a most pleasant an
assuring example of, the historical force of ideas.[46] In the 195
lecture, 'The Origins of Israel', Berlin concludes with thes
thoughts:

> Israel is not a large-scale experiment. It occupies a very small portion c
> the earth's surface; the number of persons comprising its population i
> relatively small. But its career confutes a number of deterministic theorie

---

[42] 'The Cost of Curing an Oyster'.   [43] 'The Origins of Israel', 213.
[44] Ibid. 220.   [45] 'Chaim Weizmann', in *PI*, 32–3.
[46] 'Zionist Politics in Wartime Washington', 8–9, 57–67.

of human behaviour, both materialist, and the fashionable brands of anti-materialism. And that, I will not deny, is a source of great satisfaction to those who have always believed such theories to be false in principle, but have never before, perhaps, found evidence quite so vivid and quite so convincing of the hollowness of such views. Israel remains a living witness to the triumph of human idealism and will-power over the allegedly inexorable laws of historical evolution. And this seems to me to be to the eternal credit of the entire human race.[47]

The Tragedy of Israel

Yet the triumph is uncertain, as is the credit. Berlin reminds us that Israeli national security remains precarious, and that it is a nation like any other, with vices as well as virtues. Fortune has cursed it with hostile neighbouring states. And domestic problems abound, in particular the tensions between Jewish ethnic groups, and the Jewish–Palestinian conflict inside Israeli territory.[48]

The electoral gains of the right in Israeli politics disappointed and saddened Berlin.[49] Since the election of Menachim Begin in April 1977, the secular and left-liberal foundations of Israeli political culture have begun to fracture. The 1992 electoral victory of Labour promises political change, but Israeli society remains divided none the less. After forty years of national struggle, reports now identify authoritarian and vicious factions pitted against moderate groups. And ethnic divisions within Israel are deeper now that Israeli Arabs have begun to support the *intifada*. Currently, Israel is a 'truly divided' country, like Ireland.[50]

Clearly Berlin's principles stand against the policies of the right in Israel. As an advocate of collective self-determination, it follows that he accepts the legitimacy of the Palestinian claim for national liberation. In fact, he does consider himself a man of peace. He opposed the 1982 invasion of Lebanon and continues to advocate a negotiated settlement of the Palestinian problem. In general, he supports the Israeli Labour Party and accepts the possibility of trading land for peace. To promote these views he has become a

---

[47] 'The Origins of Israel', 220–1.
[48] 'A Nation Among Nations', 34; and 'The Cost of Curing an Oyster'.
[49] Correspondence (30 Nov. 1990).
[50] Correspondence (5 Jan. 1991), 2.

member of Peace Now, the Israeli and international association that advocates negotiations with Palestinians.[51] He has signed public letters critical of Israeli policy, in particular with respect to violations of human rights.[52] But in general, he prefers to express his views privately; no doubt in order to give as little support as possible to those who wish to destroy the State of Israel.[53]

This left-wing and dovish political stand follows from his beliefs and writings, which have always held to a secular and humanitarian approach to politics. Indeed, Berlin supported the creation of the State of Israel because its formative principles were left-liberal and secular. His sense of nationalism and support of communal spirit have always been tempered by a humanist and liberal sense of justice and limited government. Religious politics, intolerance, repressive measures, torture and forced evictions of minorities cannot figure in the kind of statecraft inspired by his moral vision. The rise of the right and the growing force of religious factions in Israel, and elsewhere in the world, show how illiberal and repressive communitarian and nationalist politics can become. Berlin knows the danger.[54] While he considers that the 1992 election of Rabin and his Labour government promises better policies, the situation remains precarious.[55] The fifteen years of Likud government showed the fragility of Israeli political culture. However, Berlin remains optimistic about wedding liberal principles to communitarian and nationalist sentiments, including in Israel.[56] To quote a recent statement of hope: 'I do not wish to abandon the belief that a world which is a reasonably peaceful coat of many colors, each portion of which develops its own distinct cultural identity and is tolerant of others, is not a utopian dream'.[57]

This was also Herder's ideal. Berlin admits that it may be naïve to hold to such hopes, but finds no other course for humanity if we

[51] Conversations (21 May and 11 June 1990), Oxford; and correspondence (18 Mar. 1991 and 30 Nov. 1990).
[52] See 'Israeli Solution', (letter) in the *Independent* (28 Sept. 1988), 19; and with others, 'The Detention of Sari Nussiebeh' in the *Independent* (4 Feb. 1991), 18 (also in *New York Review of Books* (7 Mar. 1991), 4).
[53] See Anon., 'Between Two Worlds: Sir Isaiah Berlin at Eighty' in *Jewish Chronicle* (9 June 1989), 30.
[54] See 'Two Concepts of Liberty' in *FE*, 154–62.
[55] Correspondence (8 July 1992).
[56] He claims to remain 'irrationally optimistic' on this score (correspondence, 30 Nov. 1990, 2).
[57] 'Two Concepts of Nationalism: An Interview with Isaiah Berlin', 21.

are to be faithful to liberty, pluralism, and the value of belonging to one's culture.[58] It is a testimony to Berlin's honesty that he faces such a dilemma; it flows naturally from his pluralism. Certainly some ends are incompatible in moral life. But Berlin is confident that modern nations can, if they are fortunate and well governed, accommodate the desire for belonging with individual liberty. The question is finding the right mix, of inventing and making the necessary trade-offs that avoid 'intolerable choices' between extreme positions and options.[59] The problem in Israel lies with the choices not made to preserve the right mix.

Conclusion

Sufficient evidence has now been presented to support without reservation the claim that Berlin is unlike most contemporary liberals. He argues for liberalism in specific ways, drawing from the unjustly neglected strand of French liberalism and focusing on a theory of moral pluralism. As his Zionist writings demonstrate, his pluralism accepts the importance of belonging; communal sentiments are taken by him to be part of the set of basic human needs. Methodologically and substantively he avoids any of the failings of contemporary Anglo-American liberal thought, such as inattention to existing cultures and to the actual behaviour of individuals. There is not a trace of social-contract methodology, nor disdain for nationalist thought in his work.

But this does not lead to a blind or romantic endorsement of all communitarian and nationalist movements. As discussed in Chapter 6, Berlin is critical of extreme democratic theories. And as this chapter shows, he is a secular humanist and a liberal, directly at odds with theocratic or aggressively nationalist political orders. In this sense he is very much part of the tradition of British thinkers, left-of-centre, sceptical of abstractions and ideologies, and supportive of humane social policies.[60] While he understands the need for belonging to a culture, he knows that few political societies are

[58] Ibid. 20, 21–2.
[59] 'The Pursuit of the Ideal' in *CTH*, 18.
[60] Berlin credits British empiricism with giving him a sense of what is feasible, just, and decent (see the Jahanbegloo interview, 111–14; 'The Three Strands in My Life', 6).

fully integrated, containing no minorities.[61] And there remains the question of recalcitrant individuals, those who even within an integrated society would prefer to live 'against the current' of tradition and public opinion. To be called free and decent, a political society must grant sufficient room to such individuals, as well as to cultural minorities who live in most nation states. While there may be loss to a way of life when such a course is followed, the price according to Berlin is small compared to the damage to the human fabric wrought by attempts to fit all persons into one order of life proclaimed to be the best and sanctioned by the use of force.[62]

Throughout his work Berlin persists in calling for the application of liberal principles, for tolerant politics, accommodation when possible, and the pursuit of social justice. Whenever it is a question of the legitimacy and moral worth of a nation state, he demands a mixture of negative and positive liberties, of personal freedom, collective self-determination, and social justice. Not all states can maintain such standards, or such balance between conflicting principles. The tragedy of many nations is that their political constitutions and political cultures may be insufficiently flexible to easily accommodate the values of both liberty and belonging.[63] For this ideal balance we need to fight and struggle.

---

[61] It is rare that state boundaries perfectly fit ethnic groupings. Only a few cases can be cited, such as Portugal, Italy, possibly Japan (correspondence, 5 Jan. 1991). In fact, the history of empires and modern states is one of ethnic diversity (see William H. McNeill, *Poly-ethnicity and National Unity in World History* (Toronto, 1985)).

[62] Correspondence (15 Apr. 1991).

[63] 'Two Concepts of Nationalism: An Interview with Isaiah Berlin', 21.

8

HISTORY, PLURALISM, AND LIBERTY

I . . . remain, an incurably sceptical liberal, a convinced gradualist.

(Isaiah Berlin, 'Zionist Politics in Wartime Washington: A Fragment of Personal Reminiscence')

The first public obligation is to avoid extremes of suffering. Revolutions, wars, assassinations, extreme measures may in desperate situations be required. But history teaches us that their consequences are seldom what is anticipated; there is no guarantee, not even, at times, a high enough probability, that such acts will lead to improvement. We may take the risk of drastic action, in personal life or in public policy, but we must always be aware, never forget, that we may be mistaken, that certainty about the effect of such measures invariably leads to avoidable suffering of the innocent. So we must engage in what are called trade-offs—rules, values, principles must yield to each other in varying degrees in specific situations. Utilitarian solutions are sometimes wrong, but, I suspect, more often beneficent. The best that can be done, as a general rule, is to maintain a precarious equilibrium that will prevent the occurrence of desperate situations, of intolerable choices— that is the first requirement for a decent society; one that we can always strive for, in the light of the limited range of our knowledge, and even of our imperfect understanding of individuals and societies. A certain humility in these matters is very necessary.

(Isaiah Berlin, 'The Pursuit of the Ideal')

Isaiah Berlin is not a systematic thinker. As Michael Walzer puts it, 'system is not his style'.[1] However, there are common themes,

---

[1] Michael Walzer, 'Introduction' to Berlin's *The Hedgehog and the Fox* (New York, 1986), [vii].

leitmotifs, various *idées maîtresses*, that run throughout his work
He knows many things, exposes many points of views, but keep
to one vision, focused by one core set of values.[2] These include
moral pluralism, the importance of freedom for a decent life in
society, the need for understanding amongst individuals and
cultures, balanced and moderate judgement, belief in the open-
ended nature of history, and the necessity of historical understanding
not only in order to deepen our self-knowledge but to allow for
tolerance of differences and the avoidance of past mistakes.

Being a member of the British establishment has not turned him
into an intellectual conformist. Even if he supports British
institutions and liberalism, he has done so in novel ways, and by
unearthing new or long-forgotten ways of thinking. If we are to
believe him, his Jewish origin, more so than his Russian side, has
made him somewhat of an outsider. Perhaps this is the source of his
ability to understand others, including outsiders, and convey their
messages in the language of a dominant intellectual tradition; and
also to play the maverick in traditional fields of study such as
history and philosophy where he chose to make his mark
Whatever the causes, his intellectual achievements are now gaining
greater currency because they speak to problems facing many
contemporary societies, such as increasing ethnic and moral
diversity and the demise of grand ideologies, be they scientific
progressivism, Marxism, or even liberalism itself. In such context
we need an empirical, sceptical, prudential, nuanced, tentative
kind of thinking. This seems the best course available, given the
lack of overarching principles to govern our modern, or postmodern societies.[3] Berlin has always asserted the need to proceed
humbly, to be less assured of our intellectual powers. His anti-
utopianism, his critique of the Ionian fallacy prepared the ground
for what we now must face in the post-cold-war era, when political
ideologies are not fixed and self-evident.

---

[2] In this sense he is both fox and hedgehog, to apply his famous distinction to
himself. See I. Berlin, 'The Hedgehog and the Fox' in *RT*, 22–81; and Morgenbesser
and Lieberson, 'Isaiah Berlin' in *Isaiah Berlin: A Celebration*, 28–30, 216 n. 20.

[3] For the work that started these debates, see Jean-François Lyotard, *La condition
postmoderne* (Paris, 1979). For links made between postmodernism and Berlin's work
see John Gray, 'Postscript: After Liberalism' in his *Liberalisms* (London, 1989),
239–66; and Richard Rorty, 'The Contingency of Language', 'The Contingency of
Selfhood', and 'The Contingency of Community' in *London Review of Books* (17
Apr., 8 May, and 24 July 1986), 3–6, 11–15, and 10–14, respectively.

While the practice of liberal government, if not of liberal economics, has survived the cold war, political liberalism remains in need of theoretical support and revision. Liberal thinkers face ever new challenges to their practice and values: from the ideologies of new social movements, such as feminism and environmentalism, and from the strident claims of fundamentalist and some nationalist movements. Moreover, the basic conditions for a decent life have yet to be established for the vast majority of people on this earth. In this sense, the history of justice and liberty is not over; the project, if taken to be genuine, remains incomplete.

Berlin's defence of political liberalism offers advantages in the current context. As a pluralist, he does not claim that all polities need to be liberal–democratic, similar to the ones of Western Europe.[4] However, he does point to the minimum of liberty needed for a society if it is to be humane and decent. Beyond this minimum, he admits that polities can, and should, accommodate various goods other than liberty. The minimum set of values, or common core of values, is derived from a model of human nature and society. This model includes the following:

(a)   We are social and cultural beings, language users, reflective and rational, endowed with inner lives.
(b)   As moral beings, we have free wills.
(c)   We are purposive, expressive and self-transforming beings.
(d)   Our moral condition is complex and pluralistic.
(e)   We live and develop in specific social and historical circumstances.
(f)   We have a need to belong to particular communities.

Clearly this model allows for a great deal of moral and political variety. None the less, it has enough that is common to allow for a level of understanding and unity across cultures and time. As stated in Chapter 2, Berlin holds that our ability to understand other cultures and past eras points to some common human interests and shared moral concepts and categories.

---

[4] In *Post-Liberalism: Studies in Political Thought*, 283–328, John Gray develops this very point about the plurality of justifiable regimes.

Yet as I pointed out in Chapter 3, universal models of human nature, and natural law theories derived from such models, *underdetermine* the moral codes present in societies and polities. We may all agree that killing people for sport is beyond the boundaries of human civilization, but within such limits, civilizations differ greatly. Customs, mores, traditions, the historical heritage that forms a large part of our self-identities, cannot be captured by universal statements about human beings *qua* natural beings, *qua* moral beings. It is this recognition of the limits of abstract theory in ethics which puts Berlin, at least until very recently, at odds with most Anglo-American political theory. The latter had been about, and in many instances still is concerned with, working out universal moral principles and decision procedures in ethics, following either utilitarian or deontological traditions. Berlin's recognition of the limits of grand moral theory is no doubt due to his belief in moral pluralism, in the incompatibility and incommensurability of values. Yet Berlin never wrote systematically about value-incompatibility and value-incommensurability. This has now been left to others, such as Charles Taylor, Steven Lukes,[5] Charles Larmore,[6] Joseph Raz, John Gray, and Bernard Williams. Berlin's influence has been that of a teacher, rediscoverer of eccentric and challenging thinkers, and pioneer of current debates. Along with those whose thought he has reanimated, he has been a thinker and scholar running against the current of the Western rationalist tradition.

As I have tried to show by reconstructing his model of human nature and society, there is a great unity of purpose in Berlin's work and thought. For example, liberty and pluralism are the linchpins of his model of human nature and society. In his various works, he has in effect written a history of liberty and pluralism in Western civilization. In this respect he follows in the tradition of Vico, Kant, Sismondi, Macaulay, Hegel, and Croce. Many of his studies are versions of 'the story of liberty'. In this story he replays the old debate between the ancients and the moderns. The scenes of action include the French and Russian Revolutions, the rise of the resistance to Soviet Communism, the coming and passing of

---

[5] Steven Lukes, 'Making Sense of Moral Conflict' in Nancy Rosenblum (ed.), *Liberalism and the Moral Life* (Cambridge, .Mass., 1989), 127–42.

[6] Charles Larmore, *Patterns of Moral Complexity* (Cambridge, 1987).

Nazism, and the birth of Israel. Heroes and enemies of the cause enjoy gains and suffer defeats. Lessons are drawn from the beliefs and ideologies, and achievements and failures of historical actors.

In this sense his work has some teleological aspects, but here again, he is restrained and modest. Unlike most Enlightenment thinkers (Hegel, for example), Berlin does not claim that historical development will of necessity liberate human beings. In fact, he claims that history has no determined, linear course. Yet he is convinced that in Western civilization human beings have progressed, materially and morally.

Notwithstanding the wars and holocausts of the century, people enjoy more power over their lives than in the past (at least those living in Western industrial societies). Many evils, such as torture and slavery, have been reduced if not eliminated altogether and some progress can be detected. Furthermore, there is no stepping back from this liberation: most people in most corners of the world want to follow along this path.

To this story of liberty, Berlin has added 'the story of pluralism'. Along with material, social, and political liberation, our self-consciousness and understanding of society have shifted in modern times. According to Berlin, 'the greatest transformation in Western consciousness' occurred in the latter part of the 18th century with the rise of Romanticism and the counter-Enlightenment. Thinkers such as Vico and Hamann undercut the faith in natural law and in the existence of universal canons in moral, political, and aesthetic matters. The result, Berlin argues, is that we are now the inheritors of two traditions. One sees the world, the human and the natural worlds, as a uniform whole, with prescriptive ends and necessary final purposes. The other, post-Romantic view sees human beings (and at times, nature), as purposive but without fixed ends. Today we are torn between these two views, one monistic, the other pluralistic. In the end, we must operate with both views.[7] In the study of human nature and society, we find both 'uniformity' and 'multiformity'.[8] There is no stepping back from this transformation in Western self-consciousness.

'There is no stepping back'—either from the liberation of the individual or from the recognition of pluralism. This is a crucial

---

[7] I. Berlin, 'Romanticism and Social Change', Audio Learning Discussion Tape (HUA013) (London, 1974).   [8] Athenaeum interview.

historicist point. Berlin claims that patterns of thought and action are specific to certain periods and civilizations, and that as ways of life, these patterns are intransitive. We cannot relive the past, we cannot import most ancient beliefs and practices into present culture. The fallacy of anachronism refers to modes of being; it is not just a principle of textual interpretation. It points out the historical limits to political and social practice. In this sense there are contingent but unavoidable differences between the ancients and the moderns which cannot be eliminated. Two such differences are the modern notions of individual liberty and moral pluralism, neither of which is present in ancient thought. Both are the result of increasing social differentiation, literacy, growth in self-consciousness, and social and geographical mobility.

This historicist point raises several questions: what political order is adequate to our self-knowledge and understanding of society? Which political order fits which period? Which political order fits which social and cultural conditions? Which political order best represents our *universal* and *particular* interests?

In asking these questions I am pressing the historicist point; but am I coming close to relativism? I think not. Berlin can hold to the point that liberty is a widespread, universal good, something that all moral actors need, and still claim that the maximization of liberty, of this good, is needed for modern civil societies to flourish. Moreover, pluralism is a fact of moral life. Moral diversity and moral conflict are unavoidable facts of social and cultural life. (This was true of ancient life even though ancient theory did not appreciate this truth.) We can argue that a liberal order is the least dismissive of this truth and the least repressive of various life-styles. Liberal democracies remain sufficiently open-ended ideologically and tempered by the rule of law to avoid moral despotism and pogroms. In this sense, the principles of liberal democracies are truthful, and their practices humane. Stated this way, the argument seems circular. One sets up the conditions that must be respected in the light of the political order one wishes to justify; or one justifies the politics that exist by what today's politics are about. My way of posing the problem can also be viewed as positivistic. Am I, and is Berlin, merely accepting the facts of modern life without criticism? Does acceptance of these facts predetermine our judgement about political liberalism?

These questions in turn beg fundamental questions concerning method. I have argued that Berlin is an empirical and historical political theorist. He does not believe that moral and political theory can be formulated without a great deal of background information about what we know to be true of human nature and society. Such knowledge will include descriptions of our fundamental needs and interests, as well as of the development of persons within particular civilizations. Berlin's methodological point seems to be that theorists cannot dismiss the totality or major portions of historical development, *and still remain accurate vis-à-vis the facts and relevant to the problems at hand.* Nor can they selectively eliminate the needs and interests of actual, existing human beings, *and still remain true to the facts, to human nature, human interests, and particular cultural preferences.* As a sympathetic critic puts it:

If Berlin has an ontology, it is the doctrine that that which exists most indubitably, and of which we have the most direct incorrigible knowledge, is human beings in specific historical circumstances—myself and others, concrete, individual, unique, self-directing and in various degrees responsible and free; possessed of inner lives consisting of thoughts, feelings and emotions, consciously forming purposes and principles, and pursuing these in our outward lives; and that to attempt to reduce these to the less intelligible, because merely causal or statistical, terms and laws of the natural sciences—or, for that matter, to seek to transform them into functional components of any abstract monist system, metaphysical, teleological or mechanistic—however convenient this may be for practical purposes, diabolic, human or divine, is ultimately to deny too much of what men know immediately and most vividly to be the truth about themselves, and all too often in our day to frustrate, maim, and possibly crush unique and vibrant human beings in the name of dead abstractions.[9]

As a matter of method, therefore, Berlin holds that political theory must be historical and empirical, realistic and practicable. It must deal with what exists, and not suspend contemporary conditions abstractly, by some theoretical bracketing. This methodological tack is taken for moral reasons: to be anything but concrete and historical is to risk prescribing the sacrifice of living people to theories, to abstractions. Once this is made plain, the charge of positivism is less damaging. The charge begs the question of correct method in political theory. To the charge of positivism,

---

[9] Roger Hausheer, 'Berlin and the Emergence of Liberal Pluralism' in P. Manent, *et al.*, *European Liberty* (The Hague, 1988), 77.

Berlin need only retort: Do you wish to do political theory and forget about human nature as we know it and our knowledge of our fundamental needs and particular wants? Can you do political theory and forget social development in history? If you try, the Berlinian will argue that you will fail to be adequate to the task of political theory; you will not be speaking to people as we know them, according to how they act, and what their political practice is. To suspend these things is to miss the mark, and forget your charge as a theorist of practical affairs.

Berlin's whole work is there to show that one cannot suspend the course of history and human development and remain anything but witless, absurd, even very dangerous. Of course one may criticize modern morality and preferences, lament our follies and imperfections. One may even wish for radical changes in the content of our socially acquired characteristics, of our 'second nature'. But to criticize everything and offer little or nothing in return, or worse, to offer mere theories, is vain, irresponsible, and barbaric.

Much of Berlin's work is critical of this dualistic attitude, whether it be of the utopian and revolutionary variety, such as found in Marx and Sorel, or the kind of doleful romanticism inspired by Rousseau.[10] Rather, the tendency in his thought is to look at persons as they are, not as they should be according to some theory. If there is one lesson he draws from history, it is the error of seeking to sacrifice today's liberty, or any fundamental values, for putative rewards tomorrow. It is this kind of utopian and revolutionary logic that his pluralism, critique of utopianism, and empiricism guard against. Hence Berlin is responsive and responsible to the complexity and uniqueness of moral phenomena. For political society he recommends a blending of human qualities and worthy ends. In this sense, he is a sober moralist with a classical sense of balance and proportion. His understanding of politics, of judgement about regimes, is similar to Aristotle's view of polity: a practicable and good polity is a mixed regime. With Berlin this mixture includes an ongoing accommodation of the various capacities and qualities of persons, as they have developed in

[10] See I. Berlin, 'George Sorel' in *AC*, 296–332. Berlin credits Alexander Herzen with first working out a critique of dualism in utopian thought, see 'Herzen and Bakunin on Individual Liberty' in *RT*, 82–113 at 89, 94, 103, 105, 111–12. One doleful romantic, inspired by Rousseau, is the American political theorist, Benjamin Barber, whose work I deal with below.

history and continue to unfold within existing political societies. His political prescription includes a mixture of goods and interests and kinds of liberty, of social justice, and conditions for freedom.[11]

With regard to kinds of liberty, Berlin seeks to accommodate our desire to be independent and our will and need to govern ourselves collectively. As Constant argued, to unite individual liberty and positive liberty under representative forms of government is the unique achievement of modern polities. This is the ongoing accommodation we designate when we call our polities 'liberal democracies'. To have such a sense of proportion precludes romantic yearnings for ancient forms of liberty. The reason is that ancient liberty was not mixed with individual liberty, with the whole constellation of social, institutional, and cultural factors that we inherit as modern civilized persons. In short, unalloyed ancient liberty does not fit modern conditions. It is this sense of what fits when and where that typifies Berlin's political thought. It is based on his strong historical sense, and is the major methodological carry-over from the history of ideas into his moral and political theory.

Of course there is loss in history. A good example is positive liberty. In modern societies there is a loss of social solidarity, corporate unity, political participation, and senses of belonging. But much has been gained: moral rights, personal liberties, the rule of law under principles of fundamental justice, a rich civil life, and so on. To seek the reinstatement of civic man is to prescribe the evisceration of this heritage. It was for this reason that Constant charged Rousseau with Procrustean intentions, and wild and irresponsible metaphysical fantasies. Berlin and most liberals concur in this judgement. Unfortunately, this tendency in political thought has not passed. Rousseau continues to have many followers. Recently, Benjamin Barber has tried to revive a Rousseauian theory of civic politics. To achieve this revival, he has to dismiss much of the complexity of modern social and moral life. To be consistent Barber must assume that local, national, and international democratic movements can contain the totality of civil existence. Indeed, he must hope that modern mass

[11] For a development of Berlin's idea of a mixture of individual and social goods, see Amartya Sen, 'Individual Freedom as a Social Commitment' in *New York Review of Books* (14 June 1990), 49–54.

communications, if well structured, can recreate direct forms of legislation.[12]

But it is not obvious that an electronic democracy is preferable to representative institutions; or that most people would gain if they traded in their private pursuits for civic ones. Yet Barber thinks otherwise; he does not hesitate to claim that: 'Without participating in the common life that defines them and in the decision-making that shapes their social habitat, women and men cannot become individuals.'[13] The problem with this view is that it concludes from the assumption of sociability that *civisme* is the highest and best form of human interaction. Common to Aristotle and Rousseau, this view holds that self-realization can only occur in face-to-face political relations, in some kind of central public place, some *agora*.[14] To be fully human one must live and operate in a *polis*. Yet the conclusion does not follow from the premiss. That we are social and political animals does not entail that we are truly human in only one particular kind of polity.[15] Nor does it follow that individuality is of necessity fulfilled only in democratic activity. If this were true then Diogenes, Leonardo, Gauguin, and Einstein were neither full individuals, nor part of the set of individuals living a good life. Both conclusions are absurd.

Berlin's knowledge of history and sense of pluralism militate against claims that there is only one form of the best life, one form of liberty, one kind of individuality, one good polity. His vision saves us from such conformist and monistic judgements. Moreover his senses of history and political realism guard against the democratic nihilism of a Barber who tells us that 'no knowledge is certain, no grounds absolute, and no political decision irrevocable'.[16] Berlin knows, as we all do, that political decisions can kill thousands, that democratic and authoritarian politics do not contain their own limits, that many political decisions are irrevocable. (Many death sentences and many decrees for mass extermination have been

---

[12] See Benjamin R. Barber, *Strong Democracy: Participatory Politics for a New Age* (Berkeley, Calif., 1984), 261–311.   [13] Ibid. p. xv.

[14] Aristotle of course thought that a still higher life was possible for man beyond politics: the contemplative life.

[15] Bernard Yack makes these points most cogently in his essay, 'Liberalism and its Communitarian Critics: Does Liberal Practice "Live Down" to Liberal Theory?' in C. H. Reynolds and R. V. Norman, *Community in America: The Challenge of Habits of the Heart* (Berkeley, Calif., 1988), 147–69.

[16] Barber, *Strong Democracy*, 217.

irrevocable. Once the blade fell, not even democrats could give Louis back his head.) For Berlin, the historical examples of the Terror and Nazism merely confirm Plato's view that democracy and tyranny are similarly unlimited and immoderate. In short, the most effective critic of contemporary civic humanists is the history they fail to consider.

Unlike such theorists, Berlin shows how we have knowledge of goods and evils, of history, of life and death, of what makes up good lives, and what is inimical to them. We use such knowledge to judge how best to organize our polities given the circumstances we face. We use such knowledge in ranking nation states, in saying that on balance life is better in Holland and Canada than in the Soviet Union and the Albania of the 1980s. Specifically, Berlin has always been concerned with defending free institutions against usurpers and other foes, be they theorists, technocrats, or thugs. Throughout his career he has denounced fascists, communists, and other dictators. In the period from the 1930s to the 1960s such stands were not universal; they were constested by a variety of intellectuals, both of the right and left. 'Negative liberty' became his banner against all those who believed that a polity could sacrifice all civil liberties for other goals, such as economic equality or democracy or revolutionary solidarity or purity of the race, *and then call it the pursuit of freedom.*

Today no one can deny that his stand was a just one.[17] But apologias of revolutionary politics and violence were common well into the 1970s, especially on the left, as the cases of Jean-Paul Sartre and C. B. Macpherson demonstrate.[18] It was not until the mid-to-late 1970s that the French intelligentsia, the last bulwark of this kind in the Western world, overcame its romantic illusions about communist states.[19] Today, anti-communism is a commonplace

[17] Richard Rorty offers some good defences of cold-war liberalism in 'Thugs and Theorists: A Reply to Bernstein' in *Political Theory*, 15 (1987), 564–80 at 566–7, 576 n. 11, 578–9 n. 25.
[18] On the vicissitudes of Sartre's affiliations, see Ronald Aronson, *Jean-Paul Sartre: Philosophy in the World* (London, 1980). For Macpherson's apologia of Soviet-inspired regimes in Africa, see *The Real World of Democracy* (Toronto, 1965), 12–22; for his later and slightly qualified apologia of vanguardism and revolutionary violence, see 'Berlin's Division of Liberty' (Oxford, 1973), 106–7, 114–17.
[19] For this story see George Ross, 'The Decline of the Left Intellectual in Modern France' in Alain G. Gagnon (ed.), *Intellectuals in Liberal Democracies* (New York, 1987), 43–65.

attitude; history has failed the 'scientific' theory it was supposed to serve.

Context is one thing, continuing relevance, another. My claim is that Berlin remains relevant today because of his pluralism and the way he defends political liberalism. Nothing about his defence is doctrinaire, or a priori. Everything he claims about the importance of individual liberty, for human life, for modern living, is tested by experience. He often argues in the negative, saying that the *known* alternatives to liberal democracy are worse—hence saying that it behoves the critics to come up with a better and real example to supplant liberal–democratic regimes. It is experience that matters to him, not theories. Hence empirical pointers complement his normative claim that liberty is central to our moral nature, and fair because it allows persons to choose how to live their lives in a world typified by a plurality of goods and ways of life. Together, normative and empirical or historical reasons make his defence of political liberalism particularly well-grounded in our moral ideals and sentiments, and in our understanding of what is prudent and wise given the history of Western culture and modern politics.

As a political theorist, Berlin comes armed with concerns of logical consistency, explanatory import, and sympathy for traditions, conventions, and basic intuitions about what is right and good for human beings. He gives us no original contractors and no hypothetical contract, unlike early liberals and some contemporary advocates of the social-contract doctrine. In moral and practical affairs he sees debates involving, of necessity, both universal rules and particular conventions and sentiments. Most of his work explores what Stuart Hampshire calls the second face of morality— that which is historically specific, parochial, individual, and unique. It is openness to the pluralism of ends, conflicts of goods, historical specificity of mores, and plurality of institutions that characterizes modern social and political life. Unlike the rationalist tradition, Berlin is not disdainful towards the complexity and heterogeneity of moral life. This explains why he offers no fixed rules on when and how to limit liberties. He simply does not think that such rules offer much guidance when ethical decisions need to be made. This focus on the second face of morality presents us with a challenge. Certainly universal norms, legal codes, constitutional principles, and ultimate commitments all give us various rules of priority. But all these are open to interpretation and differing application depending on the circumstances at hand. In this sense, Berlin's style of political thinking encourages moral and political debate. In matters relevant to the public order, it is only informed political debate that is up to the task of judging the worth of particular liberties. Beyond the establishment of a liberal-democratic constitution, there is much that needs to be debated and done. Rather than precluding democratic debate, Berlin's sense of the importance of accommodating goods, of meeting a variety of needs, and of enacting redistributive schemes, encourages such debate. Only a society without moral conflict and injustice could do away with philosophy and politics. Short of this perfectibilist dream, philosophical and political debate, accommodation, compromise, losses and gains, are the order of the day. In fact, it is the monistic theorist who hopes to eliminate philosophy and the need for political choice. In the end the monist, the rationalist, the religious fundamentalist, is an anti-intellectual and anti-political thinker. Berlin, on the other hand, takes pluralism and thus debate and the need for choice, including political choice, to be constitutive of our moral condition. He is anti-monistic, but not anti-political.[20]

Lack of system and hard-and-fast rules nevertheless carry a price. Beyond 'basic' liberties, how are we to resolve conflicts amongst liberties, or amongst liberty and other values? Basic liberties are often compatible with many different regimes. A great deal of negative liberty could have existed in some feudal cities, or in ancient Persia for example. Berlin admits this much.[21] But this changes little; feudalism is over and ancient Persian empires are long buried in the sand. We have to accept some limits to political choice, and one of them is the time in which we find ourselves.

But what about liberal democracies? My argument so far has been to respond that such regimes fit modern social, historical, and cultural conditions. We have to accept some contingency in political theory. It may be just a contingent, but unavoidable, requirement that liberal democracies grant a great deal of liberty to their citizens in order that they may flourish in civil society. And

---

[20] Some early critics argued that because Berlin is committed to negative liberty, he is correspondingly an apolitical or even an anti-political thinker. This can neither be inferred from his work, nor is it implied by it. For examples of the early criticism, see B. R. Crick, *Freedom as Politics* (Sheffield, 1966); and Marshall Cohen, 'Berlin and the Liberal Tradition' in *Philosophical Quarterly*, 10 (1960), 216–27.

[21] See 'Introduction' to *FE*, pp. lvii–lviii.

this is probably Berlin's point: in such matters, it is the contingency of affairs, of historical arrangements, that is central. As he says: 'Total patterns of life must be compared directly as wholes.' The subject matter of politics itself is vague; it is difficult to divide into logical, conceptual pieces and to put to formal tests of validity.[22] A great deal of interpretative leeway is needed, and most judgement will be based on historical narratives which are themselves disputable. However, one would be hard pressed to state that we need to jettison most, or even all, social and cultural conditions in order to have a different kind of politics. Claiming, in the abstract, that such a trade would be beneficial seems hardly plausible. In short, an appeal to historical and cultural facts is inescapable. This does not aid us in deciding between liberties and other values. The weakness of Berlin's work is due to the fact that he never worked out the limits of pluralism, or the preferred balance between negative and positive liberties, or what is part of the common core of human values and what is not. Instead he points out the difficulty in making these kinds of measurements and comparisons.[23] He offers only the prescription to make workable trade-offs when values conflict. Consequently, his contribution remains underdeveloped.

   None the less, he does tell us what we need in order to go forward on his path. What is required is the best knowledge that the empirical sciences can give us of human nature and society; knowledge of human needs and interests, and of human development in history—knowledge which should always be taken as fallible. Hence universal and comparative knowledge about individuals and societies are the beginnings of political theory. Then we must proceed with clear conceptual thinking, scepticism of the facts, some basic principles, and a give-and-take attitude in moral and political debate. We must never fail to seek knowledge and enlightenment; never give up the virtues of common sense, decency, civility, fair play, kindness, liberty, justice, measured judgements, and gradual approaches to hard problems. A sense of balance and proportion, of what fits when and where, is crucial to the theory he enjoins us to practise.

   One thing is certain about Berlin's thought. Utopian thinking, eschatological hopes and revolutionary practice have done more

---

[22] 'Two Concepts of Liberty', 130 n. 1.   [23] Ibid.

harm than good. With the collapse of the Soviet Union, possibly
the last empire built on a grand ideology, the era of utopian
thought seems over. The times call for reasonable and practical
thinking, not theoretical hubris. This attitude has long been
practised by Berlin and other empirically minded and prudential
liberals. We should follow their example.

Bibliography

Works by Isaiah Berlin[1]

1. Collected Essays and Books

(Only those articles directly referred to in the present volume are listed.)

(1939), *Karl Marx: His Life and Environment* (Thornton Butterworth, London; 4th rev. edn. Oxford University Press, Oxford, 1978).

(1956), *The Age of Enlightenment* (Houghton Mifflin, Boston, Mass.).

(1969), *Four Essays on Liberty* (Oxford University Press, London).
    'Introduction'
    'Political Ideas in the Twentieth Century'
    'Historical Inevitability'
    'Two Concepts of Liberty'
    'John Stuart Mill and the Ends of Life'

(1976), *Vico and Herder: Two Studies in the History of Ideas* (Hogarth Press, London).
    'Introduction'
    'The Philosophical Ideas of Giambattista Vico'
    'Herder and the Enlightenment'

(1978), *Russian Thinkers*, eds. H. Hardy and A. Kelly (Hogarth Press, London).
    'The Hedgehog and the Fox'
    'Herzen and Bakunin on Individual Liberty'
    'Fathers and Children'

(1978), *Concepts and Categories: Philosophical Essays*, ed. H. Hardy (Hogarth Press, London).
    'The Purpose of Philosophy'
    'Verification'
    'Empirical Propositions and Hypothetical Statements'
    'Logical Translation'
    'Equality'
    'The Concept of Scientific History'
    'Does Political Theory Still Exist?'
    'From Hope and Fear Set Free'

---

[1] For the most complete and up-to-date listing see Henry Hardy, 'A Bibliography of Isaiah Berlin' in the most recently revised impression of Henry Hardy (ed.), *Against the Current: Essays in the History of Ideas* (Clarendon Press, Oxford, 1991).

(1979), *Against the Current: Essays in the History of Ideas*, ed. H. Hardy
    (Hogarth Press, London; revised impression, Clarendon Paperback,
    Oxford, 1991).
    'The Counter-Enlightenment'
    'The Originality of Machiavelli'
    'The Divorce between the Sciences and Humanities'
    'Vico's Concept of Knowledge'
    'Vico and the Ideal of the Enlightenment'
    'Montesquieu'
    'Hume and the Sources of German Anti-Rationalism'
    'The Life and Opinions of Moses Hess'
    'Benjamin Disraeli, Karl Marx and the Search for Identity'
    'The *Naïveté* of Verdi'
    'Georges Sorel'
    'Nationalism: Past Neglect and Present Power'
(1980), *Personal Impressions*, ed. H. Hardy (Hogarth Press, London).
    'Chaim Weizmann'
    'Felix Frankfurter at Oxford'
    'L. B. Namier'
    'J. L. Austin and the Early Beginnings of Oxford Philosophy'
    'Einstein and Israel'
(1990), *The Crooked Timber of Humanity: Chapters in the History of Ideas*, ed.
    H. Hardy (John Murray, London).
    'The Pursuit of the Ideal'
    'The Decline of Utopian Ideas in the West'
    'Giambattista Vico and Cultural History'
    'Alleged Relativism in Eighteenth-Century European Thought'
    'European Unity and its Vicissitudes'
    'Joseph de Maistre and the Origins of Fascism'
    'The Apotheosis of the Romantic Will:
        The Revolt against the Myth of an Ideal World'
    'The Bent Twig: On the Rise of Nationalism'

2. Essays and Published Letters

(1929), 'Pelican s'en va-t-en guerre: a tale of war and peace', *Pelican
    Record*, 19: 34–6.
(1930), (as Albert Alfred Apricott), 'Music Chronicle', *Oxford Outlook*, 53
    616–27.
(1930), 'Some Procrustations', *Oxford Outlook*, 10: 491–502.
(1949), 'Attitude on Marxism Stated: Dr Berlin Amplifies His Remarks
    Made at Mount Holyoke', letter to the *New York Times* (8 July), 18.
(1949), 'The Anglo-American Predicament', *Listener*, 42 (29 September),
    518–19, 538 (Letters: 20 October, 681 and 10 November, 813–14).

(1952), 'Jewish Slavery and Emancipation', *Hebrew University Garland*, ed. N. Bentwich (Constellation Books, London), 18–42.

(1952), (as O. Utis), 'Generalissimo Stalin and the Art of Government', *Foreign Affairs*, 30: 197–214.

(1952), 'Lament for Lipatti', *House and Garden*, 7: 91–8.

(1952), 'Dr Chaim Weizmann', *The Times* (supplementary obituary) (17 November), 8.

(1954), 'Men Who Lead', *Jerusalem Post* (2 November), 5, 6.

(1954), 'Realism in Politics', *Spectator* (17 December), 774–6.

(1957), (with Miriam Rothschild), 'Mr James de Rothschild', *The Times* (supplementary obituary) (13 May), 15.

(1957), 'The Silence in Russian Culture', *Foreign Affairs*, 36: 1–24.

(1958), 'The Origins of Israel', *The Middle East in Transition*, ed. W. Z. Laqueur (Routledge, London), 204–21.

(1961), 'What is History?', letter to the *Listener* (18 May), 877.

(1961), 'What is History?', letter to the *Listener* (15 June), 1048–9.

(1962), 'The Biographical Facts', *Chaim Weizmann*, eds. M. W. Weisgal and J. Carmichael (Weidenfeld & Nicolson, London), 17–56.

(1962), 'Mr Carr's Big Battalions', letter to *New Statesman* (5 January), 15–16.

(1962), 'The Road to Catastrophe', *Times Literary Supplement* (30 March), 216.

(1964), 'Hobbes, Locke and Professor Macpherson', *Political Quarterly*, 35: 444–68.

(1964), 'Rationality of Value Judgments', *Nomos* 7, *Rational Decision*, ed. C. J. Friedrich (Atherton Press, New York), 221–3.

(1964), 'Portrait of Ben-Gurion', *Jewish Chronicle* (25 December), 7, 22.

(1966), 'Preface' to H. G. Schenk, *The Mind of the European Romantics* (Constable, London), pp. xiii–xviii.

(1966), 'A Generous Imaginative Idealist', *Meyer Weisgal at Seventy*, ed. E. Victor (Weidenfeld & Nicolson, London), 89.

(1967), contribution to *Authors Take Sides on Vietnam*, eds. C. Woolf and J. Bagguley (Simon & Schuster, New York), 60–2.

(1970), 'Weizmann as Exilarch', *Chaim Weizmann as Leader* (Hebrew University of Jerusalem, Jerusalem; two lectures, one by I. Berlin and one by Israel Rolatt), 13–21.

(1970), 'One of the Boldest Innovators in the History of Human Thought', *Molders of Modern Thought*, ed. B. B. Seligman (Quadrangle Books, Chicago), 41–56.

(1972), 'Dr Jacob Herzog', *Jewish Chronicle* (14 April), 28, 43.

(1972), 'Zionist Politics in Wartime Washington: A Fragment of Personal Reminiscence', Yaacov Herzog Memorial Lecture (Hebrew University of Israel, Jerusalem).

(1972), 'Giambattista Vico', *Listener*, 88 (28 September), 391–8.

(1972), 'Foreword' to Friedrich Meinecke, *Historism: The Rise of a New Historical Outlook*, ed. and trans. J. E. Anderson (Routledge, London), pp. ix–xvi.

(1973), 'A Nation Among Nations', *Jewish Chronicle* (colour magazine, 4 May), 28–34.

(1974), 'Go There to Find Your Identity', *Jewish Chronicle* (supplement, 16 April), p. i.

(1975), 'General Education', *Oxford Review of Education*, 1: 287–92.

(1978), 'Corsi e Ricorsi', *Journal of Modern History*, 50: 480–9.

(1978), (with others), 'Is a Philosophy of History Possible?', *Philosophy of History and Action*, ed. Y. Yovel (Reidel, Dordrecht), 219–25.

(1979), 'Professor Scouten on Herder and Vico', *Comparative Literature Studies*, 16: 141–5.

(1979), 'The Three Strands in My Life', *Jewish Quarterly*, 27: 5–7.

(1980), 'A Tribute to my Friend' [J. L. Talmon], *Forum*, 38: 1–4.

(1980), 'The Incompatibility of Values' and 'Virtue and Practicality', *Ethics in an Age of Pervasive Technology*, ed. M. Kranzberg (Westview Press, Boulder, Colo.), 32–3; 193.

(1981), *For Teddy Kollek* (The Jerusalem Foundation, Jerusalem).

(1981), Reply to H. Aarsleff, 'Vico and Berlin', *London Review of Books*, 3 (5–18 November), 7–8.

(1983), 'Reply to Kocis', *Political Studies*, 31: 388–93.

(1985), 'On Vico', *Philosophical Quarterly*, 35: 281–90.

(1986), 'The Cost of Curing an Oyster', *Jerusalem Post* (10 February), 8.

(1986), 'Greetings', *Secular Humanistic Judaism*, 1: 2.

(1988), 'Israeli Solution', letter to the *Independent* (28 September), 19.

(1990), contribution to 'The State of Europe: Christmas Eve 1989', *Granta* 30 (*New Europe!*) (winter), 148–50.

(1991), (with others), 'The Detention of Sari Nussiebeh', Letter to the *Independent* (4 February), 18 (also in *New York Review of Books* (7 March), 4).

(1992), 'Reply to Ronald H. McKinney', *Journal of Value Inquiry*, 26 (1992), 557–60.

3. Wartime Despatches

(1980), H. G. Nicholas *Washington Despatches 1941–1945: Weekly Reports from the British Embassy*, ed. H. G. Nicholas with an Introduction by Isaiah Berlin (Weidenfeld & Nicolson, London).

4. Audio Tapes

(1965), Six Mellon Lectures, 'Some Sources of Romanticism', given at the National Gallery, Washington, DC, June and July. Now held in the

National Sound Archive, the British Library, London. (These lectures were rebroadcast on the BBC during June and July 1989 in celebration of Sir Isaiah's 80th birthday.)

(1974), talks with Roy Pascal, 'Romanticism and Liberation' and 'Romanticism and Social Change', Tape HUA013, Audio Learning Discussion Tape, London.

5. *Interviews*

(1982), with Magee, B., 'An Introduction to Philosophy: Dialogue with Isaiah Berlin', *Men of Ideas: Some Creators of Contemporary Philosophy*, ed. B. Magee (Oxford University Press, Oxford; from interviews at the BBC, 1978), 2–27.

(1988), with Galipeau, C. J., 'Interviews with Sir Isaiah Berlin' (unpublished transcripts of taped recordings), 23 May, Oxford, and 1 June, London.

(1990), with Galipeau, C. J., Untaped interviews, 21 May and 11 June, Oxford.

(1991), with Jahanbegloo, R., *Recollections of a Historian of Ideas: Conversations with Isaiah Berlin* (Charles Scribner's Sons, New York).

(1991), with Gardels, N., 'Two Concepts of Nationalism: An Interview with Isaiah Berlin', *New York Review of Books*, 21 November, 19–23 (with corrections by Berlin in a letter to the *New York Review of Books*, 5 December 1991, 58).

6. *Unpublished Letters*

To Galipeau, C. J.: 19 September, 17 November 1988; 30 November 1990; 5 January, 18 March, 15 April, 16 May 1991; 8 July 1992.

To Polanowska-Sygulska, B.: 24 February 1986.

Secondary Works on Isaiah Berlin

1. ˙ *Books and Articles*

AARSLEFF, H. (1981), 'Vico and Berlin', *London Review of Books*, 3 (5–18 November), 6–7.

ANNAN, N. (1980), 'Introduction', *Personal Impressions*, ed. H. Hardy (Viking Press, New York), pp. xii–xxx.

ANON. (1959), 'Silhouette: Sir Isaiah Berlin', *Jewish Chronicle* (5 June), 77.

ANON. (1989), 'Between Two Worlds: Sir Isaiah Berlin at Eighty', *Jewish Chronicle* (9 June), 30.

AYER, A. J. (1977), *Part of My Life* (Oxford University Press, Oxford).

BLUMENFELD, Y. (1979), 'Is Isaiah Berlin the Philosopher of the 1980s?' *International Herald Tribune* (weekend supplement) (28 December), 7w 10w.

BOWRA, C. M. (1966), *Memories: 1898–1939* (Weidenfeld & Nicolson London).

CARR, E. H. (1962), *What is History?* (Macmillan, London; first broadcast a a series of lectures on the BBC in 1969).

—— (1962), 'What is History?', *Listener* (1 June), 973–4.

COHEN, G. A. (1979), 'Capitalism, Freedom and the Proletariat', *The Idea of Freedom: Essays in Honour of Isaiah Berlin*, ed. A. Ryan (Oxford University Press, Oxford), 9–25.

—— (1991), 'Isaiah's Marx, and Mine', *Isaiah Berlin: A Celebration*, eds. E. and A. Margalit (Hogarth, London), 110–26.

COHEN, M. (1960), 'Berlin and the Liberal Tradition', *Philosophical Quarterly*, 10: 216–27.

CRICK, B. R. (1966), *Freedom as Politics* (University of Sheffield, Sheffield).

GALIPEAU, C. J. (1990), 'Liberalism and Zionism: The Case of Isaiah Berlin', *Queen's Quarterly*, 97: 379–93.

—— (1990), 'Isaiah Berlin's Liberalism: An Exposition and Defense', unpublished Ph.D. dissertation, University of Toronto.

GAY, P. (1979), 'Freud and Freedom: On a Fox in Hedgehog's Clothing', *The Idea of Freedom: Essays in Honour of Isaiah Berlin*, ed. A. Ryan (Oxford University Press, Oxford), 41–59.

GRAY, J. (1989), 'On Negative and Positive Liberty', *Liberalisms: Essays in Political Philosophy*, J. Gray (Routledge, London), 45–68.

—— (1993), *Post-Liberalism: Studies in Political Thought* (Routledge, London), 283–328.

HAMPSHIRE, S. (1991), 'Nationalism', *Isaiah Berlin: A Celebration*, eds. E. and A. Margalit (Hogarth Press, London), 127–34.

HARDY, H. (1978), 'Editing Isaiah Berlin's Writings', *British Book News* (January), 3, 5.

—— (1991), 'A Bibliography of Isaiah Berlin', *Against the Current: Essays in the History of Ideas*, ed. H. Hardy (Clarendon Press, Oxford), 356–80.

HAUSHEER, R. (1980), 'Introduction', *Against the Current: Essays in the History of Ideas*, ed. H. hardy (Hogarth Press, New York), pp. xiii–liii.

—— (1983), 'Berlin and the Emergence of Liberal Pluralism', *European Liberty*, P. Manent, *et al.* (Martinus Nijhoff, The Hague), 49–80.

KOCIS, R. (1978), 'Rationalism and Romanticism Redux: The Political Philosophy of Sir Isaiah Berlin', Ph.D. dissertation, University of Pittsburgh.

—— (1980), 'Reason, Development, and the Conflicts of Human Ends: Sir Isaiah Berlin's Vision of Politics', *American Political Science Review*, 74: 38–52.

—— (1983), 'Toward a Coherent Theory of Human Moral Development:

Beyond Sir Isaiah Berlin's Vision of Human Nature', *Political Studies*, 31: 370–87.

—— (1989), *A Critical Appraisal of Isaiah Berlin's Political Philosophy* (Edwin Mellen Press, Lewiston, NY).

LIEBERSON, J., and MORGENBESSER, S. (1991), 'Isaiah Berlin', *Isaiah Berlin: A Celebration*, eds. E. and A. Margalit (Hogarth Press, London), 1–30.

MACCALLUM jun., G. C. (1972), 'Negative and Positive Liberty', *Philosophy, Politics and Society* (4th series), eds. P. Laslett, W. G. Runciman, and Q. Skinner (Blackwell, Oxford), 174–93.

MACPHERSON, C. B. (1973), 'Berlin's Division of Liberty', *Democratic Theory: Essays in Retrieval* (Oxford University Press, Oxford), 95–119.

—— (1985), 'Pluralism, Individualism, and Participation', *The Rise and Fall of Economic Justice and other Essays* (Oxford University Press, Oxford), 92–100.

MARGALIT, E. and M. (eds.) (1991), *Isaiah Berlin: A Celebration* (Hogarth Press, London).

MCKINNEY, R. H. (1992), 'Towards a Postmodern Ethics: Sir Isaiah Berlin and John Caputo', *The Journal of Value Inquiry*, 26 (1992), 395–407.

MILLER, D. (1991), 'Introduction', *Liberty*, ed. D. Miller (Oxford University Press, Oxford), 1–20.

MOMIGLIANO, A. (1976), 'On the Pioneer Trail' (review article of *Vico and Herder*), *New York Review of Books* (11 November), 33–8.

PARENT, W. (1974), 'Some Recent Work on the Concept of Liberty', *American Philosophical Quarterly*, 11: 149–67.

POLANOWSKA-SYGULSKA, B. (1989), 'One Voice More on Berlin's Doctrine of Liberty', *Political Studies*, 37: 123–7.

RAPAPORT, L. (1984), 'The Hoskins Affair,' *Jerusalem Post* (23 November).

RORTY, R. (1986), 'The Contingency of Language', 'The Contingency of Selfhood', and 'The Contingency of Community', *London Review of Books* (17 April), 3–6; (8 May), 11–15; and (24 July), 10–14 respectively.

—— (1987), 'Thugs and Theorists: A Reply to Bernstein', *Political Theory*, 15: 564–80.

RYAN, A. (ed.) (1979) *The Idea of Freedom: Essays in Honour of Isaiah Berlin* (Oxford University Press, Oxford).

SANDEL, M. (1984), 'Introduction', *Liberalism and its Critics* (New York University Press, New York), 1–11.

SCOUTEN, A. H. (1978), review of *Vico and Herder*, *Comparative Literature Studies*, 15: 336–40.

SEN, A. (1990), 'Individual Freedom as a Social Commitment', *New York Review of Books* (14 June), 49–54.

SKINNER, Q. (1984), 'The Idea of Negative Liberty: Philosophical and Historical Perspectives', *Philosophy in History*, ed. R. Rorty, J. B. Schneewind, and Q. Skinner (Cambridge University Press, Cambridge), 193–221.

188 *Bibliography*

STRAUSS, L. (1989), 'Relativism', *The Rebirth of Classical Political Rationalism*, ed. T. L. Pangle (University of Chicago Press, Chicago), 13–26.

TAYLOR, C. (1979), 'What's Wrong with Negative Liberty', *The Idea of Freedom*, ed. A. Ryan (Oxford University Press, Oxford), 175–93.

WALZER, M. (1986), 'Introduction' to Isaiah Berlin, *The Hedgehog and the Fox* (Simon & Schuster, New York), [pp. i–xi].

WEIZMANN, V. (1967), *The Impossible Takes Longer* (Hamish Hamilton, London).

WHITE, M. (1979), 'Oughts and Cans', *The Idea of Freedom*, ed. A. Ryan (Oxford University Press, Oxford), 211–19.

WILLIAMS, B. (1979), 'Conflicts of Values', *The Idea of Freedom*, ed. A. Ryan (Oxford University Press, Oxford), 221–32.

—— (1979), 'Introduction', *Concepts and Categories: Philosophical Essays*, ed. H. Hardy (Hogarth Press, New York), pp. xi–xviii.

—— (1991), 'Naive and Sentimental Opera Lovers', *Isaiah Berlin: A Celebration*, eds. E. and A. Margalit (Hogarth Press, London), 180–92.

WOLLHEIM, R. L. (1991), 'The Idea of a Common Human Nature', *Isaiah Berlin: A Celebration*, eds. E. and A. Margalit (Hogarth Press, London), 64–79.

2. Unpublished Letters

From J. Gray to C. J. Galipeau, 14 March 1988.

3. Untaped Interviews

With G. A. Cohen, All Souls College, Oxford, 23 May 1988.
With L. Siedentop, Keble College, Oxford, 27 May and 3 June 1988.

Secondary Works: General

ACKERMAN, B. (1980), *Social Justice in the Liberal State* (Yale University Press, New Haven, Conn.).

ANTONI, C. (1963), *L'Historisme*, trans. A. Dufour (Droz, Geneva).

ARBLASTER, A. (1984), *The Rise & Decline of Western Liberalism* (Blackwell, Oxford).

ARISTOTLE (1948), *The Politics of Aristotle*, trans. E. Barker (Oxford University Press, Oxford).

ARONSON, R. (1980), *Jean-Paul Sartre: Philosophy in the World* (Verso, London).

BARBER, B. R. (1984), *Strong Democracy: Participatory Politics for a New Age* (University of California Press, Berkeley, Calif.).

BERNSTEIN, R. (1978), *The Restructuring of Social and Political Theory* (University of Pennsylvania Press, Philadelphia).

BULLOCK, A., and WOODINGS, R. B. (eds.) (1983), *The Fontana Biographical Companion to Modern Thought* (Collins, London).

BURKE, P. (1985), *Vico* (Past Masters Series: Oxford University Press, Oxford).

CONSTANT, B. (1872), *Cours de politique constitutionnelle*, vols. i–ii, ed. E. M. Laboulaye (Librairie de Guillaumin et Cie, Paris).

—— (1988), *Constant: Political Writings*, ed. and trans. B. Fontana (Cambridge University Press, Cambridge).

DWORKIN, R. (1978), *Taking Rights Seriously* (Harvard University Press, Cambridge, Mass.).

—— (1985), 'Liberalism', *A Matter of Principle* (Harvard University Press, Cambridge, Mass.), 181–204.

EPICTETUS (1983), *The Handbook of Epictetus*, ed. and trans. N. P. White (Hackett, Indianapolis).

FONTANA, B. (1985), 'The Shaping of Modern Liberty: Commerce and Civilisation in the Writings of Benjamin Constant', *Annales Benjamin Constant*, 5: 3–15.

FOUCAULT, D. (1989), 'Jusqu'où faut-il respecter l'autre?', *Le Monde diplomatique* (April), 16–17.

GRAY, J. (1986), *Liberalism* (University of Minnesota Press, Minneapolis).

—— (1989), *Liberalisms: Essays in Political Philosophy* (Routledge, London).

GUNNELL, J. G. (1986), *Between Philosophy and Politics: The Alienation of Political Theory* (University of Massachusetts Press, Amherst, Mass.).

GUTMANN, A. (1985), 'Communitarian Critics of Liberalism', *Philosophy & Public Affairs*, 14: 308–22.

HAMPSHIRE, S. (1983), *Morality and Conflict* (Harvard University Press, Cambridge, Mass.).

HART, H. L. A. (1967), 'Are There Any Natural Rights?', *Political Philosophy*, ed. A. Quinton (Oxford University Press, Oxford), 53–66.

HAVEL, V. (1989), *Living in Truth*, ed. J. Vladislav (Faber & Faber, London).

HAYEK, F. A. von (1944), *The Road to Serfdom* (University of Chicago Press, Chicago).

HEGEL, G. W. F. (1942), *Philosophy of Right*, trans. T. M. Knox (Oxford University Press, Oxford).

—— (1977), *Phenomenology of Spirit*, trans. A. V. Miller (Oxford University Press, Oxford).

HOBBES, T. (1968), *Leviathan*, ed. C. B. Macpherson (Penguin, London).

HUNT, L. (1986), *Politics, Culture, and Class in the French Revolution* (Methuen, London).

HYPPOLITE, J. (1946), *Genèse et structure de la Phénoménologie de l'esprit de Hegel* (Aubier, Paris).

HYPPOLITE, J. (1983), *Introduction à la philosophie de l'histoire de Hegel* (Éditions du Seuil, Paris).

KANT, I. (1948), *The Moral Law [Groundwork of the Metaphysic of Morals]*, trans. H. J. Paton (Hutchinson, London).

—— (1965), *The Metaphysical Elements of Justice*, trans. A Ladd (Bobbs-Merrill, Indianapolis).

KERFERD, G. B. (1981), *The Sophistic Movement* (Cambridge University Press, Cambridge).

KYMLICKA, W. (1989), *Liberalism, Community, and Culture* (Clarendon Press, Oxford).

DE LACY, P. (1973), 'Skepticism in Antiquity', *Dictionary of the History of Ideas*, iv, ed. P. P. Wiener (Scribners, New York).

LARMORE, C. (1987), *Patterns of Moral Complexity* (Cambridge University Press, Cambridge).

LEWIS, C. S. (1960), *Studies in Words* (Cambridge University Press, Cambridge).

LONG, A. A. (1974), *Hellenistic Philosophy: Stoics, Epicureans, Skeptics*, 2nd edn. (Duckworth, London).

LUKES, S. (1989), 'Making Sense of Moral Conflict', *Liberalism and the Moral Life*, ed. N. Rosenblum (Harvard University Press, Cambridge, Mass.), 127–42.

LYOTARD, J. -F. (1979), *La condition postmoderne* (Éditions du Minuit, Paris).

MACPHERSON, C. B. (1962), *The Political Theory of Possessive Individualism* (Oxford University Press, Oxford).

—— (1965), *The Real World of Democracy* (CBC Enterprises, Toronto).

—— (1973), *Democratic Theory: Essays in Retrieval* (Oxford University Press, Oxford).

MANNING, D. J. (1976), *Liberalism* (J. M. Dent & Sons, London).

MCNEILL, W. H. (1985), *Poly-ethnicity and National Unity in World History* (University of Toronto Press, Toronto).

MEMMI, A. (1989), 'Intégrisme et laicité', *Le Monde diplomatique* (March), 3.

MICHEL, H. (1896), *L'Idée et l'état: essai critique sur l'histoire des théories sociales et politiques en France depuis la révolution* (Hachette, Paris).

MILL, J. S. (1964), *Utilitarianism, Liberty and Representative Government*, ed. A. D. Lindsay (J. M. Dent & Sons, London).

MILLER, D., *et al.* (eds.) (1987), *The Blackwell Encyclopaedia of Political Thought* (Basil Blackwell, Oxford).

MONRO, D. H. (1976), 'Relativism in Ethics', *Dictionary of the History of Ideas*, iv, ed. P. Wiener (Scribners, New York).

MOUFFE, C. (1987), 'Le libéralisme américain et ses critiques', *Esprit* (March), 100–14.

NOZICK, R. (1974), *Anarchy, State and Utopia* (Basic Books, New York).

PLAMENATZ, J. (1960), 'The Use of Political Theory', *Political Studies*, 8: 37–47.

—— (1963), 'Liberalism', *Dictionary of the History of Ideas*, iii, ed. P. P. Wiener (Scribners, New York), 41–3.

—— (1963), *Man and Society*, vol. i, (Longman, New York).

—— (1965), 'Introduction', *Readings from Liberal Writers: English and French* (Barnes & Noble, New York), 11–18.

POPPER, K. (1945), *The Open Society and Its Enemies*, vols. i–ii (Routledge, London).

RAWLS, J. (1971), *A Theory of Justice* (Harvard University Press, Cambridge, Mass.).

RAZ, J. (1986), *The Morality of Freedom* (Oxford University Press, Oxford).

ROSENBLUM, N. (1987), *Another Liberalism: Romanticism and the Reconstruction of Liberal Thought* (Harvard University Press, Cambridge, Mass.).

ROSS, G. (1987), 'The Decline of the Left Intellectual in Modern France', *Intellectuals in Liberal Democracies*, ed. A. G. Gagnon (Praeger, New York).

ROUSSEAU, J.-J. (1966), *Du contrat social* (Garnier-Flammarion, Paris).

—— (1971), *Discours sur les sciences et les arts/Discours sur l'origine de l'inégalité* (Flammarion, Paris).

SCRUTON, R. (1982), *A Dictionary of Political Thought* (Pan, London).

SIEDENTOP, L. (1979), 'Two Liberal Traditions', *The Idea of Freedom*, ed. A. Ryan (Oxford University Press, Oxford), 153–74.

STRAUSS, L. (1959), 'What is Political Philosophy?', *What is Political Philosophy? and Other Studies* (University of Chicago Press, Chicago), 9–55.

TALMON, J. L. (1970), *The Origins of Totalitarian Democracy* (Norton, New York).

TAYLOR, C. (1985), *Human Agency and Language: Philosophical Papers*, vol. i (Cambridge University Press, New York).

—— (1985), *Philosophy and the Human Sciences: Philosophical Papers*, vol. ii (Cambridge University Press, New York).

VERNANT, J.-P. (1975), *Les origines de la pensée grecque* (Presses Universitaires de France, Paris).

VERNIER, D. (1988), 'La blessure de l'excision', *Le Monde diplomatique* (October), 100.

VICO, G. (1982), *Vico: Selected Writings*, ed. and trans. L. Pompa (Cambridge University Press, Cambridge).

WALLACH, J. R. (1987), 'Liberals, Communitarians, and the Tasks of Political Theory', *Political Theory*, 15: 581–611.

WILLIAMS, B. (1972), *Morality: An Introduction to Ethics* (Cambridge University Press, Cambridge).

—— (1981), *Moral Luck: Philosophical Papers 1973–1980* (Cambridge University Press, Cambridge).

WILLIAMS, B. (1985), *Ethics and the Limits of Philosophy* (Fontana, London).

YACK, B. (1988), 'Liberalism and its Communitarian Critics: Does Liberal Practice "Live Down" to Liberty Theory?', *Community in America: The Challenge of* Habits of the Heart, eds. C. H. Reynolds and R. V. Norman (University of California Press, Berkeley, Calif.), 147–69.

Index

Index compiled by Howard Kwan